Praise for *A Fair Country*

Shortlisted for 2009 CBA Libris Awards, Non-Fiction

"Any Canadian reading the book, or learning about its content, will think of Canada differently." —*Toronto Star*

"There's something admirable, possibly even heroic, in the earnest anger of John Ralston Saul as he bangs away at the theme of his book *A Fair Country*." —*National Post*

"A stinging assessment of public- and private-sector leaders paralyzed by a 'colonial inferiority complex.'" —*Edmonton Journal*

"Gutsy and exciting ... *A Fair Country* has the potential to change the way Canadians see themselves forever. It offers a romantic and heroic vision, and it's a stirring and unpretentious read." —*Winnipeg Free Press*

"An excellent first step to recovery. By seriously examining Aboriginal influences in Canadian history, Saul goes some way to curing the ongoing dysfunction suffered by—not Aboriginal Canadians—but by mainstream Canadians ... A consequence of Saul's vision is that Western Canada assumes greater influence in the Canadian story ... Makes a lot of sense." —*Calgary Herald*

"To anyone who recognizes the Anishnabek world view of Turtle Island, the [cover] illustration is a perfect summation of Saul's thesis. Canada is, indeed, a Métis nation. Saul's carefully constructed and illuminating argument offers us a new way of viewing ourselves, an argument with roots that stretch back centuries before Confederation. Our ties to the Aboriginal, Saul argues, are far stronger than our ties to the European.

Clearly, this makes some more than a touch uncomfortable, even angry, which will certainly lead to good debate. And isn't that the point of a great book? ... *A Fair Country* will change the way we view ourselves as a nation." —Joseph Boyden, author of *Through Black Spruce*

Praise for John Ralston Saul

"Only a handful of writers have combined imaginative literature with a serious claim to be savants ... Of this small number, the Canadian writer intellectual with the greatest claim to international influence is novelist John Ralston Saul." —*Toronto Star*

"Thank God for John Ralston Saul. At least Canada has one leading intellectual unafraid to challenge the feeble orthodoxies that seem to consume our elites." —David Mitchell, *The Vancouver Sun*

"John Ralston Saul can claim shelf space with such seminal thinkers as Harold Innis, Marshall McLuhan and George Grant." —Peter C. Newman, *Maclean's*

"With his sophisticated international perspective and blunt freedom from cant, he offers a promising persona for the future: the intellectual as man of the world." —Camille Paglia, *The Washington Post*

Saul writes as though thinking, wondering and considering are the most important things we as humans can do. They are, and he demonstrates this on every page." —*The Gazette* (Montreal)

"Saul shows his gift for bringing a fresh perspective to concepts we've come to take for granted, for unmasking absurdity and explaining the paradoxical." —*Edmonton Journal*

PENGUIN CANADA

A FAIR COUNTRY

JOHN RALSTON SAUL's philosophical works—*Voltaire's Bastards, The Doubter's Companion, The Unconscious Civilization* and *On Equilibrium*—have had a growing impact on political thought in many countries. His five novels, including the international bestseller *The Birds of Prey* and *The Paradise Eater*, deal with modern power and its clash with the individual. In 2005, in *The Collapse of Globalism: And the Reinvention of the World*, Saul confronted the dominant ideology of globalization and laid out the economic crisis that would come several years later. His thirteen works have been translated into over a dozen languages.

His work has received many national and international awards, including the Governor General's Literary Award, the Premio Lettarario Internazionale in Italy and Chile's Pablo Neruda Medal. Declared a "prophet" by *Time* magazine, Saul is included in the prestigious *Utne Reader*'s list of the world's hundred leading thinkers and visionaries.

Mr. Saul was born in Ottawa and studied at McGill University, Montreal, and King's College, London, England, where he obtained his Ph.D.

Also by John Ralston Saul

NON-FICTION

Voltaire's Bastards

The Doubter's Companion

The Unconscious Civilization

Reflections of a Siamese Twin

On Equilibrium

The LaFontaine-Baldwin Lectures
(with Alain Dubuc and George Erasmus)

Dialogue on Democracy: The LaFontaine-Baldwin Lectures
(with Louise Arbour, Alain Dubuc, George Erasmus, David Malouf and
Beverley McLachlin)

The Collapse of Globalism: And the Reinvention of the World

NOVELS

The Birds of Prey

The Field Trilogy
I. Baraka or The Lives, Fortunes, and Sacred Honor of Anthony Smith
II. The Next Best Thing
III. The Paradise Eater

De si bons Américains

A FAIR COUNTRY

TELLING TRUTHS ABOUT CANADA

JOHN RALSTON SAUL

PENGUIN
CANADA

PENGUIN CANADA

Published by the Penguin Group

Penguin Group (Canada), 90 Eglinton Avenue East, Suite 700, Toronto, Ontario, Canada M4P 2Y3
(a division of Pearson Canada Inc.)

Penguin Group (USA) Inc., 375 Hudson Street, New York, New York 10014, U.S.A.
Penguin Books Ltd, 80 Strand, London WC2R 0RL, England
Penguin Ireland, 25 St Stephen's Green, Dublin 2, Ireland (a division of Penguin Books Ltd)
Penguin Group (Australia), 250 Camberwell Road, Camberwell, Victoria 3124, Australia
(a division of Pearson Australia Group Pty Ltd)
Penguin Books India Pvt Ltd, 11 Community Centre, Panchsheel Park, New Delhi – 110 017, India
Penguin Group (NZ), 67 Apollo Drive, Rosedale, North Shore 0632, New Zealand
(a division of Pearson New Zealand Ltd)
Penguin Books (South Africa) (Pty) Ltd, 24 Sturdee Avenue, Rosebank, Johannesburg 2196, South Africa

Penguin Books Ltd, Registered Offices: 80 Strand, London WC2R 0RL, England

First published in a Viking Canada hardcover by Penguin Group (Canada),
a division of Pearson Canada Inc., 2008
Published in this edition, 2009

1 2 3 4 5 6 7 8 9 10 (WEB)

Copyright © Towards Equilibrium Inc., 2008

Excerpt from "The Social Worker's Poem" by Alden Nowlan copyright © 1974.
Reproduced with permission from House of Anansi Press.

Excerpt from "History Lessons" by Jeannette Armstrong used with permission of Theytus Books, Penticton, B.C.

Manufactured in Canada.

LIBRARY AND ARCHIVES CANADA CATALOGUING IN PUBLICATION

Saul, John Ralston, 1947–
A fair country : telling truths about Canada / John Ralston Saul.

Includes bibliographical references.
ISBN 978-0-14-316842-3

1. National characteristics, Canadian. 2. Canada—Social conditions. 3. Native peoples—Canada—
Politics and government.
4. Elite (Social sciences)—Canada. 5. Equality—Canada.
6. Canada—Politics and government. I. Title.

FC97.S37 2009   971   C2009-903586-3

Visit the Penguin Group (Canada) website at **www.penguin.ca**

Special and corporate bulk purchase rates available; please see
www.penguin.ca/corporatesales or call 1-800-810-3104, ext. 477 or 474

for
Adrienne

Wen net ki'l
Who are you?

—Rita Joe

CONTENTS

THE POWER OF A STORY

A dancer who describes himself as a singer will do neither well.

To insist on describing ourselves as something we are not is to embrace existential illiteracy. We are not a civilization of British or French or European inspiration. We never have been. Our society is not an expression of *peace, order and good government*. It never was.

To accept and even believe such fundamental misrepresentations of Canada and Canadians is to sever our mythologies from our reality. Playwright and novelist Tomson Highway points out that "Languages are given form by mythologies." To accept a language that expresses neither our true selves nor our true mythologies is to disarm our civilization. It is to cripple our capacity to talk and to act in a way that reflects both our collective unconscious and our ethical standards.

And so there are actions—creative acts—we believe we should take. We feel it would be right for us to act in a particular way, a way right and true to ourselves. Yet these beliefs and feelings have something inchoate about them, because our mythologies and our organized language do not support them. Thus, we find it almost impossible to take such actions or to act in a way true to ourselves. Or we find the process leading to action so difficult, so tortuous, so dragged out that by the time we arrive at the act itself, it is no longer what we had intended.

We have problems we know must be solved. They do not appear unresolvable, certainly not for a well-intentioned, well-educated population of citizens. Yet we seem rarely able to solve them. At best we stitch together bits and pieces, as if we were paupers in a rag yard.

We imagine ourselves playing particular roles at home and abroad, yet we rarely play them, or only do so in a narrow, hesitant short-term manner.

The outcome of all this is an increasingly dysfunctional elite, ill-tempered to the role it is meant to play. As for the citizenry as a whole, we show signs of uncertainty and frustration, as if we feel ourselves adrift.

At the core of these difficulties is our incapacity to accept who we are. There may be many explanations for this. But the first is that we have shrink-wrapped ourselves into a very particular description of our civilization and how it came to be. We have wrapped ourselves so tight within that description that it has become a straitjacket that expresses the history of another people, a history that would have produced a very different civilization than the one we have.

We are a people of Aboriginal inspiration organized around a concept of peace, fairness and good government. That is what lies at the heart of our story, at the heart of Canadian mythology, whether francophone or anglophone. If we can embrace a language that expresses that story, we will feel a great release. We will discover a remarkable power to act and to do so in such a way that we will feel we are true to ourselves.

PART I

A MÉTIS CIVILIZATION

What Shaped Us

We are a métis civilization.

What we are today has been inspired as much by four centuries of life with the indigenous civilizations as by four centuries of immigration. Perhaps more. Today we are the outcome of that experience. As have Métis people, Canadians in general have been heavily influenced and shaped by the First Nations. We still are. We increasingly are. This influencing, this shaping is deep within us.

When I dig around in the roots of how we imagine ourselves, how we govern, how we live together in communities—how we treat one another when we are not being stupid—what I find is deeply Aboriginal. Whatever our family tree may look like, our intuitions and common sense as a civilization are more Aboriginal than European or African or Asian, even though we have created elaborate theatrical screens of language, reference and mythology to misrepresent ourselves to ourselves.

Our leaders endlessly mull over our institutional and cultural inheritance from British parliamentary democracy, British and French justice, the Enlightenment, British liberalism, Western individualism with its important variations, U.S. populism, Judeo-Christian moral questioning, Athenian principles of citizenship and democracy, Western European philosophy, Western social democracy, Western capitalism, in particular its U.S. form. Frankly, once you get below the surface, I see very little in the way we use all of these that would ring familiar bells in Britain, France or elsewhere in Europe or in the United States.

Then, as if to offset all of these efforts made to conform intellectually, emotionally and structurally to the Western canon of ideas and actions, we set aside some time to praise ourselves for the great mix of cultures with which we so comfortably live. We point out that our friends and allies around the world are having trouble with similar situations. This talent, we seem to be saying, for living comfortably with diversity, is our particular contribution to Western Civilization. Yet we never seriously asked ourselves how that came to be. After all, if our civilization has been built out of the Western inheritance, how is it that the rest of the West is struggling precisely where we find the challenges quite easy?

Stranger still, in this process of examining our Western inheritance, and vaunting it, there is scarcely a nod, let alone a meaningful nod, in the direction of the First Nations, the Métis, the Inuit. There is no intellectual, ethical or emotional engagement with what their place might be at the core of our civilization. On the single issue of immigration and citizenship diversity, we seem unable to notice the obvious—that it is a non-racial idea of civilization, and non-linear, even non-rational. It is based on the idea of an inclusive circle that expands and gradually adapts as new people join us. This is not a Western or European concept. It comes straight from Aboriginal culture. But then, why bother to invoke the First Nations idea of the circle as a concept of inclusivity when you can fall back on Kant or John Stuart Mill? At best we manage a pro forma phrase about Aboriginals as one of our founding peoples.

Of course, we do worry about their situation from time to time; that is, we feel sympathy for them, particularly their children, some guilt about them, them over there, outside of our lives in small, isolated, unsustainable communities, usually reserves, or the poorest parts of our cities. But then we remind ourselves that these difficulties, even tragedies, are all caught up in complex negotiations involving civil servants and lawyers over money and land—land most of us have never seen, will never see. We are careful not to ask ourselves whether those indigenous people over there want our sympathy or are interested in our guilt. We don't ask ourselves whether sympathy and guilt are appropriate reactions. Of course, the Canadian government was right to apologize in 2008 for the destructive residential school system. It should and could have done it in the 1980s or 1990s. And Canadians were right to believe that the apology should be made. It was an act of dignity as befits an adult nation. Yet we don't seem to find it odd that non-Aboriginals concentrate, when it comes to Aboriginals, only on what doesn't seem to work, so that we have no idea what or how much does work or how well. As Sandra Laronde of Red Sky Theatre puts it, "We are more than our issues."

Perhaps sympathy and guilt are inappropriate and paternalistic and insulting. Perhaps our sympathy is just a cleaned-up version of the old racist attitudes.

Perhaps those people, those Aboriginals, aren't over there at all because we ourselves are in the same place. Perhaps in some way or many ways, we also are Aboriginal. I don't mean in any legal sense. Perhaps the sympathy and guilt expressed toward Aboriginals are actually signs of non-Aboriginal self-denial—the sort of denial that makes us dysfunctional because we cannot embrace who we are. In colonial terms, this sort of denial is an expression of self-loathing.

And so through a maze of what non-Aboriginals believe to be problems, failures, poverty, communities out of sync with our urban view of ourselves, we see them over there, as we have for a century. We see them insisting on old treaties and bad land, which we forget that we made sure they signed and lived on. And when that land turns out to involve oil or some other wealth, we use every legal and administrative tool available to limit their ability to benefit from it. How could they possibly benefit, being such failures? Lost in this maze we cannot see how much of what we are is them, how much of what we think of as our way, our values, our collective unconscious, is dependent on what we slowly absorbed living with them or near them over the centuries.

Throughout the Western world in the second half of the nineteenth century, middle-class, pew-chained and empire-obsessed civilizations gradually slipped toward the paranoid fears of the twentieth century. Fear of what? Fear of the loss of purity—pure blood, pure race, pure national traits and values and ties. This delusionary indulgence in a purity that had never existed went further in some places than in others. But it flowered everywhere, and gradually, from the late eighteenth century on, it led to an infantile rewriting of history as one of singular peoples—singular and exceptional. These singular peoples were therefore exempted from ethical principles when it came to dealing with impurity, that is, with people not of their pure clan. Even that proved an impossible challenge, given the reality of racial impurity. And so children of the Enlightenment around the world wrapped themselves in the psycho-sexual pleasures of fear. They turned their back on the central premise of humanist philosophy and set about fearing *the other*, then killing *the other* in a multitude of ways. The mixing of the Enlightenment and nationalism throughout the Western-dominated nineteenth century produced something that swelled like a planetary boil, because a handful of empires dominated everywhere. And then we lanced it in a killing frenzy of two world wars followed by a multitude of localized but equally violent clashes.

Was there a particularity to Canada's participation in this experience? Behind the fears of Protestants versus Catholics, English-speaking versus French-speaking, those who imagined themselves as pink or white versus all of those Ukrainians and Jews and Chinese and Japanese, was there a deeper, unspoken fear? Did those Canadians who had got hold of so much of the country—both physical and mythological—fear above all the possibility of a real *other* whose place this was and in whose shadow they—and eventually we—would have to find our reality? In spite of the posturing and myth manufacturing of those who dominated for approximately one century out of our four, perhaps that real *other*, the Aboriginal, was as present as ever, with us, within us. And were we not so much one of those singular European races, but something quite different? Perhaps *the other* we denied and feared was actually the possibility of becoming something more complex, an integral part of that *other*.

So it is both curious and troubling that we cannot bring ourselves to talk about how profoundly our society has been shaped over four centuries in its non-monolithic, non-European manner by the First Nations. Our immigrant society was fragile, tiny and poor everywhere in Canada until well into the nineteenth century. This was true even of the concentrated older enclaves of francophones and anglophones in the

Maritimes and the Canadas, people who had long before stopped thinking of themselves as immigrants. In some areas it was still fragile late into the nineteenth, even into the twentieth, century. In part because of this reality, the relationship between the First Nations and the immigrants varied from region to region. And so the new Canadians, even those who had been here for two or three centuries, were in different ways still dependent on the First Nations for their survival.

Over the first two hundred and fifty years of settler life in Canada, the newcomers had at best reached the level of partnership with the Aboriginals. New France, the Hudson's Bay Company and the North West Company consciously built their place here on the indigenous ideas of mutual dependency and partnership. The Loyalists were part of that process. In more northerly parts of the country, that general idea of partnership went on well into the twentieth century. In the Arctic, our mixture of dependency and partnership was never completely extinguished. And already the Inuit are more or less back in control.

2

Marrying Up

There is a perfectly straightforward foundation to these four centuries of shaping Canada. Anyone whose family arrived before the 1760s is probably part Aboriginal.

I'm not making a racial argument that links blood and character. Nor would any Aboriginal. After all, the idea of racially defined peoples was imported by the Europeans. As power shifted in the nineteenth century, it involved carefully written, legally binding racial definitions, which included some enumeration of rights but above all created limitations on rights for specific minorities to such things as land and the franchise. These racial definitions may at first have been aimed at Aboriginals, but they gradually spread to hive off anyone who arrived in Canada from outside the magical European enlightened and rational gated community. If today's land claims, treaty rights and membership in particular First Nations seem to be dependent on definitions of race, that is entirely the outcome of a European-imposed approach, one that had nothing to do with the Aboriginal idea of expandable and inclusive circles of people. To take their idea of society as an inclusive circle and apply it in the twenty-first century, you have only to use words such as *non-monolithic* or *diversity*.

All I am pointing out is that the constant physical intermingling between First Peoples and newcomers—with the accompanying sea of desire, love, human relations from their best to their worst, children, families, consecrated in an Aboriginal manner or Christian or both or merely in what we would call affairs—had myriad effects. Some were conscious and intended. Others, as with most relations, were the outcome of life. Some descendants slipped toward Aboriginal society, others to that of the settlers. Others became Métis. But in all cases, even if these origins would eventually be forgotten or denied, the effect was nevertheless there, in the way children were brought up, in the expectation of social and political behaviour. As a result, "we have a subconscious Métis mind," novelist Guy Vanderhaeghe said to me. And even as this physical mixing shrank in some parts of the country, it continued to grow in others. All of this over four hundred years. Today it continues as part of the general racial mixing that has developed into a characteristic of the country, one of which we are rightly proud.

We have no problem today with the reality that intermarriages break down barriers, weave together our attitudes toward *the other* and theirs to us, and so help to change how our society functions. This cannot be measured, but the resulting society shows the effect.

In our big cities we talk constantly of groups learning to live together. The assumption is that a healthy percentage of these people will live together in the full sense.

It was only gradually in the nineteenth century, mainly in the second half, that monolithic nationalism, with its ideas of racial purity and the European inheritance, began to throw whole layers of our society into denial of our past. Suddenly our press, poetry, novels and political discourse were advancing arguments that didn't match our real past built upon a continuous mixing of people and, more broadly, of cultures. But why believe that the one hundred years of politicized denial that followed could eradicate real attitudes developed over the preceding two hundred and fifty years? Besides, this artificial Europeanization of Canada, destructive though it was to Aboriginals and chosen groups of immigrants, was never complete. Throughout this dark time, there was a multitude of exceptions, the sort of insistent exceptions that showed how alive our underlying civilization was.

There was one other element in the first two and a half centuries of mixing peoples and cultures that was central to what we would become. By marrying into the indigenous world, most of the newcomers were marrying up. They were improving their situations socially, politically and economically. They were improving their conditions of life—food, clothing, even the suitability of their housing—and thus their health, their power, their status, their mobility, their safety, their cleanliness, the odds that their teeth wouldn't fall out.

They were indeed marrying up. After all, who were they? At best, minor colonial officials from France and Britain or managers of trading posts. Many of the latter were young, penniless, hardly educated men from northern Scottish islands. Many others were French-Canadian farmers, even less educated, with small land holdings, usually subjected to a seigneur, owing him regular payments. Neither the Scots nor the Canadiens were fully free men. They were subject to strict contracts. Others were simple soldiers or adventurers, hoping to make their way. They were by every dispassionate social measurement of the time the social inferiors of those whom they married.

Champlain said, "Our young men will marry your daughters, and we shall be one people." I can't think of a European governor—French, British or other—making such a policy statement in any other colony from the sixteenth to the nineteenth century. With this sentence, he reveals the nature of the First Nation–European relationship—at the very least one of equals. His masters in Paris sent him constant instructions to subject the locals to French control, to assert European racial, cultural and political superiority. He was on the spot. He knew better. He knew what reality required. That he made such a declaration suggests that he felt his colony's position to be weak. But it also suggests that he believed such a mix of the two civilizations could work.

And this was not a short-lived ploy, a beachhead strategy. Throughout the life of New France, one-third to one-half of the men were involved in the fur trade and so lived a second life in that vast, seemingly border-less world beyond the tiny colony. A good percentage of them followed Champlain's advice. Historians tend to look at parish records to discover how common this was and therefore conclude that the numbers were limited. But again, the focus of their measurement assumes that those tiny, poverty-stricken European settlements were the core of Canadian society. That so many Europeans were absorbed into Aboriginal civilization is a partial answer to that assumption. In other words, if you look at it the other way around, at the creation of the Métis people, who were half Catholic francophones and half Anglican anglophones, or at the levels of absorption of Europeans into First Nations communities, the numbers are quite different.

These marriages were not a Scottish or New France particularity. The strength of the Acadians came in part from how close they were to the First Nations. The British, during their ongoing campaign to gain control of Nova Scotia, noted this and at one point tried to catch up by offering a stipend to any soldier who married an Aboriginal. The Hudson's Bay Company built its networks—for more than two hundred years one of the world's largest commercial and political structures—in good part through interracial marriages. A company factor who was lucky enough to be allowed by a chief to marry one of his daughters gained influence in the region and stability for his trade. As with arranged marriages anywhere, the husband sought a financial advantage. In this case, it was access to a trade infrastructure. His wife—multilingual and at the heart of local politics—often became a key player.

Okanagan Valley novelist and cultural leader Jeannette Armstrong says that in the nineteenth century the Syilx leadership in that long valley used these marriages as a "shrewd" and "systemic subversion of the colonizer's distanced gaze and detached modus operandi." This was "calculated to mediate" their relationships, "to indigenize" the settlers in the valley. And indeed, in the late nineteenth century many of the wives and daughters of these mixed-race ranching and farming families wrote about the effects of the cultures on each other.

The constant point is this. Throughout the country and over the centuries, marriages were carefully negotiated between the daughters of chiefs or of other leaders and strategic players among the newcomers. On one side—the First Nations—this was a traditional way to build alliances. On the other—the newcomers—it was a policy aimed at improving their lives and at stabilizing and controlling the fur trade. Later these marriages related to occupying land and putting communities on a solid footing.

To understand how far our mythology has gone to strip away this reality, think of the phrase *going native*. Here is a classic bit of imperial language that was meant to be a denigrating insult, implying the loss of superior European and middle-class standards. In reality, those who went native were improving their status and their lot.

Marriage aside, the foundations of the relationships between the First Nations and the Europeans can be seen in the most basic details. The newcomers were welcomed. They were taught how to survive by the Aboriginals. How to dress. How to eat to avoid scurvy, which simply killed those who wouldn't adapt. The most important Canadian business—fur trading—was reliant on a close and steady relationship with the First Nations. The other major businesses—fishing and whaling—got their start with First Nations help.

We don't think of ourselves that way simply because the mythmakers of the late nineteenth century were busy writing out Canada's past and writing in the glory of the British Empire and the British. And the Ultramontanes were busy writing in the glory of the anti-democratic Catholic Church.

The capacity to adapt to reality is a sign of intelligence in any civilization. In the Arctic, one of the principal causes of death among the British and U.S. explorers was their refusal to dress, act or eat like *savages*. From the 1830s on, they deliberately chose to ignore the example and the advice of voyageurs, Métis and Inuit. It was only late in the nineteenth century that they came to terms with their own inferiority and comic or tragicomic self-absorption. All it took in the end was one naval officer breaking ranks to spend the winter with the Inuit. He came back to the ship in the spring—healthy, happy, well fed—to find the usual collection of sick shipmates and the usual roll call of the dead. The fundamental difference was the refusal of *civilized* Englishmen to eat raw meat, which contained the necessary vitamins. Unlike the *savages*, they boiled theirs until everything healthy had been removed. These sort of comic stories need to be told because they highlight how insistent we have remained on seeing our country through the eyes of these *explorers* rather than through the eyes of those who already lived here. The explorers' stupidity and incapacity to adapt has been recast in this European interpretation of Canada as a drama, a human tragedy. Not stupidity.

What's more, we tend to see the country through the eyes of those who did not adapt, or did so as little as possible and with resentment or snobbery—the Susanna Moodies, or John Richardson and his *Wacousta* viewpoint of dangerous *savages* in a dangerous country. Theirs are so much less interesting, less relevant and less accurate than the stories of the vast majority who were eager to adapt and saw the First Nations and the country quite differently. The Acadians are among the few groups in Canada today to say openly that they would not have survived without the Mi´kmaq and the Maliseet.

How important then was the marrying-up part of this relationship to the future nature of Canada—the Canada of today? To answer, you must step back from the idea of measurement—so flawed by the measurer's point of view, by what is measured, by what elements are included, what are left out. Instead we must try to get a sense of what our society looked like or felt like.

One strategic example revolves around the Johnson family. Sir William Johnson was the senior British player on the northern edges of the American colonies in the decades leading up to the fall of New France in 1760. He was an Irish gentleman without money who had come to make his way in the Americas. His second wife was Molly Brant, Six Nations aristocracy, which gave him enormous influence in the territory struggled over during the Seven Years' War.

From the fall of New France to the Declaration of Independence by the Thirteen Colonies, Johnson was the most powerful non-Aboriginal figure in the vast uncertain lands that lay between those colonies and British North America. He died abruptly on the eve of the rebellion while speaking to thousands of First Nations leaders. He was rallying them to the Crown. His widow continued that work, as did his son by his first marriage. Sir John Johnson and his son-in-law Guy Johnson, in partnership with their stepmother's brother, Joseph Brant, would be the Crown's most successful military leaders after 1776. Eventually they would all retreat to Canada as Loyalists and, in a manner reminiscent of the Roman Empire, settle their soldiers and their families along the most exposed portions of the borders of Canada—Joseph Brant and the Six Nations along the Grand River, and the Johnsons along the St. Lawrence River with their followers, a mixture of Aboriginals, German religious minorities and Scots. Molly Brant went to Kingston with her daughters. The Brants and the Johnsons remained the most influential link between Aboriginal and non-Aboriginal society for another half-century, playing a role, formal and informal, in the organizing of Upper Canada.

Peter Lougheed was one of the most interesting and successful premiers of Alberta, holding power from 1971 to 1985. In 1883, his grandfather had arrived in Calgary, a small, bustling town. He was a young Ontario lawyer, ambitious, without reputation, money or connections. However, he married into southern Albertan aristocracy—Bell Hardisty belonged to a leading Métis family that combined a local Aboriginal network with the classic Hudson's Bay Company background. Lord Strathcona was one of his wife's uncles. Another of her uncles was a senator. She had been educated at a girls' school in Hamilton. The family structure tied Lougheed to the Canadian Pacific Railway and to possible land development. He had indeed married up and he went on to be knighted, to sit in the Senate and to become for a long time the most powerful Albertan in Ottawa.

A few years before Lougheed arrived in Calgary, Sir James Douglas, himself a mix of black and white—a Scottish West Indian—was at the height of his powers as governor of British Columbia. His wife, Amelia Connolly, was the daughter of a First Nations woman and a chief Hudson's Bay Company factor. The era of empire worship was in its first stages, the sort of worship that would require, if it were to succeed, the erasing of our long-established models of racial complexity.

The long-time governor of the Hudson's Bay Company, George Simpson, had begun his career following the tradition of close personal relations with the First Nations. This included fathering several children. But as he rose to power, he gradually came to believe in the new Victorian credo—which was nothing more than the colonial version of imperial self-congratulation dressed up in the accoutrements of the English middle class. Emily Carr described this creed in her *Book of Small*. Or rather, she described her father, who arrived from Britain in this period with everything he would need to create a little England on Vancouver Island, from the correct cooking pots to the correct garden plants. His life was an assertion that you could pretend you weren't where you were. The impossibility of any sort of social partnership with Aboriginals was a given. He couldn't even imagine a partnership with other Europeans or religions. We can look back and laugh, but damage was done in this futile attempt to remake a civilization already two and a half centuries into its methods and habits.

James Douglas found, as the fierce racism of the newly arriving English slowly hemmed him in, that he had to be more circumspect about his mixed-race family. George Simpson used his authority to try *to clean up* the personal relationships of his employees all across the country so that the company would resemble a distant reflection of the grand little Britain he was building around himself in Montreal. People such as Governor Simpson and Mr. Carr certainly succeeded in the short term and partially remade the Canadian myth. Yet it could never really work. The country stumbled badly but stumbled onto where it is now—comfortable with complexity. Nevertheless, we are still missing the conscious and original language with which to explain that comfort to ourselves and to others.

One thing is clear—the persistence of the Victorian description of Canada's past lies at the heart of many of our difficulties today. That Victorianism came late, was not a force for democracy, tried to drag us into imperial wars, blocked the sense that we had paintings to paint and books to write that expressed our reality. It is the root of that same Victorianism that still makes many Canadians think the Aboriginal situation is a situation and a problem. And it makes us feel that this country must always be the supplicant of some great power. If not one, another will do.

But in communities throughout the near, the middle and the high north, a shared pattern emerged. Fixed settlements tended to begin as trading centres. Factors solidified their positions through First Nations marriages. Gradually, Métis families came to dominate the communities. They were the natural leaders in part because they stayed where they were, in part because they controlled the business. The First Nations spent the summers in particular out on the land. They were following a set geographical pattern of seasons and geography. The local officials, such as the Royal Canadian Mounted Police (RCMP), later the teachers and nurses, came and went from one posting to another. The Métis stayed and ruled. Then gradually, as schools and nursing centres were established, the First Nations moved in and became the majority force in these settlements.

And Emily Carr painted her profoundly non-Victorian images of truth about this place. And George Simpson died in 1860 only to be replaced by the husband of Sir James Douglas's daughter, a lady out of the Métis elite. The complex web of these stories and thousands of others are invisible reflections of myriad experiences throughout society.

3

Double Denial

In this same period, across the prairies there was growing poverty and suffering among First Nations as their ability to feed themselves was destroyed and the government's recent treaty promises were broken. But this was not true everywhere. On the West Coast, in spite of smallpox and the other European diseases that decimated their population, some Aboriginals grew rich from the fishing and canning industries. And in spite of the desperate situation on the prairies, there were great leaders, such as Big Bear and Poundmaker, who manoeuvred, delayed, argued and put forward complex alternate approaches to how the vast plains should be organized as the settlers poured in. These and other chiefs were constantly laying out a vision of the land very different from what was happening. It was a vision of how to live there, sharing the land over the long term. In the short term, their approach was a tragic failure. But it is now the vision we are slowly coming to.

Then in 1885 came the moment of breakdown and violence provoked by the growing pressure to treat land and culture in Canada in a monolithic manner. It produced the Northwest Rebellion led by Louis Riel and Gabriel Dumont as well as the parallel confusion among prairie First Nations, who had signed treaties in the 1870s only to be put through that decade of poverty and starvation. None of it need have happened. And not all Canadian leaders were in agreement with the conviction of the new settlers that they should be allowed to sweep all before them. I suspect that had George-Étienne Cartier, who had put in place the mechanisms for Canada's expansion to the West, or the great

Nova Scotia leader, Joseph Howe, still been alive, it would not have happened. They had laid out quite different approaches a few years earlier. Had Charles Tupper been in Ottawa, not representing Canada in London, he might well have been able to calm emotions and batten down both the political extremism and the race-based land hunger of the Orangemen.

There was a great deal more to it than the Orangemen, but they were the driving force in what we did wrong. They arrived in growing numbers through the middle and late nineteenth century with their Protestant extremism. The old Catholic enemy in Ireland was transformed into the Catholic French-Canadian enemy here, and that was extended to any non-conforming minority who got in their way. It was as if, by becoming the voice for loyalty to the Queen and the Empire, they could pass for the voice of a majority that did not exist.

We'd be wrong to think of 1885 as a rebellion by a small group of Métis. It was a major crisis in how Canadians would think of themselves and, therefore, how they would act. We can now see that this was the lowest moment in our history—lower than the Quebec City anti-conscription riots of 1917 or the Winnipeg General Strike riots of 1919 or the constitutional divisions of 1995. Why? Because 1885 saw the fullest expression of the European–U.S. monolithic view of how to run a country. It was all about applying old European prejudices in a new place. The stronger party acted as if physical strength were moral virtue and therefore justified any sort of action, as if any weaker party, any minority, could be swept away at will, as if Canada could be forced into the monolithic model so dominant elsewhere in the Western world. The reason Canadian debates keep coming back to the tragedies of 1885 is that they represent the clearest warning shot we have of how not to act. Here was the model that we must always avoid.

After all, it had led us to violence. The idea of reconciliation had been buried for almost a century. The active memory of the historic relationship with Aboriginals was erased. The sense that treaties could be used duplicitously was encouraged, along with the idea that the First Nations were dying out. This was a classic example of *colonialism*, a word generally used in a vague manner. Its meaning is actually quite precise.

Colonialism is a denial of the reality of self in favour of an imaginary special position inside the mythology of someone else's empire. That special position can never exist because empires have their own purpose.

And so, within a few months of the 1885 crisis, some of the greatest leaders Canada has produced—Big Bear and Poundmaker—were in prison and broken; the most powerful prairie leader, Gabriel Dumont, had fled to the United States; and Louis Riel had been hanged. All of this was happening just a year after Belle Hardisty's marriage to James Lougheed, a symbol of the continuity of the old complexity. Yet with 1885 it seemed that the three founding pillars of our society— Aboriginal, francophone and anglophone—could no longer stand together, and certainly not through personal relations. The idea of balanced relationships, of shared ideas, of an inclusive circle, seemed to have been destroyed forever. If the foundation were so faulty, the whole idea of Canada was dubious.

Poundmaker surrendered by offering his hand to the British general who had led the expedition to put down the uprising. Middleton refused it, turned his back and had the captive chained. That's what imperial generals did to non-compliant natives. It was one of those existential moments when the monolithic model, represented by this British general, showed how shamefully unsuitable it was to a complex place such as Canada.

A century later, the famous general is a forgotten footnote. Poundmaker's ideas and those of Big Bear are increasingly invoked when we discuss the long-term view of how to build a successful society. Their ideas link inclusion, complexity, diversity and living with the place, not simply trying to dominate it. As for Riel, his statue stands centred outside the Manitoba Legislature to remind us that he is the founding father of the province. Schools, public buildings and streets across the prairies are named after him. And Gabriel Dumont is admired as the mythological prairie leader of the pre-settler period, as the great elected head of the Métis and as a remarkable exponent of irregular warfare.

Like the British general, the triumphant Orangemen seem to have evaporated. They have changed or keep their heads down. And John A. Macdonald's handling of the whole crisis is increasingly seen as his single greatest failure, a failure with long-term implications for the country. To this day our national weaknesses are exposed along the fault lines Macdonald allowed to open by acting without precaution, without generosity and without attempting to imagine *the other*.

At the heart of this country's long and slow evolution over the century and a quarter since the Battle of Batoche lies an unfortunate truth. Even with some goodwill at work over the last half-century, we have continued to see ourselves and *the other* in a deeply misguided manner. Yet we constantly demonstrate our desire to escape our weaknesses and our misunderstandings. The way out is tied to finding language that accurately expresses this desire. After all, what is our language striving for today? Diversity. Inclusion. Complexity. We are gradually returning to attitudes that predate the racially based, European-driven divisions of the late nineteenth century. At the same time, we miss the deep historic roots of diversity, inclusion and complexity in Canada by merely attributing them to our current society and to recent immigration patterns, to a new and more open society. In this way we fail to understand that they represent the undercurrent of Canadian civilization. Yes, there are new, positive factors at work. But the collective unconscious carries centuries of experience with complexity and diversity and inclusion.

Part of reconsidering ourselves today is to think about our unbroken past here and those tens of thousands of experiences of métissage and their influence on what we have become. And beyond those physical experiences is the long history of Aboriginal ideas and ways of life mixing in with those who arrived from the sixteenth century on.

Today we continue to expend great energy on desperately searching for meaningful connections to the ideas of Voltaire or Disraeli, the Enlightenment or the American Revolution, European socialism or liberalism or U.S. prairie populism. Meanwhile the words and actions of the Brants or Johnsons or Hardistys or Douglases or Big Bears or Poundmakers or Dumonts are kept on a back burner. Even the words of Louis Riel are usually cited as evocations of his tragedy, instead of as brilliant conceptualizations of what contemporary Canada wishes to be. "[In 1870 the Manitoba Métis population was small,] but in its smallness it had its rights. The other was great, but in its greatness it had no greater rights than the rights of the small, because the right is the same for everyone."

All of these are famous names, but they are part of something much larger. The social patterns of those mixed ranching families in British Columbia's Okanagan Valley or the thousands upon thousands of other families like them are the background to what we are doing today, yet we have forgotten to enter them into our image of ourselves.

Because our real history is not part of how we describe ourselves, we live in denial of our reality. Joseph Gosnell, who led the Nisga'a People of British Columbia to success in a quarter-century-long treaty fight, calls it a double denial. We deny our own history and as part of that seem to deny that the Aboriginals really exist—that is, exist in a way that matters to society as a whole. Renée Dupuis, chief commissioner of the Indian Claims Commission, argues that "the history of North America has not yet been written. It is still written in English from an anglophone point of view, with its colonial origins, in French from a francophone point of view, etc. One of the reasons we are blocked is that we seem unable to look at our roots in a collective manner. We are stuck on the colonizing roots."

Yet the ability of a civilization to survive and grow lies in its ability to describe itself. I don't mean in some factual or pseudo-factual or scientific manner. Author Thomas King: "The truth about stories is that that's all we are." Or Tomson Highway: "Languages are given form by mythologies." Neither is being a romantic. This is one of the rare rock-hard truths of civilization. Again, Guy Vanderhaeghe: "The narrative is how you think of things." And how you think of things will shape much of what you do or what you want to do or how you understand what you shouldn't do. The single greatest failure of the Canadian experiment, so far, has been our inability to normalize—that is, to internalize consciously—the First Nations as the senior founding pillar of our civilization. The most obvious demonstration of this is the concentration, by those who consider themselves non-Aboriginal, on Aboriginals at worst as a problem, at best as people facing problems and asking the rest of us for land, money, special rights. In a normalized or internalized situation we would find ourselves asking Aboriginals their opinion, their advice on what they think Canada should look and sound like. To put this in the straightforward language of Jack Sissons, the first judge of the North: "They have much to offer Canada." The rest of us act as if this is not the case.

Much to offer. What does that mean? There are a thousand answers. But take the practical initiatives that came out of the Arctic between the 1950s and 1970s via the judgments of Jack Sissons, then his successor, William Morrow. The "traditional marriage" of the Inuit, at first legally opposed by the southern legal administration but supported by the two northern judges, is now more or less the model for half the southern population of Canada. We call it common law. Comprehensive legal aid began in the Arctic as the logical requirement of a society not based on money. John Turner, then a young justice minister, came north and flew around on circuit with the court. He came to understand this idea that law could be constructed outside of legal fees and thus brought the legal aid idea into existence. At the heart of the concept was the particularity of Inuit society. The idea that legal cases might be more cultural than criminal had been around for a long time. But Sissons and Morrow turned it into a reality through a series of cases dealing with how the law should work in Inuit culture. In 1969, the Supreme Court invoked John Diefenbaker's Bill of Rights to support a Morrow case, the first time they had done so, demonstrating the link between Canada's idea of justice and Aboriginal approaches.

I give these historic but practical examples because, as Thomas King points out: "non-natives romanticize natives; I don't think there's anything else you can do, given the kind of cultural material that's out there that we're fed, you know, from childhood." Either we are lost in some version of "cowboys and Indians" or in the supposed tragedy of a lost people—"either the noble or the ignoble savage." The idea of the native as a normal person in his or her own right or the idea of an inclusive, fair sense of history are so blurred as to be almost erased.

How has this happened? The simplest explanation tells us everything and nothing. In the late fifteenth century, there are thought to have been seven to ten million Aboriginals in North America, two million of them in Canada. By the end of the nineteenth century, two hundred and fifty thousand were left in the United States, one hundred thousand in Canada—a depopulation of 95 percent. On the Pacific Northwest coast, there had been some 100,000 at the time of contact in the 1770s. By the 1920s, there were 20,000 left.

How? Why? First, there was the slow removal of a way of life and of the land necessary for prosperity. In many areas, particularly on the prairies, the result was malnutrition and starvation. Child mortality skyrocketed. Birth rates plummeted. South of the border, wars also played a major role. And then there were our diseases—wave after wave of them imported over two hundred and fifty years. Before the Iroquois massacred the Huron on the south shore of Georgian Bay in 1649, there had already been several attacks of mortal disease delivered along with God by the Jesuits. The Haida on Haida Gwaii off the West Coast were reduced by the early twentieth century from somewhere between 10,000 and 20,000, perhaps as high as 30,000, to 588. This was one of the great warrior nations of the Pacific, one of the sources of Canada's greatest sculpture and epic poetry. They could not know what was killing them. Death came as if from nowhere, from outside of all their experience. There are stories of them running along the rocky coasts away from their villages, prosperous only months before, attempting to flee from the grip of death, dying as they ran.

The newcomers—carriers and observers of this tragedy—gradually concluded in the second half of the nineteenth century that these were dying cultures. With regret, indifference or joy, they concluded that the time of the First Nations was over and so made plans simply to assimilate the survivors. At some level this suited the European idea that other cultures were inferior, and their religions wrong and therefore bad, probably evil. Certainly uncivilized. Assimilation, which would involve the disappearance of these religions, along with the supporting culture and languages, was therefore an act of generosity on the part of the new rulers. This was the underlying theory of the residential school system.

In reality, this idea of assimilation was a conscious attack on the self-confidence of the Aboriginals. That was its purpose. In the words of

Mi´kmaq poet Rita Joe: "I lost my talk, the talk you took away." In 1996, the Royal Commission on Aboriginal Peoples described how this desta-bilization "invaded whole communities." "The failure of family functioning can be traced in many cases to interventions of the state deliberately introduced to disrupt or displace the Aboriginal family." The commission spoke of "a psychological castration complex, cultural self-shame and cultural self-hate." Two Inuit elders, Mariano Aupilaarjuk and Emile Imaruittuq, respectively: "[The priest] told us our Inuit traditions were not good and we had to stop using them. It felt like we had to stop listening to our parents. It was like we entered a void." "If Christianity had not preached that our culture was evil, maybe a lot of the people that committed suicide would still be alive today." Quite calmly, somehow putting aside the emotional forces at work, they concluded that "we should be joining together the good parts" of both cultures. In other words, they called for a return to the balanced relationship that had developed through the first centuries of our shared history.

When non-Aboriginals are being honest with themselves, they admit that the denial of indigenous culture destabilized the Aboriginals. This is accurate. What is not discussed is how, by destabilizing one of the three pillars upon which our society is built—the senior part of our founda-tion, the one that provides us with a real relationship to this, our place — we also destabilized the other two pillars and therefore the whole civilization. At first this was not apparent. The immigrant pillars accumulated wealth and power. And yet today many Canadians—francophone, anglophone—across the country are confused about their direction, uncertain of the meaning of their place in this place.

Besides, history does not play the same game as mortals. In less than a century, and in spite of intentionally destructive policies justified by apocalyptic conclusions about their disappearance, the Aboriginal population has rebounded. The national figure in 2007 was 1.2 million—twelve times more than at the low point. There are now more First Nations in British Columbia than at the time of contact. The Haida are up to more than four thousand and growing quickly. There are far more Inuit than ever before in history. The historic national Aboriginal population level will soon be overtaken. With the highest birth rate in the country, simple demographics suggest they will be dominant players in the Northern two-thirds, if not three-quarters, of Canada. That Northern three-quarters is precisely where all our national resource wealth lies. Those are the natural resources on which our lazy elites have decided we must once again be dependent.

The result—the ironic result—is that Canadians as a whole will be increasingly dependent—once again—on a healthy relationship with Aboriginals and upon the stability of the Aboriginal cultures. There is great danger in anyone's taking a romantic view of this situation. At every level—whether philosophical or utilitarian—the Aboriginals do have much to offer the rest of us. The last half-century has been marked by historic moments when those with power might have ignored the advice of the Department of Indian Affairs and of the federal and provincial lawyers and instead made a great leap forward to re-establish the original egalitarian relationship—the one aimed at partnership and mutual dependency. In most cases, the opportunity offered by those moments was ostentatiously spurned by the non-Aboriginals and the governments they dominate. The most foolish refusal to engage seriously came with the delivery of the report by the Royal Commission on Aboriginal Peoples in 1996. Here was a vast and complex analysis that could have been seized upon immediately to help get us back on track. How often do countries offer to themselves the privilege of a great intellectual and human re-examination of themselves? How much more irresponsible of those with power not to find the courage to pick it up openly and engage? What frightened the authorities? I think it was the reappearance of the concept of Canada as an ethical pact built over centuries rather than an administrative power arrangement in which whoever has the power today gets to believe that they can run it as they wish. The managerially minded almost always opt for today. They can only be certain to have power in the present. People wonder why history is so marginalized in our society. A partial answer is that managers fear the past and the future and are terrified by the idea of a combination of the two. Yet this delaying can only work for so long. "Treaty promises were part of the foundation of Canada, and keeping those promises is a challenge to the honour and legitimacy of Canada."

There is a clarity in the commission's report that is part of its power. And so in spite of the official silence, its principles have begun to make their way into public policy: the Nunavut agreement, which in 1999 cut the Northwest Territories in half to give the Inuit a self-governing territory; the Nisga'a Agreement, which in 1999 established a new approach to First Nations settlements; and perhaps most strategic, the Supreme Court's 1997 *Delgamuukw* ruling, which introduced, or rather reintroduced, oral culture into the heart of Canadian law. Twice in his ruling, Chief Justice Antonio Lamer based his argument, which gave precedence to oral memory over written text, on the arguments of the royal commission. This great document is slowly making its way because it is the most important statement we now have of our reality—one that embraces "a relationship of mutual trust and loyalty" and deals with the real role of the Aboriginal peoples in Canada.

4

Why We Stumble

Why do we continue to stumble and resist and deny when it comes to this Aboriginal role in Canada? The most obvious answer is that we don't know what to do with the least palatable part of the settler story. We wanted the land. It belonged to someone else. We took it.

We then dressed up our right to this land, along with our shoddy disrespect for the treaties, in a heartfelt conviction that the original owners were dying off. Why? Because they were inferior to the remarkably pure-blooded and intelligent Europeans. Historians such as Francis Parkman, François-Xavier Garneau and Abbé Groulx, along with the poet and Indian Affairs official Duncan Campbell Scott and many others, provided the supporting intellectual arguments. In a full flight of nineteenth-century romanticism, they presented their opinions as scientific or utilitarian or historic determinism. Their message—stated or implied—was that if this race was disappearing, it followed that to mix with them was to dilute pure blood. Mixed races were thus weak, sly and untrustworthy. All of this was imperial cant, based on a belief in monolithic culture and a fear of social complexity. It justified this sort of language: "Shall we allow a few vagrants [the First Nations] to prevent forever industrious settlers from settling on unoccupied lands?" That was Amor de Cosmos, soon to be premier of British Columbia.

The two Riel events—in 1869–70 on the Red River and in 1885 on the South Saskatchewan—demonstrated clearly that the driving force behind these attitudes was a hunger for land and power. The aim was never religious conversion or a civilizing mission or Europeanization.

After all, the Métis were already fervent Catholics and Anglicans. Their social attitudes and their policies were those of fervent Christians. As with the Maori Parihaka movement in New Zealand in the same period, the leader of the Métis was intellectually sophisticated in a Westernized manner. In both cases, the communities were economically successful, peaceful and organized around clear and stable rules. The Métis were already on good terms with both the established traders and the established settlers in the area and were looking forward to co-operating with their government in Ottawa. The terms for co-operation were, they imagined, the sort of peace, fairness and good government the newcomers applied to themselves. Just as Riel had, the Maori leader Te Whiti turned the Christian and Western arguments on those who swore by them. He presented peaceful co-existence with the settlers in an entirely Christian context. His people were better at agriculture than the newcomers and took full advantage of Western machinery.

To be faced by people who had not abandoned their culture, but rather had grafted onto it a moral and ethical European purpose, merely infuriated the newest settlers. The Métis, like the Maori, were still missing one key element to make them deserving—the appropriate race.

The Aboriginals nevertheless spoke up repeatedly, clearly and eloquently with their own vision and their understanding of civilization, rights and treaties. Joseph Brant, the great Mohawk Six Nations leader, was constantly arguing in the late-eighteenth and early-nineteenth centuries that there were real civilizational choices at stake. And he usually did this with irony. "In the government you call civilized, the happiness of the people is constantly sacrificed to the splendour of empires. Hence your codes of criminal and civil laws have their origin; hence your dungeons and prisons. I will not enlarge on an idea so singular in civilized life. Among us we have no prisons."

Throughout the nineteenth century, virtually every chief used every meeting and every negotiation with the government to lay out in depth their concepts of how society should work and how their relationships should be organized. On the prairies, from the 1850s to the mid-1880s, Big Bear, Poundmaker and Sweetgrass were particularly famous for their complex exposés on the land and the relationship of people to it, the necessity for stable coalitions among First Nations, the importance of their own spiritual beliefs and above all the nature of ownership. They kept pointing out the impossibility of anyone owning land in the sense that Ottawa asserted. They explained that no one could have unlimited rights to do what they wished to the land. A series of court rulings over the last quarter-century, as well as government land claims settlements, are gradually taking us in the direction of that indigenous concept. Big Bear was alternately unflinching and funny. He was wary of the easy seductions central to most negotiations. In 1875, he rebuffed the federal negotiator. "We want none of the Queen's presents; when we set a fox-trap we scatter pieces of meat all around, but when the fox gets into the trap we knock him on the head." The formal *Memorial* presented by B.C. chiefs to Prime Minister Wilfrid Laurier in Kamloops during his 1910 Western tour was powerfully written, founded in history and law, and built around the force of ethical standards. They laid out the history of their relationship, first with the "real whites"—the French-speaking Canadians, with whom they had had a good relationship—then with the "other whites"—the English-speaking Canadians who had gradually imposed their way, lying at each stage about their intent. The central guilty party, they said, was increasingly the B.C. government.

The continuity in Aboriginal arguments has been remarkable. In the 1970s, Grand Chief John Kelly pointed out to a royal commission that "We have proved that we will not be assimilated. We have demonstrated that our culture has a viability that cannot be suppressed." But then he went on to make the broader argument that indigenous leaders have been making for four centuries. "[A]s the years go by, the circle of the Ojibway gets bigger and bigger. Canadians of all colours and religion are entering that circle. You might feel that you have roots somewhere else, but in reality, you are right here with us." In 2008, Tomson Highway was making the same argument in order to introduce a new opera, *Pimooteewin*. He was talking about the non-linear nature of pantheistic or animistic cultures that "function according to a circle as opposed to a straight line." And that function is all about inclusion, balance and complexity.

Through the centuries, Aboriginals have never lacked for supporters — often the farmers living nearby or church leaders or politicians. In fact, they had always had supporters. John Mills Jackson wrote a public treatise in 1809 attacking the Family Compact in Upper Canada in part for their "shoddy," "ungrateful treatment" of the First Nations, a "fine and loyal people." In 1911, a year after the B.C. chiefs and their tribes had presented their *Memorial* to Laurier in Kamloops, a delegation of their non-Aboriginal friends went to Ottawa and petitioned the prime minister on their behalf. Laurier agreed to try to get the B.C. government to the negotiating table. A century later, they are only just getting there. Throughout the last two centuries, many francophones, anglophones, Loyalist descendants and others have spoken up to condemn the self-interested drivel of those who sought to destroy the Aboriginal position.

Somehow these more noble arguments did not carry the necessary political weight. They were neutralized by a twisted and deformed political discourse. Why? Because we had never pursued the intellectual idea that Canada worked thanks to a very different approach to nationhood, that it was the product of a long history of arrangements that were generated locally. There are endless examples of people acting as if this were so and advancing elements of a broader possible argument. But these elements were never converted into a conscious mythological driving force, as was done with very different ideas in France, for example, or the United States, to explain their own cultures. And so, in a self-destructive expression of colonialism, the dominant intellectual current in common use in Canada, whether among anglophones or francophones, remained the European, with its fear of complexity, its idea of linear progress and its racial underpinnings. It remains today the dominant intellectual current.

This was a contradictory situation. The signals flashing out of the Canadian experience simply didn't match the public discourse they ought to have been illuminating. It wasn't surprising then that the idea of First Nations civilization as inferior and therefore destined to disappear ran parallel to the apparently contradictory view that we newcomers were the logical successors to this great old civilization. As successors we were to inherit their natural relationship to this place—the mythological aspect of what we call ownership. In some ways this was the benign theme of the summer camps to which so many children were—and are—sent.

In this inheritance scenario, the *Indians* were our Greeks—our Athenians, our Spartans. Like the Romans, we were mere farmers or, more recently, manufacturers, paper-pushers, service industry workers, increasingly cut off in real life from this remarkable land. And there they were, our predecessors, in Thomas King's words, "wild, free, powerful, noble, handsome, philosophical, eloquent, solitary." And romantic though this image might be, it was attached to a certain reality. In the 1880s, the poet Charles Mair, who had passed part of his life on the prairies when the two civilizations were manoeuvring for power, found he had to defend his epic poem *Tecumseh* because of the noble language he had put in the native leader's mouth. "I have never yet heard the Indian speak but as a sensible, intelligent man, fully alive to his interests and conscious of his rights, expressing himself always in language of remarkable vigor and directness." Of course, Mair didn't get along with the Métis. Perhaps it all came back to the idea that the Athenian must be of pure blood.

The added essential element was that Tecumseh had had the good grace to die in battle in the War of 1812 in defence of what could be seen as the Canadian ideal. He had tried to hold what would become part of Canada's border. He had been betrayed and abandoned by the British Army. From the point of view of nineteenth-century Canadian nationalism, it was a superbly noble death—a reminder that you can't become someone's Athenian unless you die and do it with grandeur.

The problem with all these attitudes toward the Aboriginals was that they assumed the inevitability of their disappearance and, in the meantime, the disappearance of their culture and thus their voice. Yet somehow, mysteriously, there they were in the First World War, carrying much more than their share of the nation's battlefield burden. To all intents and purposes, they did seem to be defending their country. This country. And again, between the wars, in spite of the mistreatment of their returning veterans, there they were, speaking up in protest, with dignity, as their population began to make a comeback. And again, there they were, carrying more than their share in the Second World War; and from the 1950s on, growing ever faster, finding new ways to speak up, getting back the vote, occupying a growing space in the public discourse.

Somehow they just didn't understand the inevitability of Western Civilization's victory sufficiently to fade away gracefully into a grand and noble myth for us to inherit.

I sense that the evil perpetrated in the residential schools—the deadly health conditions, the banning of language and culture, the sexual degradation and physical violence, the disruption of families—was the expression of a deep and growing Euro-Canadian anger at the refusal of the noble ancestor to reach for his full apotheosis by disappearing. The last organized expression of that anger came with the 1969 Ottawa White Paper on indigenous questions that, behind a rhetoric of rational modernization, was designed to integrate Aboriginals out of existence. Advancing as if blindfolded on narrow rails, it met the returning force and speed of the indigenous communities head-on and was derailed. What this demonstrated was how profoundly out of touch our political and emotional structures were with our reality.

Derailed or not, no new Canadian point of view has yet been put into place. And so Thomas King asks with dark irony: "What is it about us that you don't like?" The answer is that, like Socrates or the warriors at Thermopylae, you're supposed to have disappeared so that we can put up some statues, write some poems and get on with our lives as your anointed successors.

It is the courts that are gradually forcing Canadians to deal with their historic obligations. And the voices of goodwill in the population at large are stronger than they have been for perhaps a century and a half. But the consciously stated philosophy of our country still has not changed. In place of any organized *disappearance* policy, we have that new racism I have already mentioned—that which focuses us on Aboriginals as people in trouble with drugs, drink, abuse and so on. We have trained ourselves not to see the Aboriginal nature of Canadian society. And we have developed blinkers to avoid seeing what does work in Aboriginal communities. And a great deal works well.

We don't talk about the seven thousand Aboriginal students in universities and colleges in Saskatchewan and the thousands in other provinces. Or the experiment with radically decentralized government in Nunavut, which is dependent on high-tech communications. Or the success of the Makivik Corporation in Nunavik, where the Inuit have used their James Bay Settlement money to build the largest business empire in the North. Or myriad experiments with new approaches to education across the country. Or the remarkable success of the Haida in slowly getting Haida Gwaii off the old pulp and paper treadmill to forest extinction. In 2007, they convinced the B.C. government to co-operate in transferring yet another large chunk of the archipelago to a very non-Western land-use model. This put about half of Haida Gwaii onto a circular approach that their elected president, Guujaaw, says will bring cultural, environmental and economic interests into balance.

In general we talk of Aboriginal leadership only when something goes wrong. Yet in my experience they have a solid phalanx among the younger generations of some of the finest leaders in the country. The Aboriginal response to the sympathetic pessimism of most Canadians has been a growing refusal, as cultural leader and novelist Jeannette Armstrong puts it, to be portrayed as victims. Jack Anawak, one of the founders of Nunavut and until recently Canada's circumpolar ambassador, refutes the entrenched linking of youth suicide to some vaguely traditional *Inuit* way. He puts it down instead to the recent social crisis and reminds people that the core of the Inuit way has always been not suicide but survival in a very difficult landscape. These examples of indigenous *pushing back* are part of a broad movement to counteract the pessimism this new racism feeds. In its place there is a growing concentration on traditional indigenous ways—spiritual training, healing circles, religious ceremonies, schools bending Western education into Aboriginal forms. This is not a retreat into the past. You have only to look at indigenous theatre, art and film. These traditional ways are reasserting themselves because they are alive, flexible and not locked into the past.

That we are still having this sort of argument—non-Aboriginals still struggling with denial of their own reality, Aboriginals still struggling with the effects of profound destabilization—is a great failure of our society. But we could also see this uncertainty and disquiet as a sign of how central the Aboriginal pillar is to our civilization. The writer Octavio Paz argues that "In the United States the Indian element does not appear ... the United States was founded in a land without a past. The historical memory of Americans is European, not American, [while] exactly the opposite is true of Mexico, land of superimposed pasts." Canadian society is very different from Mexican, yet they resemble each other in this complexity of superimposed pasts far more than they resemble the nation lying between them. It is the difference between a country built upon the conquering and cleansing of its territory and two in which tough circumstances forced different civilizations to figure out how to live together.

We have not yet developed a broad Canadian view that re-establishes Aboriginals in their full and central place. Yet something must be happening because the old habits of denial don't seem to work anymore. Those who are still wedded to the exclusionary view have more and more trouble whipping up widely shared expressions of anger and rejection. Again and again we are told there will be a hot summer with roads blocked in British Columbia or Ontario or Quebec. When the moment comes, there are a few ugly flare-ups, a few persistent local running sores, a few overreactions by a few politicians or police officers who still haven't understood that appropriate action in their own society means trying to understand *the other* and seeking to talk your way through the problem in order to resolve the problem.

But there's also a tendency by Canadians as a whole to back off from any attempts to create yet another crisis between Aboriginals and non-Aboriginals. We are increasingly less trusting of those who see the fundamental problem as lying on the Aboriginal side. We don't quite know what to do, but we back off just to be safe, while looking for a different, more constructive track.

5

Learning to See Ourselves

How we might lay out a Canadian point of view that matches our reality is complicated. But what we need to do, how we need to act, is not so difficult. Ideas, intellectual concepts don't always come first, but they can't lag far behind existential action. The results of such actions, on the other hand, are impossible to predict, let alone design. What I am talking about is the need for an interim stage. Either we stumble on, ever more frustrated that our society doesn't function as it should, or we start to rethink our history, to re-examine it. If we look, we will discover the First Nations, the Métis and the Inuit at its core. We have to learn how to express that reality, the reality of our history. I am not talking about a passive projection of our past, but rather about all of us learning how to imagine ourselves differently. And this is not something that we must do—we, the people who don't think of ourselves as Aboriginal. It's something we have to do *with* Aboriginals. Otherwise, it will be just another romantic delusion.

Nor do I mean that this is just a matter of utilitarian action. That would be insulting to all parties. Indigenous peoples are already there, at the core of our civilization. That is our reality. Our challenge is to learn how to recognize what we have trained ourselves not to see. We must remove the imaginative and historical veils that we have used to obscure this reality. That means trying to identify the elements that make this Aboriginal presence real to both non-Aboriginal and Aboriginal.

And this is not primarily about thanking or apologizing or admitting wrong or settling outstanding accounts. All of that needs to be done.

What I am talking about is a quite different stage—one in which we learn how to see ourselves, to identify ourselves and, finally, to describe ourselves. Then we would be able to talk to each other in a language that makes sense here, a language that is not yet another tortured attempt to apply European or U.S. concepts to a very different reality.

How would this happen? Some of it is deceptively simple. In the National Gallery in Ottawa a few years ago, the curators reimagined their Canadian galleries and began to integrate Aboriginal art of the equivalent era alongside those paintings and sculptures we used to think of as mainstream. In other words, the Aboriginal work is no longer treated as ethnographic or marginal or even as distantly parallel. They exist in the same rooms together. And as soon as what was thought of as the art of separate worlds is hung together, you begin to view our society differently—in a more holistic way. The Glenbow Museum in Calgary is now doing the same thing. This is a small first step. But art—culture in general—is never really a small step. It is the sign that we are getting ready to think differently—that we are starting to imagine ourselves in another manner.

Some of this change is much more deceptively complex. Our Supreme Court has now given serious weight to oral culture through a series of judgments focused on indigenous questions. In fact, it has ruled that it is willing to believe oral evidence over written. Our universities, which ought to be in the same philosophical and cultural universe as our highest levels of justice, are instead entirely designed to deny the importance of the oral. At the core of higher learning in Canada lies an obsession with the written and a concept in which learning means written. The higher your studies go, the more they are built around narrow, exclusionary ideas of truth, tightly tied to a world of people footnoting one another. And so our intellectual class, whether lawyers or social scientists or those who teach literature, is constituted to deny the centrality of the Aboriginal cultures. The intellectual class exists to deny any particular Canadian approach toward culture. They write it out, marginalize it, even when ways are found to give the oral written form.

Many would say there is no alternative. Yet the historic basis for most of what is taught in the humanities was oral or largely oral for thousands of years.

Of course, separating out elements in a complicated world is a valid intellectual activity. It must be done. But the capacity to see how the elements fit together is a completely different form of intelligence and is of equal if not greater importance.

It is that horizontal, inclusive approach to thought that will allow us to see what we have trained ourselves not to see. If we suffer from an imaginative blockage, it is all about generations of tightly argued assumptions. We no longer remember that many of our contemporary *facts* are merely the expression of political assumptions from the late nineteenth and early twentieth centuries. Our studies may be immersed in modern methodology, but their intellectual base remains an old-fashioned, imperial view of the world. After all, it is the intellectual idea of the rational human that has made it so difficult to focus on a balanced use of natural resources. It is the nineteenth-century concepts of individualism that have made it so difficult to maintain social co-operation. It is the eighteenth-century idea linking science and progress that has made it so difficult for us to judge our technical initiatives.

If we begin to look directly at those assumptions, what we find is remarkably inaccurate. For example, the idea that the Europeans discovered a poor, backward culture here, one of mere hunters and gatherers, remains in place even if not expressed in such a direct way. The reality was quite different. In technical, Western terms, four hundred years ago, the Europeans arriving in Canada and the indigenous peoples they met here could both be described as belonging to medieval civilizations. Each had certain advantages. Western advantages such as guns and metal implements were quickly adopted by the Aboriginals. These were advantages in the same way that computers were a Western-produced advantage in Asia a few decades ago. Technical advantages last at best a decade. The advantages of the Aboriginals, on the other hand, were all about living and moving in this place. Both the French and the British adapted to Aboriginal ways, first to survive and then to do well. In fact, the newcomers became an adapted form of hunters and gatherers in order to become wealthy. And the reign of the Aboriginal advance lasted not a decade, but centuries. This raises a central question about our idea of stages of progress.

First, Aboriginals were not poorer, did not eat less well or live roughly when compared to the newcomers. They considered the newcomers poorer in part because they dressed so inappropriately and ate so badly that they died of scurvy or lost their teeth, then hair. And part of this had to do with the great class differentiations in European civilization. Aboriginals considered any society that was intentionally so unfair to so many to be inferior. That someone would insist on eating in a particular way because it was appropriate to their class even if it was bad for their teeth, or be obliged to dress a certain way by others because of class, was a sign of limited intelligence.

The idea of egalitarianism that we have today is far closer to that of the seventeenth- or eighteenth-century First Nations than it is to that of the newcomers of that period. And if this were untrue, why did both colonial armies have a problem with men deserting to the Aboriginals? These men escaped to a world in which they ate better, lived in greater comfort, were healthier in the winter and were cleaner. And if the Aboriginal civilization was not attractive, how did we all together come to create a whole new race—the Métis—in such a short period of time?

Tied to such basic realities is the concept of exploration. The newcomers did not discover the interior of Canada. They were shown it, thanks to alliances, treaties and commercial agreements. And most of it was shown to them by canoe. Writer John Jennings has demonstrated that Canada is the only country invested in by the Europeans in which the local means of transport and much of the way of life was maintained. Everywhere else the Europeans introduced their own boats, carriages or horses. The wheel was one of those strategic tools of conquest and occupation pretty well everywhere, except in Canada. The canoe in all its forms and sizes, sometimes slightly altered for specific purposes, was to be used as our principal means of transport—personal, governmental, military and commercial—for several centuries. Why? Because the First Nations had developed the appropriate means of transport for our road system, that is, our rivers and lakes. It wasn't until the middle of the nineteenth century that we seriously set about developing metallic rivers—railway tracks. Even these could take you only so far. It was thanks to the canoe and to the First Nations that, in moving across the country through the waters, we became a financially viable society. The fur trade was our first source of wealth. It set the pattern for an endless sequence of raw materials upon which we are still dependent. Farming for a long time was the poorest of options until we began to develop hardy crops.

If this enormous space was shaped and held back long enough from the manifest destiny of our neighbour to evolve into a country, it was largely thanks to Aboriginal alliances and Métis prowess. It was the Maliseet-Acadian alliance that held the New Englanders at bay for decades, long enough to produce the unintended result that there was a place to which Loyalists could come in the 1780s. It was the Métis and the Cree, among others, who held the prairies to a latitude not far off our Canadian border. The new country appropriated and solidified that line. The First Nations were central to holding the borders of Ontario and Quebec. The most famous turning point in ensuring the long-term existence of what would become Canada was probably the Battle of Queenston Heights in 1812. A surprise invasion across the Niagara River gave the U.S. troops a key strategic position. Had they held on to the Heights long enough for reinforcements to join them—one night would have been sufficient—their advantage would have made it difficult for the divided Canadian forces to reverse. It was John Norton, Joseph Brant's successor, commanding a coalition of Aboriginal forces dominated by the Six Nations from the Grand River, who led a guerrilla-style attack, destabilized the U.S. position and so turned the battle.

The simple question is this: How many times did the First Nations or the Métis defend, save or help save the space that would become Canada? Queenston Heights is a strategic example. The Battle of Grand Coteau in 1851 in North Dakota, in which the Métis defeated the Sioux coming from farther south, was just as important, but is even less understood. It was a victory that solidified spheres of influence. These spheres were taken over by the Canadian and U.S. governments and thus settled the border to within a few hundred kilometres. There were hundreds of other smaller military incidents, each of which contributed to shaping this country. The life of the great Métis guide Jerry Potts is a perfect example of the way we misunderstand how we came to develop this country. He made it possible for the North West Mounted Police to establish themselves in Alberta. In the most basic terms, they had little idea of where they were. He was central to First Nations–government relations and to the relative peace among First Nations during the Riel Rebellion. Had he been white he would have been bemedalled and much statued. He is remembered, but more as a colourful figure than a builder of the province. Yet the existence of Alberta owes more to him than to the standard shortlist of policemen, politicians, land speculators and other businessmen who are often cited as provincial heroes.

This indigenous military role was not an accident. From the beginning, the European strategy in the northern half of North America was to govern and defend via patterns of alliances with Aboriginals. This was the New France strategy and the Hudson's Bay Company strategy. It became the British-Loyalist-Canadien strategy after 1759, and then the Canadian strategy until almost two decades after the War of 1812. In other words, this was the Canadian strategy for two and a half centuries.

The broad reality was an integrated First Nations role, central to the shaping of this country, which went on for twice as long as Canada has existed as a Confederation. It was military, civil and commercial. We never really ask ourselves why so many of our provinces, cities and towns, our rivers and lakes, have Aboriginal names, as do our animals, birds, fish, pieces of clothing and means of transport; why there is an Aboriginal presence in the cadence of much of our popular music, particularly in Acadie and Quebec; why Aboriginal art seems to fit us like a glove. These are not names, images, sounds, objects chosen in flights of romantic fancy—tributes to a disappearing past. These are the marks of our reality.

And this reality means that we need to examine the language most of us use to be certain that we understand what we mean. After all, both English and French are understood in different ways in different countries. Here our sense of both languages has been subtly shaped by Aboriginal assumptions. I'm referring to our practical use of these languages but equally to the philosophical, ethical and metaphysical.

For example, we struggle endlessly with the concept of *sovereignty*. Why? Because the concept we are searching for is not part of the Western tradition. What we are after is an indigenous idea with which we have centuries of experience. The Mohawk call it tewatatowie. It is all about being able both to help yourself and to look at yourself: "Sovereignty is harmony achieved through balanced relationships." This is very different from the England-U.S. English meaning or the France-French meaning. In the European tradition, sovereignty is built around all sorts of rigid legalistic implications defining borders and the application of laws.

Yet it is this European sense that dominates in our universities, our standard legal theory and our civil services. It stands directly in the way each time Aboriginals attempt to explain what they mean by sovereignty or self-government. Why are we so eager to use this European intellectual approach? After all, it has a long, tired history of bloodied conflicts produced by a particular idea of the nation-state. This is the sort of conflict we have more or less avoided. What's more, the Europeans themselves have been slowly abandoning their own meaning as they construct the European Union. But their changes are quite naturally developed as intellectual amendments to their own meaning. We are having a great deal more difficulty because we are using their language to describe our very different experience and reality. Meaning in language is an evolution. For us to try to get intellectually to where we are physically by following the Europeans' political evolution is ridiculously tortuous.

This is one way of understanding the continuing frustration over the place of Quebec in Canada—frustration both from within Quebec and in the rest of Canada. It comes from our confused sense of concepts such as sovereignty. We feel it to mean one thing but intellectually oblige ourselves to explain it to mean another. We may feel or sense differently because of the long-term Aboriginal influence. Because we have not consciously accepted that this influence exists, we have not developed the intellectual mechanisms—the appropriate language in English and French—to express that difference. And so in our collective unconscious an idea such as sovereignty may be close to the Mohawk, but we contradict this intelligence with our conscious intellectual explanations, which have not been adapted to this place. They are imported, as if they were static international terms. At most we fiddle about with the surface details, leaving the core meaning the same.

For that matter, after four centuries of functioning together, we don't even look at French and English as if they have had an influence on each other. How could this long co-existence not have led to very different senses of understanding and intention in each language? Of course, they have profoundly influenced each other. And we know this. And our politics and our laws actually try to express these influences, as do some of our music and plays and poetry and novels.

But there is almost no formal discussion of the implications of such influence. Our universities—anglophone and francophone—are largely constructed as pale imitations of European models led by language. And so ideas—to say nothing of literature and history—are separated out by language, as if that were the ultimate statement of meaning, as if an Algerian novel had more to say to a francophone or a Sri Lankan novel had more to say to an anglophone just because it was written in *their* language, even if the experiences and influences are completely different. That is the way culture is taught in our universities. I'll come back to the question of the colonial mind later, but it is hard to think of anything more colonial than to deal with civilization as if it unfolds principally via a language, the shape of which is set elsewhere. Even when there is much protest about the importance of Canadianisms in English and French, it is almost always treated as a linguistically limited phenomenon. In other words, these particularities are seen as derivatives from the motherland English or French, but not as meanings derived from two linguistic groups living and working together and so influencing each other's tongue.

If we have difficulty accepting the profound meaning of this English-French crossover, it is even less surprising that we don't deal with the Aboriginal influence on both. And yet, if we accept the idea that our civilization has been built upon three pillars and so has a triangular foundation, that must mean something. And the central meaning must be the effect on our thinking.

Was Parti Québécois (PQ) founder René Lévesque's sense of sovereignty closer to the Mohawk sense or to that expressed in theoretically international dictionaries such as *Le Robert* or *Oxford?* Was his sense expressed accurately anywhere in our studies of political philosophy? Again, this whole field is treated in Canada as if it were centred on international norms, which are actually neither international nor norms. One of the great tricks of today's virtual empires—in which communications and corporations replace the occupying of vast territories around the world with troops—is that they present the meanings produced by their personal experience as being disinterested and geography free. And they use their long historic catalogue of writers and thinkers as the footnote proof of their neutrality. What we are often dealing with are simply concepts developed for circumstances very different to ours. And if this question of meaning was never clarified in French, it isn't surprising that the confusion is even greater in English.

When you look at how our federalism works at its best, as opposed to how we formally describe it, the Mohawk idea of how things should be done—harmony achieved through balanced relationships—seems much more accurate than the linear, carefully measured, theoretically rational assumptions of common or civil law. Equally, the European-derived laws have great difficulty adapting their defined concepts to different eras. Yet in the Aboriginal manner Canada seems to have eased its way into a relatively flexible approach.

It is that history of Canada, that Canadian experience, which our courts, and in particular our Supreme Court, have gravitated toward, both in their interpretation of Aboriginal rights and treaties, but also in their approach to justice for the country as a whole. It is as if we are slowly rediscovering a reality about ourselves that was swept out of sight by the force of imported European-style nationalisms. And if we still have trouble recognizing this old and new connection, it is in part because we continue to be inundated by that European idea of nationalism via the constant drumbeat of U.S. films, television, magazines, indeed most details of our neighbour's beliefs.

And I notice, increasingly, debates in Quebec in favour of pure secularism or laicité. Much of what is said is mere parroting of old-fashioned Parisian arguments. This purism came out of France's very particular two-century-long battle between violently anti-democratic forces tied to the idea of a state religion versus democratic forces, equally violent and determined to destroy all hints of religious presence in any corner of public life. By the end of it, there had been many coups, dictatorships and civil wars, and a serious percentage of the population had been killed by their fellow citizens. These very French arguments about education and religion seem to have made their way into a remarkably different culture simply because the only other major French-language interlocutor is France, and France, as do the United States and Britain, advances itself as a virtual empire of universal principles and norms, which are merely the evocation of their national experience.

There are those among us who will interpret my statements as classic Canadian anti-Americanism or anti-Parisianism, and either be pleased or displeased. My statements are neither. French arguments are French arguments. They apply to a history filled with brilliant initiatives, political instability and violence, interesting democratic experiments interrupted by a variety of dictatorships, but also by remarkable successes. France simply has a different history to us. The United States has the right to its myths and its sense of itself. That it thinks of itself as the only true child of Europe and the only true child of the Americas is entirely its privilege. These are the collective unconsciousnesses of other people with their own fascinating experiences through time. It doesn't follow that a deafening drumbeat of their myths is helpful to Canadians trying to work out what is true about ourselves and our experience.

6

Progress

If we misrepresent what we are, we cannot think about ourselves in a useful way. What is a useful reflection of self? One that creates the context and the self-confidence for further reflection and action.

The European view of human progress, which includes the U.S. view, is a civilization that begins with hunting and gathering, leaves that behind for the sedentary pastoral life and in turn leaves the farm behind for the always intended destination of high civilization: urban life. In Europe, only the Romantic Movement rejected this idea of progress. Stories of people who do not follow it play an important role in U.S. mythology. They are either symbols of an ideal lost past or they are doomed rebels. But love it or hate it, they are left behind on the unstoppable road of progress.

Canadians have generally allowed this three-step view to be applied to our own studies of progress. It has always been here, nagging us, as if we couldn't understand how a proper civilization ought to be organized. Go back to the eighteenth and nineteenth centuries in French Canada. One-third to one-half of the men regularly disappeared from the pastoral village into "le pays d'en haut"—the mysterious borderless world of rivers and forests and *Indians*, to trade in furs or bring down trees. The Catholic Church and the civil authorities disapproved, in particular the church. It is usually explained that this disapproval was all about its loss of control over these men and the fear that they were *going native*.

More important is what lay behind those utilitarian fears: a conviction that civilization was an idea of progress—a progress from which these men were regressing all the way back to the primitive state of hunting and gathering. The first hint that this idea of *regression* and primitive didn't really work for Canada can be found in what made Canadians rich versus what left them poor. Until well into the nineteenth century, hunting was the central source of wealth. Farming, a theoretically more advanced undertaking, was a recipe for poverty. So by going native, these men became a little less poor and had more control over their lives.

Take this a step further. There are two elements in the Western idea of progress that don't work for Canada. These elements, if we integrate them as ours, undermine any hope we have of understanding and absorbing the Aboriginal role and therefore any possibility of describing ourselves as we really are.

First, we can never fulfill the requirements of a healthy Western Civilization by moving from nomadism to a sedentary rural life to an urban life, at which point the land retreats into a background of recreation, weekend houses and a bit of hobby farming. We can't do this because our country consists of five regions, three of which cannot alter their fundamental purpose.

Even the other two regions don't quite fit the European model. First there are our urban regions, in which most people live. They appear to fit the Western ideal. Yet the longer you look, the less typical they seem. For a start, our cities are not the inheritance of the rural. They are gradually turning into primary sites of experimentation for the mixing of races and cultures. Unlike cities in Europe or the United States, in which interesting mixtures are also being created, ours are entirely intentional experiments and are built around an initial assumption of shared citizenship. More than 85 percent of Canadian immigrants become citizens. The U.S. figure is 40 percent. The European figures are much lower. That our approach is intentional doesn't mean it is thought through or always well done. But the intent sets the pattern for the shaping of these communities.

The rural region in some ways resembles the European model. Many people have left their farms for cities. But, as in countries such as Australia and the United States, most of the rural is not a nearby hinterland surrounding the cities. It is great expanses, each with its own logic. And even though they follow the industrialized model of farming, focused on quantity and high-tech efficiency, Canadian farmers cannot function without subsidies or set production levels. This suggests that progress toward the urban and urban methods is not necessarily progress. What's more, neither the urban nor the rural have been able to turn themselves into Canada's underlying source of wealth.

What remains is three-quarters of the country—that mass of land upon which our wealth is once again increasingly dependent. There is the commodity region—a great east-west sweep of forest, rock, lake and mountain that can never be either rural or urban. But it accounts for about one-third of our gross domestic product (GDP)—forestry, mining, oil and gas. Above it is a second great east-west sweep, more or less beyond the treeline, which could be called the *barrens* or the Mid-North. It is contributing ever more heavily through mining to our GDP, and its role, too, is immutable. It will never be rural or urban. It won't even be forested. Finally, there is the Far North, the most astonishing part of our land. Few Canadians will ever go there. Yet if countries have responsibilities to the larger world, what you might call historic responsibilities, a good part of ours is concentrated in the Arctic. It is not only fragile, it is the bellwether of our environmental well-being. In this massive territory—the size of India—there are some fifty thousand people, most of them Inuit—an historic high. It is now more densely inhabited than ever before in history.

I often hear urban dwellers talking as if this North—while fascinating in a vague way—is only a distant responsibility or burden. To take too much interest in these vast, *empty* regions is to regress into a romantic-wilderness view of Canada. We are urban dwellers now, high-tech and postmodern.

Perhaps. But without these three regions—without taking them seriously as a stable purpose in and of themselves—we are hardly a country. We would certainly lose the basis of our wealth—the continuing foundation of our urban well-being. We would also lose our central role in the geographic and environmental reality of the world. To accept in any way—in particular intellectually or emotionally—the Euro-U.S.

idea of progress is to cut ourselves off from our particular reality—to cut ourselves off from ourselves, our real life in our real country.

These territories are increasingly under the stewardship of Aboriginal citizens or a mix of Aboriginal and other northerners. This is therefore our shared reality. When I say we must reintegrate the Aboriginal reality into the core of how we imagine ourselves, this includes developing a very different concept of progress. What's more, a willingness to reimagine progress would actually put us in the forefront of an international movement. That reimagining is exactly what people are reaching for in a world faced by environmental crises. In many parts of the globe, this means turning away from what had seemed to be their reality—the reality of their culture, philosophy and economics. For Canada, it simply means accepting our reality and doing something with it. In spite of this, we seem more hesitant than populations who probably have a great deal more to lose in the short term by such a change. Our reluctance reveals how confused we are.

I said there were two elements in the Western idea of progress that were problematic for Canada. The second has been laid out by the thinker Hugh Brody, who has devoted his life to trying to understand peoples such as the Inuit and their relationship to Western culture. Brody's rethinking was this. We believe in "stereotypes of *nomadic* hunters and *settled* farmers." "[O]ne society is highly mobile, with a strong tendency to both small- and large-scale nomadism, whereas the other is highly settled, tending to stay firmly in one particular area of territory." And the settled society is assumed to be more developed.

Except it is the farmers who move about and the hunter-gatherers who have always been settled. They have very carefully occupied three places in a year according to seasons—the same three, year after year, taking what they needed from each. But if you look at agriculture in Canada over the last few hundred years, you see enormous instability—areas farmed out, soil exhausted, land abandoned because it was poorly chosen in the first place or because land elsewhere has produced cheaper products. That instability continues. In other words, we have been following a short-term, highly nomadic approach to agriculture. And the same is true of commodities exploration and industry. Mines are opened, the contents emptied out, and they are closed. Nearby communities prosper, then are left to wither. Species—fish, game animals—are fished out, hunted out and the exploiters move on. Villages and towns wind down or struggle to find a new purpose. In Jeannette Armstrong's words:

> Out of the belly of Christopher's ship
> a mob bursts
> Running in all directions
> Pulling furs off animals
> Shooting buffalo
> Shooting each other
> left and right …
>
> Civilization has reached
> the promised land.

If the hunter-gatherers were stable for so long it was because they had, in Brody's words, developed a highly sophisticated "combination of detailed knowledge and intuition." They needed to. And they needed to see themselves as only "one of the reciprocal forces in a harmonious universe"—only one part of a much larger order.

This argument is not about the superiority of one culture over another or the true nature of civilization or the right idea of progress. It is about appropriate ways of life in appropriate places.

Here is a perfect example of how we can be freed to imagine ourselves if we walk away from standard Euro-U.S. concepts, which by their very assumptions make a place such as Canada impossible. Why? Because with a central Aboriginal component, two international languages, cultures that are not separate but are not intended to become one, you have a non-monolithic culture. The Western idea is all about narrowing our focus as civilizations. But once this deterministic idea of progress is rethought, the complex, non-monolithic result seems perfectly natural and appropriate.

If, for example, our agriculture were imagined differently—less as a knock-off of nineteenth-century industrial methods and more as a purpose in and of itself, functioning not as an expression of international economic theory, but as production appropriate to its place, well then, it would be less nomadic, more settled and far more profitable.

Brody's arguments were built upon decades of work by others—work that ultimately culminated in revolutionary publications in the 1960s and 1970s. The message was ignored. There was no desire in the West in general and in Canada in particular to think differently about our reality. With *The Other Side of Eden* in 2001, Brody made an attempt, brilliant and lucid, to relaunch this more sensible view of how societies work. He had an effect, although it was more underground and gradual than apparent. Perhaps now, almost another decade later, with a growing sense of environmental fragility, people are more open to accepting that the world works in a different way than that suggested by the standard Western arguments.

What could help in Canada is the amplified role of language and non-linear intellectual concepts in Aboriginal culture. After all, oral cultures are centred on *the word*—remembering the word, mixing the words of the sacred with those of the story, being able to reimagine the word through generations of fire-keepers, keepers of the words and the concepts. One of the standard complaints of the British and the Canadian officials who negotiated treaties with the First Nations was that the latter talked on and on. Had our negotiators paid any attention to *the other*, they would have realized that the First Nations leaders talked on because they were not engaged in a goal-oriented process that, like the Europeans' commercial contracts, is concluded by a transfer of ownership. The First Nations leaders weren't even negotiating owner-ship. Instead, they were putting on the table concepts of complex, inclu-sive, balanced existence on the land. The newcomers were pressed for time because they didn't have much to say and had only come to conclude what they thought of as a legal transfer. They were driven by a simple utilitarian desire for ownership. This was the straightforward, low-level stuff of Western property law described behind the grandiose and romantic idea of Queen Victoria as everyone's mother.

There was one other important element revolving around language in these encounters. The First Nations had protocols they had to follow in order for agreements with others to take a proper shape and so become real. They were not seeking opportunistic deals. They wanted balanced arrangements that could work for a long time, providing both parties were prepared to keep on discussing and adjusting on a regular basis— usually once a year—to maintain the appropriate equilibrium. It sounds just like Canadian federalism. The protocols in question were expressed through complex linguistic concepts.

In Cree alone, you find a vast array of concepts central to these protocols—concepts that describe how people can live together. These are not in the first instance about ownership or competition or control. They are about sustainable human relationships. More important still, they are about harmony in a world in which humans are only one element among a vast panoply of dynamic forces. In all of their formal sessions with British and Canadian officials, the Cree were negotiating on the basis of Witaskewin—how people, not necessarily coming out of the same nation, can live together. It is an idea of carefully negotiated and continually renegotiated peaceful co-existence. That idea of co-existence is based on a related concept of sharing, which includes the idea of sharing the space, and is dependent upon Wahakohtoin, which means relationships that work because they follow a complex, unwritten code of ethics. The outcome is intended to be Miyo-wicehtowin—good, healthy, happy, respectful relationships.

One of the oldest Inuit traditions is that "the first thing created out of the primeval chaos and darkness was a word." If anything, oral cultures are more deeply intellectual than today's reigning form of utilitarian linear society in the West. The oral tradition is constantly in search of equilibriums, while the written slips easily toward the truths of parsed details in which any sense of the whole is lost. It is toward those equilibriums expressed through the oral that our Supreme Court has been slowly making its way, while shoving the linear, parsed details to a secondary level.

In other words, we are making progress, even breakthroughs, toward normalizing these Aboriginal ideas. And we are progressing in spite of the intense resistance of our governmental and intellectual structures. What is fascinating is that the forces driving us come from seemingly unrelated worlds. For a start, the Aboriginals are increasingly effective at putting forward their point of view and making the mechanisms of power respond or adjust. Then there is the world of the arts, which at its best is attracted by new ways of imagining. Finally, there are the courts, which have taken the lead in helping the country work out how to recognize itself.

On the other hand, there is the world of formalized thought, which still presents the serious blockage of a colonial mindset. Yes, there are many within the universities who are working for a change in this way of thinking. But what remains dominant is the Western canon. Actually, what dominates is rarely broad enough to constitute the Western canon. The wilfully maintaining of barriers of language and references mean that you are usually dealing with the Anglo-U.S. canon or the French, as in Paris, canon. These surprisingly separate worlds of exclusive truth don't take serious account of each other, let alone much in the Italian or Germanic or other Western traditions, let alone anything in the Islamic, Buddhist or Confucian world. If you look at the books taught in particular places, you find they largely represent a narrow outcropping of one particular old imperial view.

If you look at the particular question of progress and how we understand it, you will find that we have begun to change our way of thinking over the last half-century, mainly thanks to people such as Brody, who work outside the academy. But no sooner did the argument that hunter-gatherer civilizations have something to contribute begin to settle in than a whole new wave built up from within the academy set on demonstrating the inevitability of the standard linear, highly written approach, with its underlying European assumptions. Rationality was, as always, much invoked as our only bulwark against the romanticism of any other approach.

Nevertheless, over the last half-century Canada has begun crawling toward a sense of the essential Aboriginal role in our civilization. The most obvious sign is the extent to which their art has burst into the mainstream of our creative imagination. West Coast and Inuit art in only a few decades have become central to how Canadians represent themselves—that is, how we imagine ourselves. The Great Hall in the Museum of Civilization in Ottawa is central to how we imagine ourselves. Inuit sculpture, whether in its art version or in tourist shops, is central to how we imagine ourselves. Inukshuks, popping up spontaneously on cliffs along the Trans-Canada, are an existential expression of that imagination. These are all conceptual images. They are a physical emanation of ideas. They are consciously attached to Aboriginal concepts of the sacred, of land, of the human role in a larger context of existence. How is it that the vast majority of Canadians, who are neither from the North or the West Coast, have slipped so easily into treating this art as images that could represent them, evocations of their inner self?

The first answer is that we find something true in this art. The second is that we have little trouble in identifying that truth, or rather identifying with it, because we are ourselves in various ways part of the same civilization. The fundamental influence of Aboriginals on our civilization is revealed in the ease with which we have adopted their art as an expression of ourselves.

7

Learning to Imagine Ourselves

This adoption of the Aboriginal image as a shared expression of us all is not the same thing as the normalizing of the Aboriginal reality. Normalizing means organizing ourselves and acting as if it is central to our whole civilization. It means rethinking our language at multiple levels and tying how we act to that language. It means linking how we informally and formally think of ourselves. Today, the formal ways in which we describe our actions—whether in politics, the arts, the economy, our social organization—have little to do with how we try to act. Why? Because we are still trying to function on borrowed language. So normalizing means uncovering what in the Aboriginal reality is central to how we actually think of ourselves at some almost unconscious or instinctual level. Once we uncover that, we will find it far easier to deal with how we imagine ourselves and how we wish to act.

The first step in this normalization involves picking out the strategic elements that shape how we imagine ourselves. We can then see whether each of these is linked to the Aboriginal nature of Canada. What are these strategic elements?

Our obsession with egalitarianism. Our desire to maintain a balance between individuals and groups. The delight we take in playing with our non-monolithic idea of society—a delight in complexity. Our tendency to try to run society as an ongoing negotiation, which must be related to our distaste for resolving complexities. Our preference, behind a relatively violent language of public debate, for consensus—again an expression of society as a balance of complexity, a sort of equilibrium.

Our intuition that behind the formal written and technical face of society lies something more important, which we try to get at through the oral and through complex relationships. Our sense that the clear resolution of differences will lead to injustice and even violence. And related to that, our preference for something that the law now calls *minimal impairment,* which means the obligation of those with authority to do as little damage as possible to people and to rights when exercising that authority.

Over the last few years, Canadians seem to have been talking more and more about egalitarianism. We seem to be asking ourselves why it is so important to this society. Some ask this sympathetically. Others ask it with annoyance, their attention turned to the pleasures of a class-based society that admires and rewards such things as private education and private health care. What I notice is that on all sides this discussion is tied to the tension between individual and group rights and powers.

Neither of these ideas of social structure—egalitarianism and the individual-group balance—comes to us from Britain. There are elements of them within the English and Scottish socialist tradition, but in both places these are tied to a very specific sort of class struggle and so has always seemed an artificial transplant when it is invoked or proposed here.

Nor do these concepts come from France, where the concept of equality is highly legalistic and played out against a society that, through structures very different to those of the English, nevertheless uses forms of class to shape power. If there is a tension in France between individualism and something else, that something else is the overwhelming power of the centralized state.

The theory and reality of the United States has always had more to do with individual opportunity—not counterweighted by a great deal when it comes to individual or group responsibility, rights and opportunities—which is quite different from egalitarianism and does not involve a tension between individual and group rights. Interestingly enough, the often highly successful attempts of the United States at social programming have been inspired if anything by the old English and French socialist approaches. And this is because the U.S. class system often seems to be a weird combination of the French and the British.

What then are the sources of Canadian egalitarianism and our strange attempt at a positive tension between the individual and groups? There is certainly some of it in the habits the Scots brought with them—in particular the northern and Highland Scots who came with the Hudson's Bay Company and with the British forces in 1759. The German religious minorities, who made up so many of the Loyalists, may also have contributed something.

On the other hand, it is not helpful to attribute our taste for egalitarianism to the functioning together of a multitude of immigrant groups. That would be reading contemporary assumptions about multiculturalism or interculturalisme—the word most often used in Quebec—into a past that was very differently organized. Besides, there were broad mixes of immigrants elsewhere in the world and yet there the outcome was quite different.

Part of it could be put down to the marginal, difficult conditions newcomers found here. Canada was poor. Population was scarce. This required great individual effort combined with group co-operation. Egalitarianism was a sensible outcome. The Family Compact idea of an English-style society was ridiculous in the circumstances. And the seigneurial class system, which dragged on in French Canada until the middle of the nineteenth century, was equally ridiculous.

That, of course, was then. Canadians no longer think of their country as poor. In part that is a positive outcome of our success. But it has also meant a return of the Family Compact, indeed seigneurial, colonial inferiority complex. It seems to re-emerge each time there is a growth of great wealth in small groups that, having made the money, have no particular long-term purpose for themselves. Some of the new moneyed class doesn't want to believe that public health care can be improved, because they want the sort of private health care available to the people they admire in the empires. Some of them want to decorate their children with the old-fashioned accoutrements of private education and private universities. Yet their numbers remain low, and most Canadians still find this kind of thinking pretentious and a waste of money. Certainly these children will not be helped in their careers by having been separated out at a formative age from a more organic and shared experience in the public school system.

When Pierre Trudeau first introduced his Charter of Rights, many felt it had a U.S.-European liberal air about it. In other words, it tended toward legalistic views of equality and individualism, which in countries such as France and the United States have produced an unexpectedly formalized class system. By the time the negotiations over the Charter were finished, its imported liberalism had been buried in a purposely unresolved tension between individuals and groups. Since then, the Charter decisions of the courts have anchored that Canadian reality ever more deeply into how we function. The individual-group tension is what marks the difference between egalitarianism and equality, that is, the predominance of individual rights versus the idea of fairness.

The fascinating missing piece in all of this is the originating concept for the Canadian approach. It is all very well to search for the explanation of human behaviour in actions forged by particular circumstances or crises. Usually these turn out to be more the traffic signals than the roadbed. New ideas—particularly new ideas about how to organize a society—don't just pop out of nowhere, even in a crisis.

The most obvious origins in Canada are Aboriginal. Again, the newcomers—the francophones from the seventeenth century on, the Scots from the late seventeenth but increasingly the eighteenth century on and the German religious minorities from the eighteenth century on— all settled here in difficult, isolating circumstances and made their way thanks to the First Nations and later the Métis. Their relationships evolved over time, often for the worse. But it was a slow evolution, a matter of centuries. Ways of relating to *the other* and ways of doing things settled in, became habit, became culture.

What was it that the newcomers experienced with the First Nations? A deeply rooted egalitarianism that included a clearly defined sense of individual responsibility—a meritocratic individualism tied to a fierce sense of independence. This was in turn tied to what might at first seem to be a contradiction. Marie Brent, from a well-known B.C. Métis family, wrote in her memoirs less than a century ago of how individual Salish—one of the many B.C. nations—had a "hatred of domination, of anything which interferes with his personal freedom." In 1623, Brother Gabriel Sagard, who lived among the Huron on Georgian Bay, described the same thing. "Huron war chiefs could not order their warriors into battle, but had to persuade them." Yet these same Huron were horrified by the division between rich and poor among the French. A society that did not look after its own suggested "unintelligent" people—"ill-balanced" people.

It is true that both the pure hunter societies and the partially agricultural, such as the Huron or the Mi´kmaq or the Nisga'a, lived in smaller groups than we do. There was no room for people who didn't carry their weight. And suffering was too close to be ignored. As Leonard Nelson of the Roseau River Anishinabe put it to the royal commission, their word for the concept of government actually means their "way of life." And that way was inclusive. The early French missionaries arrived filled with certainty that they spoke for a superior civilization. Most of them quickly altered their view as they noticed the Aboriginals' unusual sense of community and the built-in patience that meant each person had to be listened to. This balance of individualism—which could be understood as constantly proving yourself—with "the practice of sharing," and the resulting belief in group interests did not fade away. What I've just cited is a late twentieth-century Dene approach. It is very close to the Métis idea of government that took form in 1873 at Red River—the form of government that would produce Manitoba.

According to the Nisga'a leader Joseph Gosnell, his people call this the concept of "our common bowl." It is not charity, it is community. I remember being on a state visit to Latin America in 2001 when Chief Gosnell was part of the Canadian delegation. It was fascinating to watch how quickly the rest of the delegation—leading politicians, business people, creators—organized themselves so that the Nisga'a leader would be their unofficial public spokesperson. It wasn't simply that he is a remarkable man. They were all in their own way remarkable people. But he had a way of describing what they believed or wanted to point out that seemed to satisfy everyone. It was as if he were combining these ideas of egalitarianism, strong individualism and inviolable community standards without effort, as if this unusual equilibrium were natural.

That such an approach began in a civilization of small communities might suggest that it could not be applied today. Perhaps. But principles that work for small societies are not necessarily unadaptable by large groups. After all, Western philosophy is almost entirely based on theories developed in tiny communities such as Athens. How large was the society that knew the Greek myths or Socrates' arguments or the Old Testament or St. Paul or St. Augustine? Besides, the indigenous population was not particularly small, with several million in Canada before the European diseases struck. And they had complex relationships among themselves, often based on several nations summering together where rivers met.

The indigenous idea of egalitarianism balanced by a tension between the individual and the group goes back to their idea of society as an inclusive circle that can be enlarged. And if such an adaptation is handled right, all sides should be able to benefit. For example, Inuit women tended to testify to the royal commission that under the new system of Nunavut they had far more power than under traditional culture. First Nations women, on the other hand, tended to protest that most negotiations for self-government were limited by the imported nineteenth-century assumptions of the Indian Act and so gave more power to men, while the traditional system had been much more balanced.

In the territory of Nunavik in Northern Quebec, each village or town has a community walk-in freezer, stocked with food caught during the caribou migration and char run. As well, people who have killed more than they need drop the surplus off at this community freezer. Two men are in charge of each of these freezer systems and ensure that everything is neatly gutted and butchered. One section of the freezer is reserved for older people. When anyone in the community is short of meat or fish, they drop by and take something. There is no paperwork for givers or for receivers, no thank you's, no sense of guilt. This is not charity. And no one seems to abuse the situation. It is all about seeking egalitarianism through the balance between individualism and the community. The community assumes its responsibility to share. Individuals exercise their independence. And their dignity is intact. This is a reimagining for larger communities of the old concept of sharing in traditional camps. I can only think how superior this approach is to our food banks, which, although born of goodwill, ultimately come out of the old tradition of charity/humiliation. Our single-tier health-care system, on the other hand, reflects that balance of community responsibility with individual independence and dignity. Somehow the idea emerged from our long experience here. It is a non-charity, inclusive approach that is not derivative of what was done in Europe. The British National Health Service was built around their class system so that the elite would have separate, parallel health services. The French system was a more sophisticated creation. It is two-tier. But the public part contains a wonderful meritocratic structure, which simply builds in a certain kind of treatment for the dominant classes. The private part deals mainly with the softer medical needs of the elite. And the United States took the class/charity model to its extreme with its public services limited to the poor, in the nineteenth-century European tradition.

I'll come back to the way in which a part of our elite has worked over the past fifteen or so years to drag us toward a two-tiered, class-based health-care system. The point here is the originality of our single-tiered system and, in Western terms, its atypical expression of the egalitarian idea.

You find the same pattern in our non-monolithic idea of how a society can run. The relative ease with which this has developed—not without racism and exclusion, but nevertheless the relative ease—suggests roots that go beyond the classic Western immigration experience. How is it that we morph without major crises as new groups join us? Where are the real origins of what for the last few decades we have called multiculturalism or interculturalisme?

The francophones and anglophones who came here found a complex web of First Nations and learned to live as part of that web of dozens and dozens of different nations and cultures. This indigenous system had always had its fair share of wars and rivalries, although its violent clashes tended to be minimized by the idea that no victory could remove a rival.

No solutions could come out of war, only slight readjustments of relationships.

So the underlying idea was an acceptance of complexity. Put another way, the terms for living without war were based on the acceptance that clarity could not be achieved. The First Nations therefore designed relationships that used complexity to save face on all sides. It was a profoundly non-monolithic approach that carefully avoided those concepts of victory and of racial clarity central to post-medieval European politics. The Confederacy of the Five Nations, to take a single example, was based on the Great Law, which said that clans transcended the boundaries of the nations. Thus members had two personalities, belonged in two ways.

Across North America, First Nations shared the idea that people were linked primarily by relationships, not blood. Many of the nations had ritual adoption to replace people who were killed. This often involved captives taken in battle being traded as slaves to another nation, where, through difficult trials, they became someone else. This might seem a violent form of transformation to most people today. But first, among Europeans at that time, practices of torture and execution were more common than among Aboriginals and at least as violent in their details. Second, unlike the Aboriginal practices, they rarely involved any concept of redemption or rebirth. Third, European torture ended in death. The indigenous approach often included a belief that people could pass through a metamorphosis into a different form of belonging—they were not locked into a single role determined by race. They wanted the transformed person alive and active in their new role.

Beyond these trials of metamorphosis, the general approach of the First Nations to people from outside their nation was that a relationship needed to be worked out so that they could deal with each other. Relationships with people from other nations were formalized by defining a place for them in each nation's family. It was, in this state of mind that Aboriginals entered into treaty negotiations. What the Europeans treated as contractual utilitarianism was, on the First Nations side, all about creating kinship within a larger circle.

Guy Buchholtzer, an independent scholar who has long been associated with West Coast First Nations, argues that "multiculturalism is an inherently Canadian tradition." The creation of "a web of relationships between culture, language and identity" was the norm in First Nations society. On the Northwest Coast (what is now mainly British Columbia), there were some forty languages belonging to a dozen linguistic families. These nations considered themselves to be very different one from another, yet the relationships of stories, myths and economic roles linked them into a larger culture, a complex, highly textured one. "In the circle of life, the circumference nurtures the centre."

This was the dominant atmosphere within which the Europeans began to establish themselves early in the seventeenth century. The complexity we have come rightly to see as a Canadian invention was indeed the well-established setup of the First Nations. It was into this world that the one-third to one-half of the men of New France who spent time out of the small European settlements along the St. Lawrence had to fit, as well as the Hudson's Bay Company employees and a good percentage of the Loyalists.

From a Western point of view, one key element was missing. Neither before nor after the arrival of Europeans were the indigenous peoples who lived in this myriad of nations and languages linked together or separated by race, certainly not as the West understands race. The royal commission pointed out that belonging might come from "marriage, adoption, ritual affiliation, long-standing residence, cultural integration and group assistance." Rene Lamothe, of Fort Simpson, spoke of the Dene: "The Land is the boss and will teach whoever she wants." This sense of place over people or at least of place in balance with people isn't surprising in an enormous, difficult territory. That tension is still with us and it constantly undermines the classic Western human-centred world view, which in turn fed the ideas of monolithic cultures and race.

Tied closely to that sense of place over race are a series of creation myths that are the exact opposite of the Judeo-Christian ones. "We are," Thomas King says, faced by a choice between "a world in which creation is a solitary, individual act or a world in which creation is a shared activity; a world that begins in harmony and slides towards chaos or a world that begins in chaos and moves towards harmony." The first choice—the Judeo-Christian-Islamic—encourages a search for clear answers, a Manichean world of right and wrong, good and evil, winners and losers. It is a powerful base myth because people are constantly driven to re-establish the perfection of the past. The other choice—the indigenous—does not suggest that there is some possible ideal situation. None has ever existed. The Manichean is therefore both innocent and dangerous. Central mythological figures such as the Trickster contain the complexity of reality. He is not pure or a virgin or a martyr or a hero to be followed. He is us. And he, along with the basic idea of seeking an impossible equilibrium, encourages the idea of non-monolithic societies.

Canadians carry both the Aboriginal and the European tradition. We have become rich in part because of that Western Manichean drive. And ideas of exclusivity and race were certainly introduced here with a vengeance. Yet those tendencies have been limited by our other tradition. And today the delight we take in our non-monolithic society suggests that our Aboriginal foundations are rising to the surface. At the same time, the sense of discomfort in the country over environmental and economic policy shows that much of the tension between our two basic forces remains unconscious.

And so we work hard to fit our non-monolithic culture into a revised version of our European liberal monolithic inheritance. But that requires twisting ourselves into a knot in search of Western justifications for non-Western actions. Of course, there are European liberal elements in our way of life, but our deep roots are here not there; they are far more indigenous than liberal. The source of our non-monolithic—and for that matter our egalitarian—sense of ourselves lies in the structures of the Aboriginal maze the Europeans found here and into which they eased themselves over hundreds of years. You have to work hard to avoid this argument. And you have to turn your curiosity away from our local reality. Both parties were changed. Both gained. Both lost. But our deep roots are indigenous, and there lie the most interesting explanations for what we are and what we can be.

In all of this, our courts are far ahead of our political scientists, politicians and philosophers. Why? Because the courts have now understood the First Nations' assumptions at the time of the treaties. They have traced those assumptions further back through their shared history with the early immigrants. And they have based a series of revolutionary judgments on a normalization and actualization of that long history. It is difficult to describe as anything other than revolutionary the way they have disinterred our history in order to explain a quite different approach to justice.

As a result, what the judges have fixed upon are precisely the Aboriginal roots of Canadian civilization: egalitarianism, individual and group rights and obligations, balanced complexity, reconciliation, inclusion, continuing relationships, minority rights.

In 1999, in the Marshall case, the Supreme Court pointed out that "the subtext of the [1760] Mi'kmaq treaties was reconciliation and mutual advantage." Today, we stretch and deform the Western tradition whenever we talk about a non-monolithic society or interculturalisme or multiculturalism or diversity or carrying multiple personalities. Why? Because what we are talking about is reconciliation and mutual advantage. To understand this you have only to watch the difficulties our European allies are having today in dealing with what they often call migrants.

Our non-monolithic idea of society was exactly what the Cree understood when they talked of the laws governing good relations—Miyowicehtowin. They understood this and still understand it to be about ongoing reconciliation in a circle capable of including *the other*.

On June 21, 2007, just as indigenous people were about to become very visible on a national day of action by asserting control over roads and rails that crossed their land, and various populist papers and call-in shows were trying to provoke anger among non-Aboriginals, former national chief Ovide Mercredi chose to say publicly: "Our people are very conservative when it comes to political action. We would rather talk than demonstrate." He could have added, we would rather talk than fight. The warrior culture has always been present and powerful in First Nations history. But it was always separate from the tradition of talking, which was represented by the political leaders, the spiritual leaders, the elders and the fire-keepers. These were two parallel streams with separate leadership. Violence was always an available option in First Nations culture, as it was in European. But the separation of roles meant that its use would almost always be felt as a failure of the political and spiritual stream.

In Western terms, such a separation would be seen as softness. In indigenous terms, talking, negotiating, developing relationships, enlarging the circle was all about intellectual superiority, the long view and the capacity to take a non-Manichean approach. If you have to fight, you fight. But that represents a failure of relationships, a failure of foreign policy, not an extension of it, as the classic European phrase would have it.

What the French found when they first made their way up the St. Lawrence, with the Hudson's Bay Company arriving not long after, but from the North, was that they were welcomed. To welcome *the other* was all about respect, because in this non-Western culture their ancestors were assumed to be as important as yours. To welcome *the other* was a ritual of human contact.

From the beginning the French grasped enough of this to settle into negotiations and so develop oral treaties, which were effectively family relationships. Champlain's declaration that they must marry each other was an attempt to show engagement. The Hudson's Bay Company followed this example. The rituals of their yearly negotiations with First Nations people wherever they traded were lengthy, formal, filled with exchanges of information and presents, formal pipe smoking, and the leaving behind of such things as the grand calumet pipe—to be smoked again the next year as a sign of long-term continuing negotiation.

These two societies could not have had more different philosophical bases. Yet their negotiations were all about each party having "to adapt and modify their practices and protocols into a single process that they both understood and accepted." The form and style of these meetings, as well as the approach to language used by both sides, were Aboriginal, from the early 1600s to the 1860s. Most important, the bookends to the negotiations were always the indigenous theory of welcome and a balanced outcome. Even if one party was weaker—and often this was the European—the protocol of relationships meant that the result should be about an equilibrium. In December 2007, the Ipperwash struggle over the control of some Aboriginal land in Southern Ontario came to an end with the return of those lands to the Chippewas. The last stage had stretched on for twelve years. During that time we saw the shooting of Dudley George, an unarmed Cree leader, by the Ontario Provincial Police, as well as disgraceful behaviour by the premier, Mike Harris. Michael Bryant, the cabinet minister who settled the mess in 2007, did so with humility and grace, but then he was on the losing side. What I noticed were the words of Sam George, the murdered man's brother, but now the clear winner: "I and my family would like to thank the people of Ontario. By returning these [lands], by keeping a treaty promise, and by honouring the memory of our brother Dudley, we are respecting each other and it shows we can be friends." Elegance, respect for *the other*. An understanding that all agreements require a balanced outcome—an equilibrium.

There is no Cree word for justice. The closest equivalent is the word for talking. The Royal Proclamation of 1763, with its introduction of the concept of Peace, Welfare and Good Government, which I will deal with in Part II, also formalized almost two centuries of talking and working together in a particular way. Once treaties began to be put on paper, the methodology of the early negotiations was an almost exact continuation of the Hudson's Bay Company approach, which had already adopted and blended in the French methods. Both the French and the Hudson's Bay Company approaches had been shaped by indigenous approaches to how civilized people should deal with one another. Highly ritualized, lengthy, filled with formalized statements of purpose, these negotiations were not about clarity and completion. They were about ongoing talks and developing relationships.

Later in the nineteenth century, when written treaties began to be signed, First Nations leaders continued to come forward to consult and negotiate. The *modern* bureaucratic view was that there was nothing more to talk about. The relationship was now contractual and the stronger party would interpret the contract. This was an attempt to apply the European approach to relationships in which contracts redefined agreements and laid out the implications in a fanlike manner. This legal framework was *meant* to create a narrow idea of loyalty as a political weapon. If you strayed from the contracts, you were in breach of them and therefore treasonous.

To understand which intellectual tradition is prevailing in the long run, you need only note that a century later Canada is busily renegotiating nineteenth-century treaties. Even more important, examine how we have come to run Canada in general. It is a process of constant negotiation in the indigenous manner. Jean Friesen, the historian and former deputy premier of Manitoba, puts it that "we have built negotiation into our way of dealing with ourselves and the world." And as she points out, the First Nations were neither gullible nor ignorant in those nineteenth- and twentieth-century negotiations. They knew exactly what they were saying and trying to do in very difficult circumstances. They took the time to put forward their understanding of what was going on. And doing so orally, at great length and in front of large groups of people, they were creating an historical body of witnesses. On the British, then Canadian side, many people understood this.

However, those who tended to be in charge—the rather mid-level officials—either didn't understand or didn't wish to. And it is precisely their Manichean, legalistic view that over the last few decades has been discounted in favour of a view truer to that developed during the earlier centuries and orally expressed at the negotiations. In a sense this is a continuation of the legal blending that began when Champlain negotiated his first treaty in 1603 at the mouth of the Saguenay.

Renée Dupuis, chief commissioner of the Indian Claims Commission and a leading writer on how Canadian law applies to First Nations questions, puts it that the "Aboriginal roots are mixed into the roots of the two European legal systems." She points out that even in formal lawmaking, Aboriginal customary law has been mixed into the legislation, sometimes unconsciously, sometimes consciously. When we look at this approach toward continuous negotiation, which has come to be *the* Canadian characteristic, it is hard to find British, French or U.S. origins. It has become what we call federalism. And when we are not sinking into colonial posturing at the international level, it best describes our foreign policy and military approaches. Over four centuries, these sorts of federal negotiations have been tough and aggressive. They fall apart only when one party takes advantage of its strength to undermine the balance or when one party defines itself as permanently aggrieved, never taking into consideration whether it is actually doing better or doing well, or how *the other* is doing. Both of these positions—the perception of the fixed overdog versus that of the fixed underdog—are profoundly nineteenth-century European. They make this country seem ungovernable because they undermine the idea of equilibrium built into our way of negotiating.

At the heart of all our talking is the idea that consensus can be reached if positions are laid out fully and enough time is taken to fairly consider what all can see. You will find this idea of consensus in almost every description of Canadian negotiations going back to the seventeenth century. And you will also find that the opposing view—that of complex situations being forced into clear solutions, which are enforced to the letter by contract—undermines our sense that consensus is possible. During the Mackenzie Pipeline debate thirty years ago, Chief Alexis Arrowmaker of the Dogrib Dene reflected that initially the Southerners "had talked to us, but now they only give us pieces of paper. [So] we were forced to have our own paper people." The Aboriginals began to hire good lawyers and to encourage their young to become lawyers. In this way, the Dene were able to out-negotiate the governmental and oil company lawyers. But their concern and a more general concern for the country is that this Europeanization of our approach to negotiation gradually makes the existence of a place such as Canada more problematic. Curiously enough it has been the Supreme Courts, both federal and provincial—institutions traditionally associated here and elsewhere in the world with the pedantically written word—that have consistently ruled in ways that reinforce the ideas of consensus and of the oral.

The normal description of Canadian history highlights key moments such as 1763—the Royal Proclamation; 1774—the Quebec Act; 1840— the Lord Durham version of how to unite Upper and Lower Canada; 1848—the Canadian reaction through responsible government, democracy and a version of federalism; 1867—Confederation. But the other way to read our civilization is to look for deeper foundations. It could be argued that the key moment in the creation of the idea of Canada was the gathering of thirteen hundred Aboriginal ambassadors from forty nations with the leaders of New France in 1701. The result was the Great Peace of Montreal. It was here that the indigenous Aboriginal ways of dealing with *the other* were consciously and broadly adopted as more appropriate than the European. Here the idea of future treaties was born. Here an approach was developed that would evolve into federalism. Sir William Johnson's great gathering of two thousand chiefs at Niagara in 1764 had been organized in order to cement the Royal Proclamation. In many ways, this was the second act in the creation of the idea of Canada—a continuation of the Great Peace of Montreal.

The idea of both was to establish a continuous equilibrium, shared interests and shared welfare. The phrase in the Great Peace was that they would all "Eat from a Common Bowl." Which is to say that relationships were about looking after one another. This is the shared foundation for equalization payments and single-tier health care and public education. What I am describing here is not the technical footnoting of particular policies, but the origins of the mindset that made them possible. I am making an argument about culture, not about mere instrumentalism.

This profound current began to re-emerge as a conscious, that is to say intentional, approach in the last quarter of the twentieth century. You can see it happening in three pivotal Supreme Court judgments— *Guerin, Delgamuukw* and *Oakes*.

In 1984, in *Guerin*, the Supreme Court reasserted a very old idea—the Honour of the Crown. This has nothing to do with someone wearing a crown. The Crown is not a person, it is a concept. The Crown is legitimacy. With the arrival of responsible government, the Crown could no longer be presented as the legitimate will of any individual, even if ministers were doing the talking. It could no longer be represented as an expression of power, legitimate or not. Instead, it gradually became an expression of legitimate authority built upon an abstract representation of the land, the place, the people and the obligation of those in authority to the land, place and people. So the Honour of the Crown is not simply the obligation to respect formal commitments. It is the responsibility of the civilization to respect its reality. In other words, the underlying idea of the Crown has nothing to do with monarchy, any more than it does with contract and ownership. The Honour of the Crown exists whether or not there is a monarchy and it overrides both contract and ownership. At its core, it is about responsibility.

As a court case, *Guerin* was all about a low level bit of misrepresentation by public officials to Aboriginals over some land in the Vancouver area that was to be sold off for a golf course. The civil servants were, if you like, doing things by the letter of the law. They were taking a pure contractual approach. In its judgment, the Supreme Court reprimanded the Crown for trying to "hide behind the language of its own document" and condemned it for breaching its fiduciary duty. The court held the Crown to standards that rose far above written contract, far beyond the letter or even the language of the law. "The issue was not one of contract, but rather conduct."

And just as the Supreme Court made it clear that its judgment was shaped by relationships predating the Royal Proclamation of 1763, so the primacy the court gave to conduct over contract has implications far beyond differences between the Crown and the First Nations. It defines the general responsibility of the state to the country and to the people. The maintenance of the Honour of the Crown is meant to prevent particular politicians of a particular day from using a panic or a fashion to override the broad public good. To put this another way, the Honour of the Crown is our tiller and it is intended to maintain an equilibrium in society.

With the *Guerin* decision, the court brought together two of the strategic elements in our society—the roles of consensus and of the oral. Consensus in the U.S. and European tradition is used to mean agreement. If you look at statements by Thomas Jefferson or James Madison or by a wide variety of French leaders, consensus is used as an evocation of loyalty to the nation. The implication is that fractious minorities— whether ethnic groups or those with different opinions—must find ways to fall into line with the majority for the good of the whole. It's a question of loyalty. Consensus is used to describe the healthy functioning of a monolithic society.

The Aboriginal idea of consensus is quite different. Being a spatial rather than a linear concept, it has to do with there being an interrelated place for continuing differences inside the great circle. It is, if you like, the Honour of the Crown or the conduct of the Crown that makes this possible. And because the oral is also spatial and not goal oriented in a linear way, it does not readily narrow relationships and exclude differences. Rather, it gives people the time and the space to work out how to maintain or develop relationships.

And so the Maher Arar case, in which a Canadian was sent to prison and tortured in Syria by U.S. authorities with the co-operation of Canadian authorities on the basis of incorrect information that the Canadians had not bothered to verify, was all about the Honour of the Crown. There are still security *experts* in Ottawa whispering off the record about damning information too sensitive to be revealed, but they are not and never were capable of meeting the standards of the shared public good in a democracy.

Decades before, Justices Jack Sisson and William Morrow in a series of rulings refused "to place the law in a strait-jacket" in the Arctic. They believed in the Honour of the Crown. In the process, they invented new approaches to justice that are now common in the south. Their judgments withstood appeals or the threat of appeal because they reflected conduct, not contract.

The continued existence of homelessness and widespread poverty in Canada is all about selfishness and public laziness hiding behind contract—that is, defining public instrumentalism in such a way that homelessness and poverty are said to be beyond action by the state. This is the single greatest Dishonour to the Crown today—a failure of our civilization.

It is a particularly deep failure because it can be seen as such even if contextualized back through our history to those early conversations between the First Nations and the French, when the former were shocked by the acceptance of poverty in European class-based societies.

Delgamuukw in 1997 was the second judgment. Here, the Supreme Court gave oral evidence an equal weight to the written. There was no philosophical discussion about the broader implications of this decision for Canada, but the justices had in effect swept away the European concepts of progress. Why? Because the idea of *the written* is intimately linked to the idea of societies passing from an oral hunting society to a partly oral agrarian society to a dominantly written urban society. Suddenly Canada was representing itself—through that most written of things, a Supreme Court judgment—as a non-linear society, one that could contain the reality of those three stages, not as stages but as stable elements in a complicated civilization within a great circle. The justices explained that oral evidence could have the same weight as written or even greater. Why? Because it had been endlessly repeated in public and in that way constituted as a form of group memory—and therefore was capable both of exactitude and of expressing broader purpose. In saying so, they noted that oral history is not linear, not human centred. It is "tangential to the ultimate purpose of the fact-finding process at trial—the determination of the historical truth"—because it sees history and truth in a very different context. In part the Court said we must be "sensitive to the Aboriginal perspective" and that this could only be accomplished by accepting the oral.

But something much more profound was happening here. With *Delgamuukw*, we opened ourselves up to the full import of our history, so much of which was built upon oral agreements and an oral idea of how to organize and run society. Suddenly, the four centuries of inter-twined relationships with indigenous philosophy at its core was visible to us, if we wished to see. Suddenly, we had set ourselves up for the possible return of an historic perspective that makes sense of our society. Suddenly, it was possible through the most official of mechanisms to imagine that we could shove back the delusion that our society is merely a provincial descendant of European concepts.

As I write this, I realize how strange it will sound to most Canadians. This is not the sort of argument you are likely to hear at school or university. In fact, our universities are marching resolutely toward an ever more written, Euro-U.S. derivative, footnoted, theoretically fact-based future. Not even at the height of the British and French empires was there so much cringing here, so much defining of an inferiority complex as respect for meritocracy. The result is a rush to redefine local methods in order to match U.S. methods that—the inferiority complex giveaway—are called standards.

Standards do, of course, exist. But they come in many forms in varying civilizations. They are usually defined by the method and structure of particular civilizations. Different standards in different civilizations can be of equal or different value. What we are dealing with here is not an attempt to link such standards through a search for shared underlying principles. Instead we are faced by the pretence of universal standards, for example, in law or health care or in definitions of progress. What is really taking place is the adoption of one civilization's particular standards, based on their assumptions, by another civilization built upon quite different assumptions.

In this way, fearful minds can pretend they are concerned by quality when what they are expressing is nothing more than provincial worship of the empire's ways. With the schools and universities so blocked, there would seem to be no opening for such a resurgence of the oral.

And yet a half-century ago, our greatest thinker, Harold Innis, built his astonishing argument on communications around the oral. He "viewed his work as part of a multi-generational project based on the oral tradition." How did he come to such an idea? He was one of those millions of men who emerged from the trenches of the First World War with the sense that the Western idea was fatally flawed. His work as an intellectual took him first through the full Canadian past. He seemed to be looking at the fur trade. He certainly wrote about it. But he was clearly seeing something more profound and complex—a whole other concept of civilization. His ideas about the oral in turn inspired Marshall McLuhan and became the basis for a revolution in communications theory around the world.

And yet our society has still not embraced the implications of his theories. In fact, Innis's colleagues dropped his ideas about the oral. Then the next generation of colleagues did everything they could to destroy McLuhan's reputation. And the University of Toronto, home of the worldwide revolution in modern communications, led the march away from this originality, in part as a result of its unspoken sense that the measurement of such originality must lie south of the border.

Yes, there is a small group of people who work on such things as Aboriginal law. And they have tried to run with the idea. But, with a few remarkable exceptions, Canada embraces only the technical and the surface implications of orality. After the *Delgamuukw* decision, it was as if a felt cloth had been dropped over the birdcage of Canadian thought. Neither the Canadian legal community nor the academic community at large nor the activist community has digested what the decision could mean. For example, the whole environmental area calls out for a new, broad approach, one that rethinks how societies work. Instead we have stuck to the narrowest possible bookkeeper approach to such things as global warming. Had we followed such narrow and carefully written methods in the past in areas such as education and health, we would never have been able to embrace our imaginations and so take the great financial and social risks that produced public schools, public universities and public health care.

The implications of the *Delgamuukw* decision are there in its language. "In the circumstances, the factual findings cannot stand." The judgment rejects the utilitarian as a central motor of society. Something broader—culture—overwhelms the facts. Why? Because culture carries a greater truth than fact. "A shift from oral to written," the poet and translator Robert Bringhurst has said, "affects the functioning of memory, the understanding of truth, and the place of voice and language in the working of the world. It affects not just the meaning of words but the meaning of language itself. It affects the meaning of meaning." A shift from the written to the oral would be equally tumultuous.

I believe that we have always and unconsciously mixed the two. And that equilibrium has helped us build our egalitarian, non-monolithic, ever-negotiating, consensus-seeking, individual-group balanced idea of a society. But the implication of the *Delgamuukw* decision is that the oral element could be much more conscious and therefore much more central to how we develop ideas, organize policies, engage in debate. What does that mean? If you come from the oral tradition you can place yourself on "the line between myth and information." You can deal with how "oral culture blends fact and metaphor." Often we have been able to do this. But if you look at our crises—from the Riel Rebellion through

the Japanese-Canadian internments to today's disorder in environmental policy—you can also see those moments when we have been
unable to place ourselves on that line and so have committed dangerous
errors.

The oral reflex works when it makes sense to us, because it is in our
subconscious. To move that understanding into our consciousness and
therefore into our intentional actions, we need to shove the European
assumptions back. How? For a start, we need to release the full sense of
Aboriginal philosophy. It needs to flower for indigenous purposes—that
is, for indigenous society to rebuild its sense of itself. This is key to the
Aboriginal pillar of our society being able to play its full role. But the rest
of our society also needs this indigenous force to be heard and understood. It can help all of us in pushing back those imported delusions that
now eclipse our conscious sense of where we are and what we can do.

Aboriginal philosophy is key to Aboriginals being confident about
who they are. But it is just as important to other Canadians having a
sense of who we are.

Taiaiake Alfred is an Aboriginal philosopher who takes a tough line,
condemning most of our current treaty and governmental negotiations
as "the politics of pity." What he wants is "the reclamation of our dignity
and strength." This involves getting back to "the founding principles" of
our relationships. The way to get there is "a restored spiritual foundation." This idea of a spiritual foundation that links politics, family,
society and the individual together is common in indigenous
arguments. It is not about judging public life in religious terms. Instead,
it has to do with a sense of place that involves treating humans as just
one of the elements in the great circle. This is dramatically opposed to
the Judeo-Christian-Islamic fundamentalist idea that, in all three
religions, puts the god-scripture-human relationship at the determinist
core of the universe's affairs. Alfred calls for "non-violent contention" to
re-establish the indigenous way of being. A very different indigenous
philosopher, Dale Turner, calls for "a critical indigenous philosophy." He
says the treaties were part of a "slow insidious process of negotiating
away our humanity." He wants "to separate indigenous spirituality from
[this] critical indigenous philosophy." The "traditional *wisdom keepers*

or *sage philosophers*" would be separated from what he calls the "word warriors."

These two indigenous thinkers have a great deal to say to their communities, but also to Canadians as a whole. And what they are saying is far more relevant to our reality than the endless parsing of, for example, the early work of philosopher John Rawls and his liberal contractualism, with which so many of our university departments are obsessed. In Canada, this focus is part of an insecure, derivative world. Where does it lead us? Deeper and deeper into the sort of contractualism that makes Canada an ever more improbable concept. Why? Because the roots of liberal contractualism grow out of the old ideas of falsely rational utilitarianism and of the monolithic nation-state. It is a pure expression of the written and the linear. Its latest manifestation takes the monolithic for granted, and so is concentrated on the utilitarian applications of its unspoken assumptions.

We need the aggressivity of indigenous thinkers such as Alfred and Turner. We need the balanced approach they can help to push us toward.

Let me put this in other terms. Why is it that we don't build the revolutionary ideas of communications, which have their origins here, into our way of thinking about ourselves? The ideas are still here. You read Douglas Coupland, you read Thomas King, and what do you find if not the expression of Innis and McLuhan and the role of the oral throughout our history.

Now turn to how we actually study ourselves or how we think about what we can do or not do. Suddenly that originality disappears. The working assumption is that modern theories are developed elsewhere and if by chance they appear here, they must be sent away, sold off, to be fully developed. In effect, we cut ourselves off from our own creativity. U.S. thinkers make better use of our ideas than we do. They just have to take them from us and adapt them. We then take our own ideas back from them and adapt ourselves to their U.S. version. We have done this with communications theory. Our ideas on irregular warfare have now come back to us from the marines as Three Block War and the Strategic Corporal. Even at the most basic level—hockey—the NHL had to be reconceptualized in New York. The conclusion: better a money-losing franchise in cities in the southern states in which arenas must be filled with people who don't skate and don't play the game than a money-making franchise in a Canadian city of the same size. That is what we call world-class sophistication. The outside observer calls it a colonial inferiority complex.

The third pivotal Supreme Court decision involved the 1986 *Oakes* case. On the surface it had nothing to do with Aboriginal questions. Nevertheless, many people see it as part of the rising school that is taking us slowly away from contractual obsessions and the letter of the law; away from what might be called a written rational view of law. This is an approach that takes us toward an idea of law more concerned with justice and therefore balance and relevance to a more complicated world. It does this by reaching into ideas of balance such as the Honour of the Crown and more complicated ways of getting at truth, such as oral memory. *Oakes* was written by Chief Justice Brian Dickson. It might have been written by the great nineteenth-century Plains Cree chief Big Bear. Why? Because the central message is that authority must do as little damage as possible to people and to rights when using that authority. As I explained earlier, this was called *minimal impairment*.

The argument was simple. The courts could limit or override rights. But only if the objective in doing this was central "to societal concerns which are pressing and substantial in a free and democratic society." And even then, "the means should impair the right in question as little as possible." In other words, it is extremely difficult to justify a limitation, and even then it must be minimal.

This in turn was to be seen in the context of the balancing "of society's interest with those of individuals and groups." And we were to balance this with "the inherent dignity of the human person, commitment to social justice and equality, accommodation for a wide variety of beliefs, respect for cultural and group identity, and faith in social and political institutions, which enhance the participation of individuals and groups in the society." Some people would interpret all of this as an expression of liberalism. They saw Brian Dickson—a strong leader in this period, before, during and after he was chief justice—as a liberal jurist. They would be wrong. All of this is the precise opposite of liberalism, with its notions of the autonomous individual versus the state, interest-based relationships, the autonomous market and the ethical force of commercial trade. They would be equally wrong if they tried to tie it to European or U.S. ideas of conservatism, with its beliefs in the power of linear memory, of fixed social structures and of class.

What then is this idea? There are no satisfactory Western terms because these are not approaches derived from the Western tradition. Of course, there are many Western elements entwined in a concept such as *minimal impairment* and in the other concepts I've been discussing, just as even the most revolutionary of painters nevertheless draws on her predecessors.

But the point here is that these approaches are not derived in a line from the Euro-U.S. philosophy of liberalism or conservatism. They are born out of a meeting between people with a philosophy built in this place over thousands of years and a mixture of peoples who were in essence fleeing the philosophy of Europe and the United States. The result is a remarkable state of mind.

There are, of course, those who would have us believe that the Loyalists in particular were fleeing with a classic seventeenth-eighteenth-century conservative philosophical and ethical mindset. This was the argument of the anti-democratic Family Compact and their successors. Elsewhere in this book I lay out what nonsense that is.

At the same time they certainly were not fleeing with classic liberal ideas. That's what they were fleeing from. Those ideas were intimately mixed into the monolithic view dominant among the forces of progress in Europe and in the American colonies. These are the ideas of majorities. Majorities are ever eager to insist that minorities are merely a *dialect* of their own *natural* dominance. They will always say that about language, but they are talking about a great deal more than language. They are talking about its content, its culture, its social assumption.

What then did these fleeing minorities carry with them as a point of view? That of minorities. What is the philosophy of a minority?

It is fascinating just how little effort has been expended in modern Western history on the possibility that a culture of minorities was actually an idea, not a misfortune or an accident or of only marginal importance. In the absence of such an idea the only clearly articulated alternative for a minority was to turn the minority into a majority by a constant process of subdivision and cleansing. The new majority never-theless usually finds itself with the equally new phenomenon of its own minorities.

If outsiders are now looking at Canada with curiosity or apprehen-sion, it is not simply because we have overtly and rather contentedly come to see ourselves as a society of minorities. More important, it is because we have slowly begun to develop a philosophy of minorities.

The difficulty is that much of this work is being done by people whose references in political philosophy, to say nothing of sociology and economics, are almost entirely or entirely drawn from the Euro-U.S. models. The words and concept they are attempting to rearrange to support what we are doing in Canada were actually developed in the first place to do the opposite. They attempt to tack the Canadian phenom-enon onto these liberal or conservative models, and in that way abort their own process.

At the heart of this problem lies an essential missing piece. What we are trying to develop are arguments centred on a civilization of immigration—that is, minorities who arrive here in some state of need. We should be building those arguments around a non-linear indigenous philosophy.

If they—we—can find the way to draw back from these imported logics long enough to establish the role of that non-linear indigenous philosophy, we will then find the language to describe what we have done—are actually trying to do—as intentional and as imbedded in a long history. We will then see that what we are doing is developing a philosophy of minorities.

But if our elites remain imprisoned in an inferiority complex that tells them we can only do what we derive from elsewhere, and if we continue to organize our education and our research to give comfort to this insecurity, then no language will be developed to describe what we are actually doing.

And that is why I turn so often on these pages to the royal commis-sion and to key Supreme Court decisions, and to a handful of writers.

Because these are among the few places where smart women and men in positions of intellectual authority are attempting to lay out the language for an understandable Canadian way of proceeding—that is, a Canadian approach to philosophy.

At the heart of the idea of *minimal impairment* is an embracing of complexity as a strength. Learning to live with complexity and uncertainty is all about reinventing social tension as a positive. And out of that comes the idea that a clear resolution of complex situations often leads to injustice. It is wiser therefore to accept that complexity is a strength and that authority must be used in a spirit of minimal impairment.

8

The Minimal Impairment
of the Environment

To link the environment with Aboriginal culture is to risk being taken for a romantic. A chorus of *realists* stands ready to point out the problems on First Nations reserves—problems that don't indicate a happy or natural relationship with nature.

But there is nothing romantic about the indigenous idea of nature. It is a philosophy in which humans are a part of nature, not a species chosen to master it. This is now the central concept of most scientists, whether they are looking at climate, water or species. In today's language, the indigenous idea of what is now called environmentalism produced the concept of minimal impairment.

As for what doesn't work on some reserves, that has to do with the artificial imposition from outside of an urban philosophy, one in which humans are the chosen species. It is the failure of that urban view that has fuelled the environmental movement. So reserves were first pushed to integrate an inappropriate urban concept. They were then condemned, more or less by the same people, for complying.

More precisely, the southern, urban, human-centred "environmental consciousness" is, in the words of the Canadian Museum of Civilization curator Stephen Augustine, "new to Aboriginal society." Many of these isolated communities had already been struggling for decades to adjust to the bad situations in which they had had to settle because the settlers had taken their land. Then they had to struggle to make sense of the artificial and inappropriate structures imposed on their communities. Then the residential school system was imposed to destroy their societal and family structures. On top of that, the architecture and planning made available to them or simply imposed by Indian and Northern Affairs involved the worst of ideas from poor 1960s southern suburbs. These were literally dropped into the near North or the Arctic, the boreal forest, the barrens or the tundra. What then followed was a sudden influx into these small, isolated settlements of waves of urban junk and urban junk food and urban garbage. And we shouldn't forget the pretentious imposition by provincial ministries of education of a standard urban approach to schooling in communities that will never have road access, let alone be urban. All of this has been deeply destabilizing. Several generations of residential-school graduates were then expected to run their communities in large part according to inappropriate urban criteria, without any of the managerial training linked to these artificially imposed approaches.

But then again, people who concentrate on what doesn't work in Aboriginal communities usually haven't been in any. True, some are in crisis. But lots work very well. I've seen many of these. True, some have problematic leadership. But from what I've seen, the rising Aboriginal leadership is as good as and often superior to its equivalent in non-Aboriginal communities. After all, they have had to find their way through challenges and crises most other Canadian leaders have not had to face.

As for those who think the Aboriginal-nature link is romanticism, again, they usually know neither the culture nor the communities. There are lots of interesting initiatives that have come out of a deeply indigenous point of view. For example, the Haida on Haida Gwaii, which some still call the Queen Charlotte Islands, led a campaign to stop logging on the southern half of their archipelago. They won and got a national park, which they co-manage according to their understanding of the environment. They then began working for an integrated long-term strategy on fishing, offshore minerals and logging in the northern half of the archipelago. As a result, the local loggers changed sides, abandoning their allegiance with their employer, the logging company, and instead supporting the Haida demands for control. Why? Because the Haida have a credible long-term strategy. And, unlike the logging companies, they're not going to cut down all the trees and then leave. This is their home. The loggers also think of Haida Gwaii as their home. They also want to stay. So the First Nations are their natural ally. What has been particularly fascinating is the extent to which these discussions and debates among Haida, Parks Canada, the loggers, the logging companies, and the federal and provincial governments have been shaped by Haida culture. The sort of language used, the assumptions behind the debates, the non-linear arguments, the placing of people as part of the archipelago's life rather than its master has all been a constant reminder that the application of First Nations culture in a modernized form to Canadian public issues not only works but produces a different sort of outcome.

The same sort of story could be told about the Dehcho, who made the enlarging of the Nahanni National Park a non-negotiable part of their treaty negotiations. Or the Dene, who in 2007 brought about the creation of massive parks near Fort Good Hope and on Great Slave Lake. Or the Gwich'in, who have been struggling against the oil industry to protect the Porcupine Caribou herd, which migrates between the Yukon and Alaska.

The specific tactics used on Haida Gwaii or in many other places in Canada could not be more concrete and down to earth. The tactics of the Dene and others in the early negotiations over the Mackenzie River Pipeline could not have been harder edged. These tactics and others are the product of a very inclusive strategy. The concept of government as "our way of life" fits exactly with the Dene idea of "The Land [as] the boss of culture" or the Cree idea that the land, being sacred, could not be owned in the long term, only shared. As Big Bear put it in 1884: "[W]e heard that the Hudson's Bay Company had sold the land to Government. How can you sell land? When, from whom, had the Company ever received it?"

This is all part of the oral idea of history as non-linear. The environment is certainly not linear. It does not respond to human behaviour in a linear manner. In case this does not sufficiently clarify how unromantic the indigenous view is, listen to Mohawk writer Beth Brant: "We do not worship nature. We are a part of it." That could be taken as an exact statement of how we need to think in the context of global warming or the rapid loss of species or the polluting of water systems or the loss of arable land. If you see global warming as something precise that we humans have done, you are lost. If you see yourself as part of the situation, you can act.

The point about Canada and its nature and the full meaning of environmentalism is that we don't have to be prisoners of theories coming out of countries where nature has been—so to speak—conquered. The importance in understanding that we have five immutable geographic regions is that our relationship to place must be different. And the Aboriginal relationship has the great strength of being centred on place rather than humans, and of taking a holistic or balanced approach. This is not a policy. It is a world view. It is a philosophy centred on how things are interconnected, how "problems arise from interrelated causes, not a single cause, [so that] solutions must therefore be holistic and multifaceted as well." This is not romantic. It is practical and realistic. It deals with the world as it really works.

When you look at the rise of environmentalism over the last forty years, it is surprising to see how much of the movement originated here: Maurice Strong (one of the founders of the international environmental movement), Greenpeace, David Suzuki, David Schindler (the discoverer of acid rain). In part this is perhaps a simple outcome of the overpowering presence of nature here and a reaction to the role of commodities in our economy. But commodities have always provoked a Manichean view of nature. Either you accept the baronial approach—this is our land and if we want to strip it for quick wealth, we will—or you are on the opposing side—the belief that nature must be protected. This second option is certainly romantic, but not compared to the romantic optimism of the barons, who seem to believe that after they have rolled through, nature will simply pick itself up and set about reconstituting itself.

In the late nineteenth century, there was a strong reaction around the world to the visible effects of industry ripping away at the environment. John Ruskin in Britain and Henry David Thoreau in the United States were the direct inheritors of Jean-Jacques Rousseau—brilliant, essentially right about a parklike option for nature in their overwrought, already densely inhabited civilizations. They were indeed highly romantic. Theirs was a devotion to nature, but still with man at the centre—a reaction to the Industrial Revolution, not a new philosophical option. This same romanticism existed in Canada among many of our poets and painters. But here it was the romance of a non-densely populated country living through the horrifying elimination by disease of most of the First Nations population.

It wasn't until Emily Carr, the Group of Seven and Tom Thomson, Paul-Émile Borduas and Jean-Paul Riopelle that this romanticism would be broken in our images and replaced with something that was somehow an expression of the indigenous philosophy, unconsciously digested and reinterpreted. In language, there was a first turning point in 1900 when Charles G.D. Roberts, a leading Confederation poet, author of remarkable animal stories and bilingual translator of French-Canadian novels, himself wrote a wonderfully strange novel—*The Heart of the Ancient Wood*—in which a young woman enters into a natural, yet mystical relationship with animals, in particular an old bear. At first we don't know whether this is romanticism or another way of getting at how the world works. Then in a moment of straight violence the doubt is stripped away and, as writer Thomas Hodd puts it, "Romance, it seems, no longer rules the Canadian landscape." This story and Roberts's sense of our complex reality led three-quarters of a century later to Marian Engel's *Bear*.

It is strange and depressing how little these painters and writers—with the exception of Emily Carr—consciously built their work out of the Aboriginal sensibility. And yet consciously or unconsciously, that is what they were doing. The message of Canadian creativity was that place was central to our existence. It was as strong in Borduas and Riopelle as it was in Carr and Thomson. The real source of that idea is Aboriginal and is built into those first centuries of indigenous and immigrant peoples somehow existing together.

The great weakness in our mainstream approach toward the environment today is that we have not looked seriously at how these ideas came about and what the implications are. In other words, we are trying to impose the European, linear view of a human-centred world onto our more basic understanding that this is not so. We suffer from the specialization and narrow silos that dominate our education, administration and policies. Most Canadians, including many in the environmental movement, put more energy into their relationship with technology—a personal attachment to the idea of progress—than into their relationship with place. We are constantly rushing about with single-faceted solutions to problems simplistically represented. One day the solution is corn, the next it is paper bags. Of course. Why not? We take an idea such as *sustainable development* and parse it into the narrowest possible interpretation; there is no reconsideration of the nineteenth-century industrial and managerial idea of development, which has dominated the world since then and which makes humans the purpose of the planet. We know it has been in one sense remarkably successful, but it is also responsible for our environmental crisis. All ideas are contradictory. After a reasonable period of experience, sensible people reconsider the whole in order to build on what works and get rid of what doesn't. Instead, *sustainable development* is seen as scarcely more than modified industrial planning. But if *sustainable development* is merely an attempt to inject a slightly modified utilitarianism into a managed nature, then it is nothing at all.

Meanwhile, people around the world are watching us with increasing suspicion. Our leaders—governmental, private-sector, even much of the academic class—continue to talk as if we were serious environmental players. This sort of discourse, designed to distract Canadians, cuts no ice internationally. You can almost feel people drawing back from us as they realize that our approach to the exploitation of our commodities may well play a central role in any unravelling of global environmental conditions. You find well-known commentators—the Australian Tim Flannery, for example—describing us as "spectacularly—almost proudly—cavalier" about global warming and wondering whether there is "something deep and structural about Canadian society that renders it all but impotent to deal with large environmental challenges." Today, all around the world, people are watching our approach toward the development of the oil sands. We can protest all we want, but the general interpretation is that we are going about it in a European-style, nineteenth-century, mid–Industrial Revolution way. As the world moves toward deciding who owns the commodity-rich and environmentally delicate Arctic Ocean floor, our ability to convince others that we are safe custodians will be partly decided by the international view of how we handle the oil sands. The key voices will be our circumpolar neighbours, and the current probability is that environmentally sensitive countries such as Norway, Sweden and Denmark will classify us with the Russians as unreliable, perhaps even dangerous, custodians.

What is distressing is that a large part of the environmental movement here has not focused on the particularity of our situation— the presence of a dominant unmanageable place, which is the precise opposite of a utilitarian situation. Canada is the sort of place where it is impossible even to manage the forest fires. Yet there is little mainstream rethinking, even in the environmentalism world, about our alternate philosophy of place, which after all is a product of this environment and has an unbroken line of public discussion stretching back to before European contact. It should be of interest to us that this philosophy, while perfectly capable of making use of the utilitarian, is not dominated by it.

When I look at our role in the Kyoto process, I see no sign that we were able to look beyond the old, narrow, linear Euro-U.S. theories. We did no more than argue for somewhat tougher rules in an unchanged context. That some politicians are now arguing for even less is almost irrelevant. First, because no matter how you rearrange it, this nineteenth-century linear approach cannot help but treat environmentalism as a cost. Second, because this crucial discussion is taking place without a fundamental rethinking of our old-fashioned givens and no attempt is being made to use the philosophy of place that this place has produced.

We act as if we don't believe that we could have access to another approach—one that would change the parameters of the debate and of possible action. It is hard to believe when you are in a large, sophisticated society that the parameters could change. But they can. And eventually they do, whether you wish it or not. Circumstances force change upon those who refuse to deal with reality. Other people can change them in spite of your wishes. Or you can work out how to change them. What would the effect be if we attempted to rethink the environment and our society with the input of indigenous philosophy? It would allow us to act with a more complex understanding of the planet. We would find that we no longer looked at nature in such an abstract and artificial manner. One thing is certain: This would be a more intelligent and, in the true sense of the word, a more sophisticated approach. As any good military strategist will tell you, dealing with context seriously always takes more time and more effort, but it frees you to act sensibly. The result tends to be a longer-term, broader success.

The environmental situation and the debate around it illustrate perfectly how Canada limits itself through its addiction to imported myths and its denial of any historical originality. Here we were, one of the first countries out of the gate on environmental questions. Yet by never asking ourselves why that happened, or wondering about the implications of this precociousness, we have gradually slipped ever lower into provincial interpretations of methods developed by very different societies.

9

Minimal Impairment on the Battlefield

Curiously enough, we have done better at integrating indigenous philosophy into our military strategies than into our environmentalism. Perhaps this is because the ecological movement has attracted the support of the urban middle class, which is relatively cut off from the physical and historical reality of the country, while the military in Canada are always marginal. Being on the margins leaves you more room for originality.

I'm not suggesting that we have consciously constructed the nation's military strategy out of the Aboriginal experience. On the other hand, if you care to look you can find Aboriginal underpinnings in the strategies we have adopted.

What is our attitude toward war? Minimal impairment. What has it been for a century and a half? Minimal impairment. We are loath to be drawn in. We would rather talk and negotiate. We do not rise fast to nationalist bellicosity in international affairs. The two enormous exceptions—the World Wars—were seen as precisely that at the time: exceptions to a broader rule. Once in, we are pretty resistant to the standard twentieth-century strategy of straightforward, heavy engagement in hopes of a clear knockout. Perhaps it is the strong strain of egalitarianism in this society that makes it more difficult to use soldiers as cannon fodder in the manner of class-structured societies such as the United States or France or, of course, Britain. In any case, our history of warfare is filled with the use of indirection and flexible responses.

For the whole life of New France, its security was built upon a close military alliance with the First Nations. There were some professional continental troops, but they could do nothing without the Aboriginals and the Canadiens. For long periods there were no continental troops at all. As for the Canadiens, their approach to war was closer to that of the Aboriginals than that of the European regiments. The British carried on this tradition before and after 1759. In 1753, when it looked as if they might lose their Aboriginal allies, there was great alarm that "fatal consequences ... must inevitably follow from a neglect of them." The British-Aboriginal alliance had already been the strategy of Sir William Johnson. John Johnson inherited it. And from the uprising of the American colonies to 1815—a period covering the defeat of Napoleon and the end of the War of 1812—the strategy for defending Canada was dependent on "the military use and assistance" of the First Nations. As with the French regime, this strategy had a triangular foundation—Aboriginals, settlers and regular troops. Only small numbers of professional British soldiers were available. The military reality of Canada was some combination of local militia and Aboriginal forces, usually available only during emergencies. The people we now call Métis were then a more loosely organized group—a critical mass of people who were like the jam holding the slices of First Nations and settlers together. The settlers were a mix of French Canadians, including the high percentage involved in the fur trade, Hudson's Bay Company employees and retired employees who became settlers, and Loyalists. All of them treated conflict as irregular warfare. That was their experience. The whole strategy was dependent on the mobility and irregular movements dictated by our geography and dealt with by Aboriginal tactics. Mobility, irregular warfare, flexible tactics. This didn't come to an end in 1815. The formal tactics imposed by British officers during the 1885 Métis uprising were, as became obvious, unsuccessful compared to the irregular approach used by the Métis in all except the last battle. And it was the unruly or irregular tactics used by the Canadian volunteer regiments that carried that last battle at Batoche. The same was true of the Canadian troops in the South African campaign and even the tactics gradually developed by generals Julian Byng and Arthur Currie for the Canadian Army during the First World War.

Behind this taste for irregular tactics lay a foreign policy and broad strategy that at first seemed more instinctual than thought through. In part, this was because the 1867 agreement left foreign policy and foreign military engagements as a particularly cloudy area. On paper, London ran our foreign policy. In reality, Ottawa would agree to do only what it wished to and immediately began saying no to British insistent and repeated invitations to join in imperial wars. It is particularly important to understand, given the equally repeated and superficial confusing by Canadian historians and commentators of John A. Macdonald with a British Empire cheerleader, that the opposite was true. He set a tough non-engagement standard from the beginning. His very occasional pro-Empire flourishes—"a British subject I was born, a British subject I will die"—had a lot to do with appealing to the votes of waves of recent U.K. immigrants and very little to do with his actual policies. Behind the scenes, Macdonald was particularly rude about the continued attempts to involve us in imperial wars.

And so what appeared at first to be ad hoc decisions not to engage internationally soon took on the form of a clear pattern: a reluctance to be drawn into foreign wars, a preference for negotiations and a non-classical approach to warfare, which at first was simply put down to colonial unprofessionalism or toughness, or both.

Macdonald's foreign policy was continued by Wilfrid Laurier, who resisted London's continuing repeated attempts to draw us into their colonial wars. The struggle of his successor, Robert Borden, to create a Canadian-controlled force during the First World War was partly about Canadian nationalism, partly about anger over the carelessness with which the British officer corps threw away their soldiers. But it was also, at a military level, about a sense that different tactics would produce both better success rates and lower casualty figures. After the war, London again played the loyalty card to seek support for its imperial ventures. In 1922, the Chanak Crisis put Britain up against the new nationalist government of Turkey. It was just another of those imperial dramas that come and go. But it became the political focus of this period. Led by Arthur Meighen, Leader of the Conservative Opposition, those who belonged to the Family Compact tradition or the colonial tradition presented themselves as the voice of imperial and British loyalty and called for Canadian involvement. This was one of the key strategic misjudgments that would keep the Conservative Party out of power for most of the twentieth century. After the Second World War, those who led this tendency to define internationalism as loyalty to the military adventures of empires gradually switched their attachment from London to Washington. Their insecurity—which is indeed an expression of colonialism—required the certainty of being at the side of an empire. They felt relief at being overshadowed, at not being in control. It made them feel important to be at war in the shadow of a great power. Again they could not muster strong public support, and so Canada stayed out of the British Empire's last conflicts, accepted one United Nations war in Korea, drew the inexpressible enmity of Britain and France for helping to save them from themselves during the Suez Crisis, and stayed out of Vietnam and Iraq.

All along, the underlying theme was a reluctance to be used as cannon fodder through classic imperial military strategy and a strong national sense of the difference between imperial and non-imperial wars. For a century and a half, Canadians have been parsimonious when it comes to risking the lives of their citizen soldiers. That doesn't mean they fear risk or can't deal with losses. It means they are careful about the conditions in which they will accept risk and loss. And they distrust the sort of cheap nationalism that leads to unnecessary casualties.

There is an expectation that our elites will be able to use their brains and their diplomatic skills, both civil and military, to outweigh the bald use of power. Empire worshippers still feel that this means we are soft, self-indulgent, not carrying our weight. Perhaps it will help them to know that the Athenians thought like the Canadians. The great democrat and leader Pericles: "We believe that words are not barriers to deeds, but rather that harm comes from not taking instruction from discussion before the time has come for action." The conservative, anti-democratic Xenophon: "Violence, by making its victims sensible of loss, rouses their hatred, but persuasion, by seeming to confer a favour, wins goodwill."

These could be quotes from our highly experienced officers in Afghanistan. Or they could be from Big Bear or Poundmaker. The Canadian version of a Greek chorus has been: more talk, more consultation. As you stand ready to engage, seek ways to defuse engagement.

Some people will put this down to the typical survival tactics of a mid-power democracy. If so, why have the other mid-powers not followed this approach until very recently? Others will put it down to the political constraints caused by an anglophone-francophone difference of opinion. But that would be the old Family Compact/Québec bleu argument, both of which are derivative of a classic European interpretation, in which nation-states are expected to be a monolithic construction. And if they aren't monolithic, they have a real problem.

Once you focus on the Aboriginal idea that individualism and group interests must be balanced in order to produce stability and mutual benefits, another perspective appears. And if you add to this the centuries of collaboration between indigenous peoples and successive waves of newcomers, beginning with New France, the supposed anglophone-francophone division on military matters is reduced to just one element in a complex circle.

To understand the unbroken line of Canadian foreign policy and military policy stretching back four centuries, it is enough to ask a simple question. Where did the concept of peacekeeping come from? As if pulling a mysterious solution out of a hat, Lester Pearson produced and sold a way to end the 1956 Suez Crisis that was dividing the West, the North Atlantic Treaty Organization (NATO), the North and the South, the Judeo-Christian and Islamic. There are all sorts of footnotable answers to this question. Other nations were talking about creating an international force. Diplomatic histories are full of such arguments. But they miss the central point: The idea of a United Nations peacekeeping force and the sort of military diplomacy that surrounds it came from outside of the European and U.S. military-diplomatic tradition. It was an expression of *minimal impairment*. And it was a continuation of the development of a formal Canadian international strategy that had been gradually taking shape since 1867.

Look at the Canadian attitude during the formation of NATO. We kept insisting that it needed to be about more than war. We wanted "greater consultation and co-operation in non-military fields." This annoyed the United States and Britain. They wanted a simple, clear military focus. As the historian John English points out, Canadian foreign policy after the Second World War kept coming back to consultation as the basic strategy for maintaining an international equilibrium. Gunnar Jahn, the chair of the Nobel Peace Prize Committee that rewarded Pearson in 1957, said of his approach "that the basis of any negotiation on international problems must be an attempt to understand the other party and meet him half-way." In other words, Pearson was following classic First Nations negotiation strategy. The process is tough, the threat of military force real, but the outcome must be in balance so that all sides feel they benefit and appear to the outside world to have benefited.

Did Pearson believe he was using a method inherited from Canada's seventeenth and eighteenth centuries? Almost certainly not. Yet the bitter reactions of Britain and France—a bitterness that permanently changed our relationship with both countries—demonstrated just how different this method was from their tradition. As the crisis worsened, they knew that they needed a way out. And as Andrew Cohen points out in his biography of Pearson, they were almost grateful for the Canadian solution. But in the long term they were so out of sync with what was happening that they couldn't quite understand that an effort was being made to help them save face. Their idea of military diplomacy was so fixed on their old models of winners and losers that they could not even recognize the possibility of mutual benefit.

Peacekeeping in its original form comes very close to a First Nations model. Today there are endless, sterile debates among our civil and political military experts. They talk as if there is a clear choice between peacekeepers and warriors. For one side, the warrior is a reckless time bomb in world affairs and a betrayal of Canada's military heritage; for the other, the peacekeeper is a betrayal of military principles and of our

international reputation as real soldiers. That there are not more sophisticated debates is partly the fault of our various military schools. They
should have been taking the lead in the development of a language that
describes irregular warfare and how we deal with it. Until very recently
these schools and colleges were heavily focused on an engineering
approach at the university level and on warfare as a combat model based
on ideas set in place during and after the Second World War—tanks,
heavy artillery, large infantry units being manoeuvred over battlefields,
tactical nuclear weapons. You could call this strategy "battling for the
Polish plains." Their graduates were then sent straight off to war zones
dominated by irregular or asymmetric or guerilla warfare. In other words,
they were sent unequipped with any formal preparation—historic, intellectual, analytic, psychological or practical—for what they were going to
be doing. After all, there is a long history of irregular warfare and an
intense acceleration of it from the mid-nineteenth century on.

In some ways this lack of training has been a good thing. After all, our
soldiers have generally done well in these places. Freed of almost any
formal misconceptions, they have been able gradually to alter the
original peacekeeping model. And they have done this in the field. It has
been the business of middle-ranking officers on down.

So while a sterile strategic debate droned on, opposing theoretically
pure peacekeeping to *real* war, the peacekeepers were busy mutating
from experience to experience. Sometimes ahead of the curve,
sometimes lagging behind, they had to face several crises, especially in
Yugoslavia. This forced them to rethink the balance between talking and
fighting as they attempted to separate warring forces, re-establish acceptable regimes or aid in nation-building.

While our tactics have evolved over the years, the strategy and tactics
of those who use irregular warfare against us have mutated even faster.
Why? Because irregular warfare has become the mainstream form of
international conflict. To be ready for these mutations, our people need
a full understanding of the political and military realities that govern
them. Even more important, if our forces do not develop their own
language to explain what they are doing—what they can do, what they
can't do—they will not be able to explain this to governments or citizens.

And if neither of these understands, then neither will be able to form an opinion in an intelligent manner. Their support for military action will then be reduced to politics and emotions.

By the time we arrived in Afghanistan, we should have been able to talk about what might be involved. For example, our soldiers are faced by a constant conundrum. There are real battles to be fought against a real enemy. On the other hand, there are lots of young men in poor villages who have been given a Kalashnikov and a bit of money by that enemy. If our soldiers kill that teenager in combat, it may look like one less enemy, but through their success they may have lost the support of the entire village. This is one small part of the complexity of irregular warfare. To complicate matters, the Pentagon view is that this is indeed one less enemy. Now we are in desperate need of theory and language, and the military schools are turning their attention to this need.

Over half the MA theses at our senior staff college in Toronto are on irregular warfare. But in the meantime we have been cherry-picking concepts and language from the U.S. Army—a force profoundly different from ours in size, budget and tradition. It is built more around a class system and a tradition of technology-driven mass strategies. Over the last half-century it has been steadily unsuccessful in irregular-warfare situations. Its strengths lie elsewhere.

So we cherry-pick ideas such as Three Block War and the Strategic Corporal, which vaguely seem to fit but are conceptually wrong. We compound this problem by concentrating our international training experiences on training with the United States. Once you start using language that doesn't fit, you put yourself in an imaginative straitjacket. There is no natural and easy way to think about rethinking what you do because your language actually describes what someone else does. This impedes your ability to adapt in the field and your ability to explain to politicians and the public what you are doing. For example, the U.K.–U.S. anti-opium policy in Afghanistan is an unreformed version of U.S. Drug Enforcement Agency (DEA) or equivalent policies that have a sixty-year unbroken record of failure around the world. This current manifestation is already failing. Off the record, many of our military leaders believe it will continue to fail. Yet we have not developed an alternate language, argument or strategy that could be used in public.

Our forces continue to do well in the field because they now have a long tradition of adapting well below the radar of formal policy. But the more dependent they become on this new set of cherry-picked public concepts, the harder it will become to intelligently adapt. And whether we're in Afghanistan or not will change nothing. Irregular warfare is the only mainstream form of conflict today. It will probably continue to be for a long time. Wherever we send our soldiers next, under the flag of the United Nations or of NATO, the military situation will be a variation on the same theme. It makes no sense therefore not to be able to explain our long trajectory to ourselves and then to others.

We have fifty years of experience during which we have taken a simple concept—peacekeeping—and slowly adapted it to current needs. Yet what we have not dealt with is that it is an intellectual challenge—as all strategy must be. We have only recently begun to integrate its concepts into our strategic education. As a result, we haven't yet developed our own sense of our own evolution, with all the adjacent vocabulary, terms and arguments. Not to do this is to denigrate, even waste, the value of that experience and of its purpose. And now we are becoming dependent on a mismatched strategy imported from elsewhere to stand in for our own failure to give names to what we do.

What is it that has prevented us from dealing with all of this?

It is in good part the absence of any sense of our history and how this half-century of evolution is an integral part of four centuries of evolution. If you believe that what you do is the result of an arbitrary political invention in 1956 by one man, Lester Pearson, that will make you think another arbitrary political invention is just around the corner, after which you will set off in another direction. But if you understand this last half-century to be part of a continuum, which is an expression of our culture, you will feel a need to name and rename what you are doing because it is an expression of who you are.

10

Within an Ever-Enlarging Circle

Canadians, both as a civilization and as individuals, in our patterns of behaviour and belief, have been influenced by Aboriginal civilization. Indeed, we have been shaped. We still are. We will increasingly be.

If we are in many ways stymied or confused in our actions, it is in part because we are in denial of these, our own fundamental structures. In line with this denial, our approach to indigenous issues is largely ad hoc and defensive, as if we are dealing with marginal irritants rather than reflections of our reality.

David Arnot, for a long time the Saskatchewan treaty commissioner, says that Canada has got as far as rejecting the idea of assimilation, but "it is not clear what paradigm of the relationship has replaced assimiliation." Non-Aboriginals appear to be moving ever so tentatively toward reconciliation, which would be a first step toward understanding the situation differently. As always in our history, the elegance and generosity when it is a matter of reconciliation comes largely from the indigenous side, from those who have been wronged. All around us there are a multitude of negotiations and complaints and concerns. As they are resolved in a pattern that increasingly gives Aboriginals room to manoeuvre and re-establish their role as players and leaders in their own worlds, so they also gain the room to play an important role in Canada as a whole.

If you listen carefully, you will hear Aboriginal leaders trying to indicate that the purpose of winning is also to reconstruct an ongoing balanced relationship with other Canadians. You can find this attitude in every major Aboriginal negotiation speech over the last four hundred years. We just don't listen. That is what Joseph Brant said, what Big Bear, Poundmaker, Louis Riel and Gabriel Dumont said. All through the twentieth century, even in the most desperate circumstances, indigenous leaders have continued to repeat this. The idea of reconciliation is central to their idea of civilization. It was wonderfully laid out in the nineteenth-century Kyaanusili Haida Peace Poem:

> the path of vengeance and the path of feathers
>> start and end together.
> On the path of vengeance I departed.
> By the path of feathers I arrived.

Aboriginals have a pretty good idea of what they want and how to go about getting it. It is in part about reasserting their culture and their way, in part about ensuring that they are recognized as central to the idea and existence of Canada. "The Nisga'a people," in Chief Joseph Gosnell's words, "have long sought to negotiate our way into Canada." Once Nunavut had been created, I often heard Inuit say, "Now we are Canadian." In other words, now that their place and their role in the country had been properly recognized, they could consider themselves Canadian.

If there is a serious problem, a lack of perspective, it lies with non-Aboriginals. Even in an area as successful as literature—in both French and English—our remarkable creativity seems stuck on lack of a sense of self. And people elsewhere, for example, while admiring our novels, sense this confusion and hesitation. Robert Bringhurst: Our "literature remains in a state of denial, refusing to graft to the roots that it needs. So long as that's the case, this anglophone and francophone society is likely to remain in some respects just as colonial, just as alien, just as ill-at-ease in its own landscape" as centuries ago. You see this in the eagerness of our universities to soft-pedal the idea of Canadian literature, the eagerness of almost everyone to describe what is written in terms drawn from the three imperial centres, past and present, the lack of interest in seeking profound internal explanations.

David Malouf, the Australian novelist, has talked about how it was necessary to name the flowers, trees, animals of Australia before real poetry could be written. We have more than done this. But Malouf's point was more profound. You have to embrace the relationship between place and creativity. And that also has been done here. But then you must try to understand that relationship. You must learn how to name yourself as a point in the broad historic, geographic and social process. That has only very partially been done.

Those of us who tend not to think of ourselves as Aboriginal are lucky to be living in a time of such powerful indigenous resurgence. Some thirty-five years ago, Chief Dan George wrote:

> Am I to come as a beggar and receive all from your omnipotent hand? Somehow I must wait. I must find myself. I must find my treasure. I must wait until you want something of me, until you need something that is me. Then I can raise my head and say to my wife and family … listen … they are calling … they need me …
>
> I must go.

I feel that need. For myself. For the country. This is the missing key to making sense of what we have and what we feel is not being fulfilled.

That there is a strong indigenous population revival is the first step. Politicians, journalists, civil servants worry publicly about the challenge this represents, the costs, the education, health and job difficulties. The founding peoples will soon be back to their pre-contact numbers. Inuit have already gone well beyond theirs. The truth is that we need a critical mass of Aboriginal people for their role to be fulfilled. And if our elites still talk of this as a challenge and a worry and a cost, it merely reveals that they have not escaped the late-nineteenth-century assumptions about a marginalized, dying community.

Our leaders would be better to think of Aboriginal population growth as a remarkable second chance for the country. Countries, after all, are built out of challenges and you don't meet those by focusing on the negative. They need to think of costs as investments. In an aging country Aboriginals are contributing youth. What's more, in a massive country, with an unhealthy population imbalance toward the urban, half of the indigenous population is living on the rest of the land. The standard imported urban rhetoric is that these small cities, towns, settlements north of our megalopolis centres are inefficient, expensive and awkward to service, at best filled with dying industries and social problems, at worst without economic purpose. We never acknowledge that these people make our country real by living in it. A country is not a managerial program. It is a place and the people who live in it. Over some three-quarters of Canada's land, Aboriginals and other northerners are the Canadians present and established twelve months of the year, every year. They are the physical expression of Canada's sovereignty. Our weakness is that not enough people live throughout our country. Worse still, those in charge of managing the country and the provinces would prefer if even fewer of us left the efficient conglomerations of the downtown areas, except perhaps for a summer holiday.

If we paid greater attention to the growth of the Aboriginal population, we would also see the rise of fascinating new elites—tough, clear about where they come from, highly educated, interested in Canada as much more than a handful of cities.

The highest courts are relentlessly reminding Ottawa and the provinces that there will be no slipping back into the marginalization of Aboriginals; governments will be held to account to ensure that our real engagements in the past are respected. So much of the delay over land claims is really an almost subconscious belief, among today's successors to those original mid-level officials who negotiated the treaties, that if it is dragged out long enough, the assumptions of the late-nineteenth and early-twentieth centuries will return. They won't.

It is disgraceful in a democracy built around egalitarianism that so much of our historically and ethically based leadership has to come from our courts, while most politicians, civil servants and academics drag their feet. On the other hand, the considered and philosophical judgments coming out of the courts are establishing an approach to justice that goes beyond the European idea of what is fair. It is an approach that opens us up to our deep-rooted reality. And so we can if we wish rediscover that our apparently bumbling approach toward a civilization of continuous negotiation is actually historically based, intentional and effective. As part of this we find that the Honour of the Crown has to do with public responsibility and ethics. And minimal impairment is a highly sophisticated approach to the public good. Our culture in all its manifestations has been playing with the idea of our orality, but now the courts have given it a form that can affect the way the country functions.

As arguments from indigenous communities gradually make their way back into the mainstream of Canadian thought, so the original ideas of the *common bowl*—of inclusive egalitarianism through a balance of individual and group rights—find a non-ideological way into the public consciousness. As we struggle with the complexity of our society or, in another sphere, with the environmental crisis, we will gradually see how useful the Aboriginal world view is, with its sense of how the "facets of human life and the natural world are interconnected [so] that problems arise from interrelated causes, not a single cause, and that solutions must be holistic and multifaceted as well."

You never know how these old habits will find their way back to the surface. We have an instinctively different approach toward warfare, yet we have difficulty explaining it and so naming and describing it. As if out of nowhere one of the greatest modern-day war novels appears, allowing us to see ourselves and the First World War through an Aboriginal vision—*Three Day Road* by Joseph Boyden. For those who wish to see, he has created a literary vision of our warfare.

If our law and our culture are gradually finding their way toward these non-linear approaches, it must be said that in general our universities and schools are not doing their job. They have no problem delving into Greek mythology, Jung's archetypes or the Dalai Lama's ideas of happiness. But god forbid they should take seriously the nature of human relationships in our own indigenous tradition and how it has mixed into our collective unconscious and our actions. There are exceptions of course, but the central message of our education remains a derivative from the old and new imperial sources and so is provincially linear. The more they talk about meritocracy and world-class and measuring themselves against the best, the more provincial our universities become, destined to act like losers perpetually trying to catch up. When we look at our critical situations in almost every direction—from economics through the environment to social relations—what we need is a non-linear approach. In the words of James Dumont, Ojibwa elder and scholar, we need "an all-around vision" that can be inclusive, a circular approach to thinking, versus the "straight-ahead vision of modern thought."

All the ideas I have evoked—from the real meaning of nomadism to rethinking the nature of progress—are linked to our need to develop a vision of ourselves that is built upon our own foundations. At the heart of coming to terms with the Aboriginal nature of Canada is what Jeanette Armstrong calls "Indigenization: People reconciling themselves into the indigenous landscape." What does she mean? That we must try to think of this place in another way. We must step away from the conquering, owning ways of thought and move toward seeing ourselves as part of the place. All of this is contained in the idea that you are reconciled to the place and thus to *the other* by widening the circle. Each place has a truth about it. Through reconciliation you find out what that is.

If you think about immigration and fresh citizenship in these terms you begin to see how the latest wave of newcomers from Somalia or Morocco are part of a continuous process dating back to before the first Europeans. The indigenous philosophy explains far better what we are inventing here than any imported and amended European idea of citizenship.

Yet our education reflects almost none of this. Indigenous peoples are working hard to rebuild their self-confidence by building their culture back into their own education. To the extent that that schooling is designed by our departments of education, it is still more often than not constructed as a straight rejection of the Aboriginal reality. For that reason it needs to be rethought to create a balance. But we also need urgently to begin building their culture into the broad Canadian education system—into our schools and universities—for Canadians as a whole. Not simply into specialized courses, but into the ways we all look at geography, at history, at philosophy, at poetry as much as at justice.

Not to do this merely isolates us more and more from what is happening anyway. If we do not educate ourselves and think about ourselves in a way that reflects the manner in which Canada is beginning to run, it is as if we are choosing a sort of existential illiteracy.

Go back to the Berger Commission, which from 1974 to 1979 helped to uncover the Aboriginal civilization at the core of Canadian society. The direction of our economy was changed. But so was the way we deal with each other. The idea of all-powerful rationalism began to falter. Think of the Nisga'a Agreement. People thought it would be a disaster because of the autonomy and power it gave to First Nations. Non-Aboriginal locals were apparently going to suffer exclusion. From the moment the agreement was put in place, you stopped hearing about it. Why? Because it works. Think of the James Bay agreements and Nunavik, which is now officially an Inuit territory in Northern Quebec. Think of Nunavut, of *Delgamuukw*, *Sparrow*, *Oakes* and then in 2007 the *William* case. The *William* case involves four thousand square kilometres in the B.C. interior and a First Nations victory. In the aftermath, some people worried about such a small group getting control of such a large area. Would they rather the tiny board of directors of a company controlled it? At least now, if the Tsilqot'in deal with lumber companies, it will be in the context of land they do not wish to leave. Isn't it better for Canadians who want to live in a place to have control over that place?

The simple answer is that we need to get the stumbling blocks of treaty negotiations out of the way so that we can all get on with life. There is no excuse for the decades of intentional delay and disingenuous negotiations by the federal government and some of the provinces. James Prentice, a few years before he was briefly the minister responsible for Indian Affairs in the Stephen Harper government, said that "Canadian history will judge the current specific claims process very harshly." Little has changed. It is these unresolved claims that prolong the destabilized atmosphere in many Aboriginal communities. If we are to turn to the positive role of indigenous culture, we must remove this humiliating instability. The arguments against speedy and broad settlements are unsustainable. First, Canada has not fulfilled its engagements. That failure may in turn have destabilized indigenous society. But that is hardly an argument in favour of breaking the agreements. Second, we need to stop thinking in an unimaginative, linear manner that in turn causes people to think that settlements involve major concessions. If it helps, think of a reserve as a municipality or a corporation or a co-op or a big farm, then the conditions will seem normal. Third, these treaty settlements are not about Canada giving up something. They are about groups of Canadian citizens, who come from these areas and who do not wish to leave them, getting control over the land. Whatever happens, they want to stay. Surely this is better than commodities companies coming in for a decade or two, sucking out whatever wealth there is, then walking away leaving the locals to pick up the broken pieces. Surely what most of us who live in cities need are people who want to live in the rest of the country and have an indigenous philosophy of how to care for it. Here the word *indigenous* takes on its full meaning. They have a philosophy that is indigenous to this country and to the particular areas in question. Isn't it fortunate for all of us that they want to be in charge, that they want to take responsibility?

Put aside for a moment the Crown's legal obligations. Do any of the civil servants and lawyers who are dragging out these negotiations, do any of the urban dwellers who worry about Aboriginals getting control over large stretches of land, do the boards of directors of any commodity corporations involved on these lands or their CEOs or various vice-presidents, do any of them want to move to these areas, establish themselves permanently there, in order to develop multi-generational policies and infrastructures that will serve expanding communities? No. Therefore, we should be grateful that Aboriginals are willing to do so. Meanwhile, we worry about our sovereignty. There is no greater guarantee of sovereignty than citizens being in charge on the spot in those places that might be in question. Some feel the amount of money being given as part of treaty settlements is unjustifiable given that it is often going to only a few thousand people. Why don't they feel the same about a half-dozen or a dozen managers selling off corporations—that is, selling off what they don't own—and walking away with a few hundred million dollars? In other words, these six to twelve individuals are getting more in total for walking away than Aboriginal nations are getting for taking responsibility. And why shouldn't Aboriginals profit from getting back land that was unfairly taken from them?

As part of this whole process of normalizing the Aboriginal nature of Canada, we need to turn urgently to a central part of our culture that is in danger. There were hundreds of indigenous languages. We are down to about sixty, coming from a dozen or so linguistic families. And many of these are slipping away. Whether you are a unilingual francophone in Quebec City or a unilingual anglophone in Saint John or a newly sworn-in citizen from Sri Lanka living in Vancouver, these are your languages. They are part of the complexity of Canadian civilization. When one indigenous language slips away, it is as if heavy doors, once open and giving us access to a particular understanding of this place, have slammed shut, shutting us out forever. Part of our shared understanding is gone. That most of us do not speak these languages is irrelevant. Each of them is a passageway into the meaning of this place. Each one lost is a loss of meaning and possible understanding.

It would not be so difficult to ensure the revival of many of these languages. The programs and the money needed are neither mysterious nor particularly onerous. To succeed could only be a victory for Canada.

If I am right that we are a métis nation, that the underlying currents of this country are more indigenous than imported, why are we so nervous about embracing our reality? What is it that holds us back from embracing our larger self? There is no clear answer except that we remain prisoners of our colonial selves, straining to see across borders in search of imperial models and the illusion of imperial approval. The more we do this, the less we make sense to ourselves.

Part of the problem lies with the complexes that each of the founding groups lug about, each justified in different ways. These prevent us from building on each other in ways that can make more of each and of the whole. There is enormous interdependence between the anglophone and francophone communities. But daily life, daily discourse, public life, intellectual life is resolutely organized as if there were not. In other words, whatever our reality, the eighteenth- and nineteenth-century European ideas of purity and separation grind away on the surface, distracting us from ourselves.

The original party, the Aboriginal, is built upon a philosophy that has interdependence at its core. This is the opposite of such European ideas as the *melting pot*, which was picked up by our neighbour as a way of explaining how you could get a new kind of European-style purity out of a mix of peoples. The idea of difference is central to indigenous civilization. These differences are not meant to be watertight compartments, not vessels of purity. It is all about working out how to create relationships that are mixed in various ways and designed to create balances. It is the idea of a complex society functioning like an equally complex family within an ever-enlarging circle. That is the Canadian model.

PART II

PEACE, FAIRNESS AND GOOD GOVERNMENT

11

One Word

What a difference one word can make.

Peace, Order and Good Government. What could such a phrase possibly mean? This, we are told, is our *liberté, égalité, fraternité,* our *life, liberty and the pursuit of happiness.* And if it is boring by comparison, *well,* so be it. We are a careful, boring lot. In any case, this is the lot we must struggle against while, of course, remaining careful.

And if our motto seems elitist and anti-individualistic, even anti-democratic, well that must reflect our inner deferential self, democrats though we are. After all, what do these words describe except an obsession with some sort of paternalistic control over society justified by the need for efficient administration? If asked to match this motto with a country, most unknowing foreign historians would pick one of the corporatist regimes of the 1930s—perhaps Franco's Spain.

The sense we habitually give to this phrase is that it reflects our conservative roots. To be more precise, it reflects our pre-democratic Tory roots and our Tory nature. After all, the French Canadians were profoundly conservative and church-bound. And the Loyalists had fled the new United States because they were loyal Englishmen, often of a better class, who had lost to American rebels who were often Enlightenment philosophers or simple, freedom-loving farmers—modern yeomen who had taken up their rifles in the name of liberty.

Of course, neither of these assumptions about Canada's origins is true. The church was weak in French Canada until the middle of the nineteenth century. Many villages were without priests. True, the French regime had denied the Canadiens habeas corpus, printing presses and any kind of integrated economy. But within the context of a military regime, the colonials had developed their own sense of liberty. The fur trade made a critical mass of the Canadiens into adventurers. They were close to the natives and there was a good amount of intermarriage. And the farmers, many of whom were also in the fur trade, lived in a manner bred of their need for self-reliance in small, isolated communities in a tough environment. It was the kind of unstructured liberty that would have frightened the urbane grand merchants and slave-supported property owners of Boston, New York and Virginia, that is, the men who led or supported the rebellion.

As for the Loyalists, very few of them were English, let alone of a better class, let alone rich. After all, the colonial uprising in 1776 was a dispute between two types of English rulers—those in England versus those in the colonies. Either way it would end with an English victory. Glance over the signatures on the Declaration of Independence. There is no hint of a large German or Dutch population, little hint of the Scots or Irish, to say nothing of what were then called Indians or Free Blacks. Now examine the lists of Loyalists. They consist almost entirely of these minorities. About 40 percent of the Loyalist refugees who went to Upper Canada were German speaking, mainly of Rhineland origins. Scottish Highlanders, Irish, other German minorities, Dutch. There were probably more Aboriginal and Black Loyalists than there were English ones.

They fled not because they were Tories, but because they had been caught up in the meat grinder of Englishmen fighting each other. Minorities flee when majorities fall into conflict.

The myth that *Peace, Order and Good Government* was a suitable motto for a Tory, anti-democratic backwater is self-serving nonsense invented and endlessly repeated by a tiny, empire-besotted elite— English or pretend-English—late in the nineteenth century. This was their myth, not ours. These are the people we often describe as the Family Compact in Upper Canada or the Château Clique in Lower Canada. But they also had their courtiers, their propagandists, a nascent anglo-intellectual class filled with a sense of itself as the colonial voice of the Empire. What's more, rivals though they were, these colonial anglophones were comforted in their delusions by a francophone elite, linked to the church, and pleased by the implications of order, peaceful streets and decent administration. All of these colonial voices still exist. Or rather, the natural descendants of that class still exist. By not dissecting and formally rejecting their interpretation of our past, we have been stuck with it as an incomprehensible underpinning to Canadian society.

One of the characteristics of an old civilization is that it has long-lived, predictable patterns of behaviour. These usually take the form of consistent tensions. The classic Canadian example is that of a central power versus provincial power. As the centuries flow by, the power shifts back and forth, always with anguish on one side or the other, sometimes anger, and a lot of protestations about necessity and constitutional rights.

The other, more curious, more troubling tension is that between the vast majority of the citizenry, including part of its elites, and another insecure but ambitious slice of the leadership that feels it really belongs elsewhere. Even as far back as New France, the population seems to have been comfortable with the idea of the place in which they made their lives. They quickly made it real—the real centre of their existence. And they worked out how to function in this reality. Part of the elite—some of the seigneurs and traders—did the same. But a large part of them had a constant eye over their shoulder toward Paris. France was real. Canada was just a place to make money and advance their careers.

The Family Compact/Château Clique under the pre-1848 British regime was a direct spiritual descendant of that French colonial class. The Compact/Clique merely carried on from the French colonial class's idea of how power should function. And today, virtually unchanged, there they are, a contemporary version of the same insecure elite, glancing over their shoulders to New York or Washington or other *real* places in the empire of the day. The rest of the citizenry, by now deeply anchored in the reality of this place, have settled in, along with the waves of new Canadians, some three hundred thousand immigrants a year, not to parochialism or narrowness or protectionism, but to living as if here is real and the real centre of their lives. It becomes increasingly difficult for most of us to imagine that one of the underlying characteristics of elite success in Canada continues to be insecurity and their sense that reality is not here, but elsewhere, in another culture, another market, as part of another elite. The insecurity, these furtive glances, make such leaders even more insistent in their view of themselves as the natural inheritors of power, to do with what they wish. Sell it off. Compromise it. Realize whatever benefits as rapidly as possible. Why not? These are merely stepping stones to the reality that lies elsewhere. The rest of the population—whether of the left or the right—sees society as the search for some sort of fair arrangement. It is hard for them to digest the idea that others, holding a great deal of power, are not seeking such an arrangement.

How does this relate to *Peace, Order and Good Government* apart from the elite attachment to the concept? First, the phrase itself doesn't make much sense. If you have peace and you have good government, you must also have order. So this is tautology, unnecessary repetition. But by its insistence on a narrow concept of power, the phrase perfectly illustrates an insecure elite's idea of how such a society should be managed.

Second, there is little hint in this phrase of the real country—the Canada in which most of us live. There is no hint of the possibility of a fundamentally non-European culture with its indigenous core, no hint of a civilization of minorities, no hint of the power of place or the role of bilingualism or of a continuous and highly original history of immigration and citizenship. This phrase would not lead you to imagine regional differences or the existence of great non-urban, non-rural expanses that are the foundation of our wealth, or transfer payments or single-tier health care.

How could such a concept be presented as central to our character and yet be so disconnected from our reality? The answer is quite simple.

Through all of our history, through all of our legal and constitutional documents, all of the precedent-setting declarations, the phrase *Peace, Order and Good Government* has been used only twice. The rest of the time, from official documents to proto-constitutions to political instruc-tions, the phrase used was fundamentally different—*Peace, Welfare and Good Government*.

Over the last hundred years, *welfare* has gradually taken on a precise political sense. At first, with the rise of the social welfare state, it described the creation of public programs to help the poor, that is, the victims of the nineteenth-century Industrial Revolution. This idea became more precise during the Great Depression. The general effect of these programs was to remove the worst suffering and to help create our middle-class democracies. Over the long term, some of these programs, however, seemed to backfire and to hold citizens in a state of dependence on the edge of poverty. And so the word slowly took on a more negative connotation, suggesting heavy-handed government interference in people's lives and passivity among some poorer citizens.

But the real meaning of *welfare* over the preceding half-millennium was perfectly clear: faring well, well-being, bien-être, being well, fare ye well, good fortune, happiness, bonheur, felicity. Used by a government, this was a clear reference to the public good. The public weal. The welfare of the people. The welfare of the state. The welfare of the subject, who later became the individual.

All of that to say, *welfare* describes the well-being of the individual within a society. And this meaning was clear and stable from the early Middle Ages to the middle of the twentieth century.

The roots of the whole phrase in the English tradition probably lie with Henry VII. In 1489, he instructed his personal representatives spread around the kingdom—the then powerful justices of the peace—to serve "the politic weal, peace and good government" set out in his laws in order to assure "the perfect surety and restful living of his subjects … for to him there is nothing more joyous than to know his subjects to live peaceably under his laws and to increase in wealth and prosperity."

Why were these instructions necessary? Because his subjects were suffering from "the negligence and misdemeaning, favour and other inordinate cause[s]" of the local powers. This idea of the public weal had already been expressed in popular fourteenth-century myths by Robin Hood, who struggled against the Sheriff of Nottingham and his ambitious friends in the local aristocracy. The barons. What we call the Family Compact. These are people who hold power and money without responsibility. Henry VII's initiative cannot even be demeaned as paternalistic. This was the fifteenth century. He was the pre-modern, pre-linear, pre-utilitarian *good King*, who protects his subjects against the selfish barons. This is the just King, who wishes his subjects to be treated justly, who is concerned with their welfare.

12

Colonial Fairness

1763—Fair Rights and an International Experiment

For more than a century, while Canada slowly became a country, *welfare* in its public good/bien-être sense was the word used almost exclusively to join Public Peace to Good Government. There it is in the Instructions to the governor of Nova Scotia in 1749. This led to a local disagreement over the powers of the governor versus those of the colonial Assembly "to enact Laws for the *publick peace, welfare and good government* of the said Province and the People."

That same phrase is in the Royal Proclamation of 1763, in which the broad treaty rights of the First Nations are laid out. Dodge and delay as the federal government continues to do over treaty negotiations, its obligations stretch back two hundred and fifty years.

And there in late 1763 is the phrase in the public commission of the first British governor, James Murray, who "shall have full power and authority to make, constitute, or ordain laws, statutes, and ordinances for the *publick peace, welfare, and good government* of our said Government." He used his powers to treat the religious, civil and linguistic rights of the francophone Canadiens as normal rights, though this would not have been the case in Britain and he had as yet no legal authority to do so. That legal authority would come in 1774 with the Quebec Act.

The Great Peace of Montreal in 1701 and the Niagara Peace of 1764 can be thought of as the creative beginnings of the Canadian idea. The Quebec Act, along with the Royal Proclamation, could be called the legal basis for Canadian civilization. The phrase used in 1774 is *Peace, Welfare, and Good Government*. To accentuate what might otherwise be mistaken for the standard language of statecraft of the time, there is first a paragraph pointing out that there will be a need for "many Regulations for the future Welfare and good Government of the Province of Quebec, the Occasions of which cannot now be foreseen."

Why did London feel it had to insist on the unforeseen? And why do the Royal Proclamation and the Quebec Act represent the formal foundation of Canadian civilization? First because the initial two governors—James Murray and Sir Guy Carleton—knew the Canadien situation well and were sympathetic to it. They and others like them influenced the writing of the documents. And voices in Quebec and Montreal—both francophone and anglophone—were heard through those friendly colonial officials.

Second, they ensured that the religious and political rights of the Canadiens were clearly normalized in the Quebec Act. Many Quebec leaders today harp on about the fundamental secular nature of Quebec culture. They forget that language and culture rights were actually anchored first in religious rights. That decision—radical for its time—saved the language and culture of the Canadiens from what was done in France and Britain to the Bretons, the Provençal, the Irish and the Scots—in fact to almost every European minority by whatever group large enough to hold power as a majority.

Third, by laying out the treaty rights of the First Nations and the citizen rights of the Catholic and French-speaking Canadiens with such clarity, the new authorities were accepting and even asserting something very unusual. Whatever were to happen in the future in Canada, it would involve taking a very different tack from that taken in Europe. While Britain and France and the rest of Europe were rushing down a straight and narrowing road toward monolithic nation-states with one myth, one religion, one language, one race, Canada had already, with the Quebec Act in 1774, been legally described as cutting off down an unexplored path—a track untried in Europe and contrary to the fashion of the day. And this from the very first moment of its modern existence.

Given the local realities of the time—a small European population, insufficient military forces, tiny budgets and so on—these radical decisions may have seemed not so much philosophical as practical. Add to that two open-minded governors plus British war fatigue. The cumulative effect makes the unusual path taken seem not so surprising. Looking back, it seems to us ethically self-evident. Any other approach would have been foolish and unfair. But these choices were not made anywhere else. And they weren't made in the twenty-first century. In the context of eighteenth-century statecraft and international politics, this was a revolutionary departure, far more revolutionary as a concept than that of setting up, a few years later, a European-style nation-state in the American colonies.

By this royal proclamation and this act, the reality of three minorities, each one incapable of even pretending to be able to dominate the other two, was given a proto-constitutional form and a mythological expression. Canada would be a place that, in order to exist, would have to do so upon a triangular foundation of Aboriginals, francophones and anglophones. All the pushing and pulling within our society over the last two hundred and fifty years has been and still is somehow tied to that profoundly atypical beginning.

Such a complex system is difficult to maintain. Power also abhors a vacuum, and so when the Aboriginals were almost wiped out by European diseases, a vacuum was indeed created, and the anglophones and francophones, including all the new waves of immigrants, rushed in to occupy as much of the geographical and mythological space as they could. For a hundred years it seemed as if the triangle had been reduced to the merely bipolar. But the First Nations population gradually grew back through the last century. And Aboriginal leaders found ways to use the courts to reassert their rights. Then judges rediscovered the meaning of the original triangular foundation. And so this foundation, the fundamental truth of Canada, formalized in the 1760s and 1770s, has now reasserted itself.

But the return of this Aboriginal pillar is not simply the result of population growth and law. More important is the power of myth. It is there, deep within us, powerful whether we know it or not. Humans can cripple themselves by acting against what they are convinced they do not know. That is the meaning of Greek tragedy, or even of Shakespearean. If it is real, it will assert itself. That is what Claude Lévi-Strauss meant when he wrote that we cannot know "how people think in myths, but how myths think themselves in people, and without their even knowing this occurs." That was why Carl Jung had engraved over his door *Called or not, the Gods will come.*

Given the way we built ourselves through the seventeenth, eighteenth and half of the nineteenth century, we needed and need the return of the Aboriginal pillar in order to make sense of ourselves. Certainly the originality of our situation was virtually incomprehensible as an intellectual or theoretical position to the Europeans—including the British—until they had finally burnt out their monolithic obsessions of purity in the Second World War. Now, as they move ever deeper into their construction of a non-monolithic European continent, they slip toward the model we fell upon out of need—real need—in the eighteenth century.

As for the United States, it is still very much caught up in the old European idea that mixed Enlightenment principles with purity of race and culture. John Jay was a great revolutionary figure, signatory of the Declaration of Independence, and key author of the Federalist Papers. In the second of these he wrote "with equal pleasure ... that Providence has been pleased to give this one connected country to one united people— a people descended from the same ancestors, speaking the same language, professing the same religion, attached to the same principles of government, very similar in their manners and customs.... To all intents and purposes we have uniformly been one people." He went on to become chief justice of the Supreme Court.

His Manichean view of self and of the outer world may seem dated. The revolutionaries' original English project in North America no longer describes the vibrant and complex society of today's United States. Yet Jay's concept lies deep within its collective unconscious. George Bush Jr.'s years have shown how easy it is to draw that fundamental myth of one people, united against the world, back up to the surface. Jay, with his eloquent style, reminds us of just how European the intellectual and emotional project of the United States was, how deeply anchored in both the Enlightenment and the burgeoning idea of the monolithic nation-state. Its purity was justified by its destiny. That destiny did involve a concept of *welfare*, but one quite different to the Canadian. In the U.S. Constitution and elsewhere, the term appears as "the general Welfare." This concept refers to the well-being of the state. It is a reflection of the idea of central power. It means much what the British meant when they used the word *order*. And so the driving forces of Europe and of the United States have always been closely linked, even if they have been travelling in different time sequences.

This reminds us of just how atypical the Canadian experiment has been and remains. Our incapacity to digest and to accept this intentionally atypical past makes it hard for us to understand ourselves—to explain ourselves to ourselves and to others. This lies at the heart of the difficulty we have in doing those self-evident things that are necessary whenever we wish to advance our project.

We have our excuses. The road that we took in the eighteenth century was not announced with a grand intellectual debate producing a sequence of instructional formulae as it was in European countries or in the United States. It was not even an entirely conscious choice. Indeed, the very idea of a "road taken" doesn't really fit as an image here because until recently, the very idea of movement in Canada, whether physically or metaphorically, involved rivers, not roads.

But then why should it have been consciously, let alone rationally, argued if the direction we took was not clearly derivative of other Western models? There were no widely accepted intellectual indicators to help us on our way. And rivers are physically and metaphorically more complicated than roads. That makes them more of a challenge, perhaps more interesting.

Canadians, even those who more or less reject the country, have no trouble with the idea that ours is an experiment—a trip down uncharted waters. It has been an experiment on the same foundations for two and a half centuries, producing a strange mixture of audacious, intuitive leaps and rather stolid, careful public administration.

And so, whether grandly conceived or not, there was nevertheless an initial highly original choice, followed by a stream of choices, all leading in the same direction. Canada is an experiment, yes, but from the beginning an intentional one. And perhaps it is our unwillingness to accept this originality that makes it so difficult to digest. Perhaps it is the continuing colonial insecurity of our elites that drives them to seek patterns of Western conformity. Perhaps many of these choices were grandly conceived and argued, but the colonial undercurrent caused them to be quickly swept out of the domain of our shared consciousness, only to be replaced by comforting concepts imitative of the empires of the day. Perhaps that is why the idea of *peace, welfare and good government*, with all its surrounding assumptions, is discussed by a minute fraction of our elites and is unknown by Canadians as a whole.

1791—Does the Word Mean Something?

The Constitution of 1791 was designed to bring francophones and anglophones together in one Assembly. The intent of the text was perfectly clear. *Peace, Welfare and Good Government* was mentioned twice; *Good Government, Peace and Welfare* once; *Good Government and Prosperity* once. It was an optimistic document.

Some will ask: Do these words mean anything? Are they not just empty formulae copied out by colonial officials in London? The answer comes in five parts.

First, what British officials might have wanted to intend or not intend was one thing. What they generally produced for Canada was first shaped by a debate around the governor in Canada, in other words, a local debate involving local leaders. We would not now recognize this process as democratic. But nothing anywhere in the eighteenth century was democratic. The famous parliament of Pitt, Fox, Burke and Sheridan was not democratic. The new United States republic was not democratic. Revolutionary France was not democratic. What matters is that the Canadian process was local and, given the originality of the experiment launched, surprisingly influential. Throughout Canadian colonial history, the governor and other key figures made sure they were in London while the key legal documents were being shaped.

Second, in Canada there was the deep-set experience of Aboriginals and Europeans, more or less existing or living together. In this tradition, trademark phrases were taken to have great meaning. And this phrase fits neatly into indigenous concepts. A peaceful society, shared well-being, a meritocratic leadership. Those who belonged to the Aboriginal Canadien or Loyalist experience would feel at home with these concepts.

Third, how these texts were applied was largely a local decision. They came to mean what successful governors, in consultation with Canadian advisers, later with Canadian ministers, and finally the ministers without the governor were determined to make them mean. We have always had written proto-constitutions or constitutions. We have always used them as if they were largely oral. A single example: The 1840 Constitution was written against most local wishes to create a centralized, unilingual mono-state. In 1848, under the same constitution, Louis-Hippolyte LaFontaine and Robert Baldwin, the reform leaders of Lower and Upper Canada, turned it into a federal, bilingual decentralized state. The only fundamental law they had to pass in order to change the constitutional rules was one that formalized bilingualism. In 1848, the written Constitution became an unwritten Constitution.

Fourth, if you want to understand the intent of eighteenth- and nineteenth-century Canadian legal documents, read the French version. These Constitutions and instructions arrived in Canada in English. It was the job of those in charge on the spot to turn them into legal French documents. That process gave them their full Canadian meaning. Remember, the governors were virtually all fluent in French, at least up to the end of the nineteenth century. And the key politicians were either francophone or bilingual anglophones or, like John A. Macdonald, read French well.

As for the translators, they were well-known, respected intellectuals. Think of them as senior, longstanding members of the public service, the equivalent of a deputy minister. Their names appeared on the treaties and laws.

James Murray, the first British governor, had been Wolfe's number two. But he was a Catholic Scot, a great supporter of the francophones and an opponent of the Boston traders and the few new traders who arrived from England. This alliance of English-descent Protestants in Boston and English Protestants in England thought it should inherit all business in Canada—a reward for the fall of France in the Americas. They were furious that Catholics had been given citizens' rights. In England, these would have been denied.

The Royal Proclamation in its French version spoke of *la paix publique, le bien-être et bon gouvernement*. In other words, *peace* meant *public peace*, that is, *public order*. And *welfare* meant *well-being*, that is, the *well-being of the public*.

Guy Carleton, Murray's successor, formed a committee of local leaders to translate the Quebec Act, which had clarified the citizens' rights of Catholics, who happened in large part to be French-speaking. Here *welfare* became *bonheur* and *le bonheur futur*. So *welfare* meant *happiness*, in the eighteenth-century sense. That sense was the fulfillment of the self within the shared well-being of society. This was the *Happiness* of the American Declaration of Independence and the *bonheur* of the French *Declaration des droits de l'homme*.

Again in the 1791 Constitution, the word was le bonheur. In one paragraph *peace, welfare* became *la tranquillité, le bonheur*. In other words, *public peace* was not to be understood as authoritarian order or class-imposed order. Rather, tranquillité suggested a satisfaction tied to the public good, tied in turn to well-being or welfare. *Public peace* was dependent on *fair welfare* and *good government*.

The eighteenth-century idea of happiness did not pop out of nowhere. It was the expression of a Greek idea—*eudaimonia*—itself fixed on fulfillment, accomplishment, the well-being of others. Today happiness is more often treated as a Disneyland sort of infantilization, distraction or self-indulgence. Yet every study of happiness as contentment seems to show that an individual's positive sense of himself or herself grows with disinterested participation in the public weal. Today we often describe this as volunteerism, that is, doing something for others on a continuing basis. So happiness today might describe an engaged citizen or an active volunteer.

These words—peace, tranquillité, welfare, bien-être, bonheur, good government—were being used in legal documents and public debates here and there around the globe. Whether they were empty formulae or took root with real local meaning depended on the society and its situation. In Canada, they fed directly into the debate over how to build a non-monolithic and atypical system.

And the meaning here was linked to the beliefs of the first two governors, neither of whom were in any way democrats. But they were both fixed on the need for some sort of fair arrangement in Canada. Their choices for the official French version of peace, welfare and good government were a clear expression of that desire.

Oral Meaning

The fifth factor that gave life to this phrase was the oral nature of Canadian society. Ours has always been and remains as much an oral culture as a written one. Other Western societies have tipped much more heavily to the written. Our own elites are in deep denial of this orality. It makes them feel uncomfortable, un-Western. As they read these words, lawyers, professors, civil servants in particular, begin to skip on to the next section. They like the concept of *order* in part because it is reassuringly linked to the written, the managerial, the controlled and the orderly.

The classic modern monolithic nation-state has been built around the written word. This is the tool for defining meaning, narrowing meaning and asserting power. It allows public discourse to be tightened in an insular manner around definitions of loyalty to one language or to the singular mythology of the state or to the one religion or race. This emphasis on the written was central to the political strategies that drove the gradual rise to power of the Île de France (the area around Paris) over all of France and the rise of London over all of Britain. Minority languages were marginalized and wherever possible eliminated. John Jay and the Federalist Papers laid out the United States' version of the written word as a centralizing tool.

Part of the atypical nature of Canada lies in the persistence of the oral. I have mentioned how key legal documents tend to be treated increasingly as if they were unwritten and thus oral, and how, well before that, our orality emerged from the very heart of Aboriginal culture. With all its complexity of regions and, still today, some sixty languages, Aboriginal culture retains an oral core even when converted to a written form. What some will think of as a problem or a limitation can also be seen as a great strength, as it links our culture to far more than the surface or the linear.

We all understand that in the eighteenth and nineteenth centuries most Aboriginals were illiterate; they could not read and write European languages. But then neither could most francophone and anglophone Canadians. Each important new legal text had to be read to them in public, usually on church steps or other public gathering places. In the oral tradition, the whole idea of meaningless official language is virtually non-existent. The meaning of Canadian texts was digested within an oral tradition. And these texts did indeed have to be read in public because Canada had a particularly high male suffrage. As in most places, the right to vote was based on property ownership or income. Most Canadian men were property owners. Immigrants got property on arrival. So by the early nineteenth century we had a higher suffrage than in Britain. But our voting citizens were largely illiterate. Our democratic culture was therefore oral.

And this orality, mixed with the play between the two official languages and, at a more fundamental level, between the Western and the Aboriginal languages, meant then and means now that meanings are never clear. That is what keeps the importance of meaning alive. It cannot be clarified, then filed away as a given in the manner of classic written culture.

There is a willful bounce between the languages and the cultures. This produces a mix of meanings and a play of confusion. Citizens then understand language as it suits them and as their myths dictate.

The other oral element has come from the constant integration of races, cultures and languages. It began after the fall of New France with the mixing into francophone society over a mere half-century of large numbers of Hessian German soldiers, who converted to Catholicism, and Highland Catholic Scots and Catholic Irish, with their German, Gaelic and various English dialects. They all brought with them cultures imbued with minority views. It was even more complicated on the anglophone side. I have mentioned that some 40 percent of the Upper Canada Loyalists were members of German-speaking religious minorities. Within a few years, a big group of Mennonites followed them. They were pacifists, and the governor gave special dispensations, accepting their pacifism and therefore exempting them from the possibility of military service. Add to that another 20 percent of Gaelic-speaking Scots, almost as many Aboriginal Loyalists as European, a large group of Black Loyalists, some Jews, Irish Catholics and some Protestants and others. Even in the Maritimes the German and Gaelic components were both far larger than is now remembered. In other words, this is a population to which words such as *diversity, interculturalisme* and *multiculturalism* could have been applied. For decades they would have to relate to power mainly through the oral, but would also examine words as if they meant something. In the Maritimes, the Black Loyalist population was so large that, added to those who came to Quebec and the future Upper Canada, they made up 10 percent of those who had as refugees fled from the United States. To that you must add the slave population who were freed over the next half-century or simply not replaced with new slaves.

What this means is that the bounce and play of languages, cultures and understanding was not just back and forth between French and English. Poet and playwright George Elliott Clarke talks of the orality of the Black Loyalists and those who followed over the next century to Canada. Yes, there was a desire for literacy, as there was throughout society. At the same time, then as now, "the ghost of orality haunts most black writers." I think a similar ghost haunts the best of Canadian literature, whatever the writer's origins.

The energy from a growing oral complexity continued to expand through the second half of the nineteenth century, all of the twentieth and on to today as wave after wave of immigrants from other cultures and languages have continued to arrive. The growing elites—bureaucratic, journalistic and literary—have tried repeatedly to give a written form to this phenomenon. And all too often that form is derived not from what has happened or is happening in Canada, but instead from the nature of population changes in the United States, Britain or France. In spite of this, the heart of communication and understanding remains oral in Canada, in good part because most newly arrived immigrants can't help but build her or his understanding of this place in an oral manner. How else could they do it? For the vast majority of immigrants,

French and English are second and third languages. And ours is an old, complex civilization. How else could newcomers find their way except intuitively, through conversations and experiences?

Perhaps this is why the mythical reality of *welfare* has survived in our way of thinking of ourselves, while the weight of official language—including the concept of *order*—is more or less ignored by the citizenry. Perhaps this is why new Canadians instinctively support Canada's expression of itself through the public good—a single-tier health care, for example, or public schools. In French-immersion classes, the number of new Canadians is usually well above their population percentages. The cynic will say they want the support and want to get ahead. Why shouldn't they want to get ahead? We all want them to succeed in their new lives. The point is that they instinctively understand *faring well* as the public and the private concept of a society that is peaceful and must be well governed.

This persistent orality certainly makes the experts in utilitarian order uncomfortable. In the late eighteenth century, Chief Justice William Smith chaired an inquiry into the professionalism of the legal system. A central accusation was that judges applied French or English law or a mix of the two as it suited them. Smith avoided recommending change. More than two centuries later, a clever Toronto lawyer was deep into a technical argument before the Supreme Court. His position was dependent upon a close reading of the legal text and turned on the letter of the law. Suddenly the chief justice, Beverley McLachlin, leaned forward and asked the counsel if his argument also worked in French. After all, the law is the law in both languages and a loophole in one tends to evaporate in the other. Only an argument of substance stands up. The lawyer had no idea what to reply. Reality seen through two languages can protect us from the demeaning of justice by technical acrobatics. As a result, the meaning of the law in Canada always floats slightly off the page in an almost oral manner.

Harold Innis was the inventor of modern communications theory. He was the spiritual godfather of Marshall McLuhan, both of them professors at the University of Toronto. Innis argued that the oral and the written must be held in balance. This idea made most of the intellectuals around him uncomfortable. They were—are—happier slipping into the conformity of that Western thought dominated by Europe and the United States. For them, there is something not quite orthodox enough about orality as a modern possibility.

Why should we care about what is orthodox? Why should we accept that modernity is essentially written? I for one don't believe that is true. In *The Book of the Bible Against Slavery*, one of our most important early books, John William Robertson, an escaped slave who had become a Nova Scotian, wrote with a dynamic balance of the written and the oral. "[B]ut I knowed one thing that God has declared unto all men, I desire the righteousness which is of the law." What is that "righteousness which is of the law" if not an idea of welfare?

1837—Breaking the Covenant

What happened next—after 1791—was so confused as to slip into violence. The British authorities gradually attempted to impose the sort of colonial system that had led to revolution in the Thirteen Colonies. The Family Compact/Château Clique clung to the authorities and resisted democracy. An incompetent and reactionary governor added to the political frustration. A movement of protest followed, led by Louis-Joseph Papineau and William Lyon Mackenzie, then two badly coordinated European-style rebellions, failure, hangings, transportations of anglophones and francophones to Australia and gratuitous violence by another incompetent governor.

In the midst of all this, Mackenzie produced a draft constitution on November 15, 1837—the result of meetings among "Farmers, Mechanics, Labourers and other Inhabitants of Toronto." They denounced Britain's breaking of its "covenant with the people of Upper and Lower Canada" and proposed a new covenant in order "to make choice of our form of Government and in order to establish justice [i.e., *good government*], ensure domestic tranquility, provide for the common defence [i.e., two aspects of *peace*], promote the general *welfare*, and secure the blessings of civil and religious liberty...."

What followed the failed revolution and the assertion of authority was a sense of depression, a loss of purpose on all sides. Three colonial acts followed in 1838 and 1839, all offering *peace, welfare and good government* while in fact removing them. The last, the bill unifying Upper and Lower Canada in order to undermine the francophones and remove French as an official language, overcompensated for its destructive intent by laying on a thick layer of Enlightenment promises to "secure the rights and liberties and promote the interests of all classes."

This unification was intended to set Canada on the route of greater democracy, but by reverting to a classic European, indeed U.S., model of equality, that of a monolithic state in which the majority decide the fate of the minority. The bounce of complexity was to disappear. The interesting tension between individual rights and group rights was to be eliminated.

The majority of people in both provinces sensed that this could not work. A collective atmosphere of depression continued to hang over society. For the first time the imperial power, including its most democratic voices, had intentionally set out to force the colony down a route unsuited to its reality.

The challenge for the colonial reformers was one of imagination. Could they somehow reimagine the Act of Union to make it do the opposite of what was intended? This sort of alchemy is not impossible. In their case, it would require a leap into the unknown—unknown, that is, in the cannon of Western political organization. This sort of leap works best when there is a fundamental idea within a society of what works—a form of shared truth about the public good that, like an unconscious myth, guides you.

1840—The Egalitarian Manifesto

It was Louis-Hyppolite LaFontaine who managed to reconceptualize this Constitution designed precisely to harm him and his people. In 1840, he proposed a democratic, atypical, non-monolithic reimagining of how to deal with the situation. And what was unusual for Canada, with its halting, half-conscious, instinctual, oral approaches to justifying action, was that he laid out his idea in an elegant, moving, intellectually cutting-edge statement. It was a letter to his own constituents—*Un Adresse aux Électeurs de Terrebonne*. This was not an unusual way to make a major public statement. Edmund Burke's greatest contribution to representative democracy had come in *An Address to the Electors of Bristol*.

LaFontaine's letter dealt with the obvious political crisis. But he went far beyond that to propose an entire civilizational approach, including a full immigration policy, public education, the abolition of elite privileges, the creation of the St. Lawrence Seaway—which would finally be done 125 years later—and both a natural resource and an industrial policy. He mocked those who believed that you could get what you wanted from the Empire by building a special relationship with those who ran it. What you needed was an ethically and intellectually integrated strategy based upon a program for action. In other words, he reformulated the political spectrum.

Democracy was taken for granted as the essential immediate goal, but the real question was what to do with that democracy once you had it. The answer was to build a fair society. You could take his key points, exactly as he wrote them, and lay out a concept of action perfect for today. What made it work then, as it would now, is that his assumptions were not those of a European-style monolithic state. Instead, they were built upon the atypical, non-monolithic model that had emerged over the preceding century.

His concept would only work, he said, if the reformers of Upper Canada would join with those of Lower Canada. Two minorities, together they were the majority and could make the new, unfair Constitution serve the welfare of the whole population.

Within weeks the address was translated and published in Toronto. The anglophone reformers were energized. They gathered themselves around Robert Baldwin and the journalist and financier Francis Hinks, and then struck their alliance with the francophones.

The Address to the Electors of Terrebonne became the ethical and practical expression of how to build a new sort of country based on the continuity, but modernization, of the old atypical complexity.

What was it that LaFontaine found in the unjust Act of Union that could be turned on its head? First, there was the repeated invocation of the welfare of the people along with the need for *good government*. This time these words were linked in the Constitution to a promise to "secure the rights and liberties and promote the interests of all classes."

And what was it that would allow an alliance of reformers to accomplish this in a non-monolithic way? The standard answer is that the reformers joined together to use this promise to get responsible government—a now obscure concept that simply means democracy. Or rather it means one-half of what makes up democracy. The first half is the franchise. I have already explained why Canada had a broader franchise than most countries, including Britain. The essential second half was that any government must be responsible to the people's representatives, not to the head of state or the powerful families.

This simple battle, which took eight years to win, was remarkable in another way. Canada was the first colony in any empire to extract full democracy from the central power without having to go to war. I think of this as an early illustration of the manipulative skills and patient toughness needed to accomplish what we would come to think of as the middle way.

Once Canada had what passed for full democracy in 1848, the eventual disappearance of the European empires had been decided. Once London had conceded real democratic control to a colonial assembly, which in order to function required the involvement of large numbers of non-British peoples, the basic assumption of that empire or of any other had been disproved. What is the basic assumption of empires? One people, by some obscure necessity, must govern other peoples. The disintegration of the British and the French empires in the two decades following the Second World War turned on precisely that conundrum. As had been clarified in Canada exactly one hundred years before, you couldn't govern India, or Algeria, unless the citizens of those countries governed themselves, in which case you could no longer govern. This demonstration of the fallacy of empire remains as dramatic today as the United States rediscovers the same truth. But from Canada's point of view there was something more fundamental going on than the agony of imperial delusion.

The driving force behind which LaFontaine reimagined the Canadian situation was a sense of shared welfare. It was shared because of a common egalitarian approach to society. This was the strategic key that he extracted from Canadian history in order to build an alliance of reformers capable of winning power, establishing democracy and, with a flurry of new laws, laying the foundations for an atypical, non-monolithic experiment. The heart of his argument in *The Address to the Electors of Terrebonne* could not be clearer:

> Beyond Social Equality, we must have Political liberty. Without Political Liberty we have no future; our needs cannot be satisfied. In vain would we strive for that state of well being which is the promise of this continent's vast nature. With constant effort, driven by firmness and prudence towards that goal essential to our prosperity, we will secure our political liberty. They can deny us this status only if they are able to destroy *the Social Equality which constitutes the distinctive characteristic as much of the population of Upper Canada as of Lower Canada. For this Social Equality must necessarily bring us our Political Liberty. The principles of a people are stronger than the laws imposed upon them. No privileged caste, beyond and above the mass of the people, can exist in Canada.*

The only terms to be used more than twice are *political liberty* and *social equality*. Four times they are linked as the two halves of a successful Canadian civilization. Through the context of the Address he lays out how these terms are to be understood. This is not equality as an abstract theory of individual rights, as it is used in the United States and France, in the first case to suggest the autonomous individual and in the second a carefully defined code of sameness into which all individuals must fit in order to protect the state.

LaFontaine's idea is not *equality*, as the Enlightenment understood it, but *egalitarianism*. His idea of social equality was a concept that expressed the Aboriginal idea of a permanent tension between individual and group rights. That tension or balance remains central to our approach to egalitarianism. In the *Address*, LaFontaine had begun his demonstration of the essential link between democracy and social equality with the simple observation that on this continent "the greatest blessing we enjoy is social equality." Later in his address, he came back to the need to do everything possible "to equalize the ranks of society." And in a final flourish, as if to demonstrate why these two concepts must fit together, he declared that "Education is the first public good that a government can give to a people."

What happens in *The Address to the Electors of Terrebonne*, and in the anglophone-francophone alliance that follows, and in the future discussions of the public good in Canada, stretching right up to today, is that *welfare* is understood to mean something shared in the citizenry. Welfare means fairness. But we live as individuals and in groups. Only in a very abstract theoretical approach could we believe that fairness could be applied through individualism alone. That is why we are also part of groups. And that is why fairness is dependent on a balance between the two.

These two words—*welfare* and *fairness*—are not related linguistically. They come from different roots. Our history has worked its way in its bilingual manner from welfare—faring well, bien-être, bonheur, happiness, equitability, social equality and a welfare that implies difference as a strength—to social justice and what we now call pluralism. The idea of the public good that was first expressed through the Germanic/British term of welfare and the French equivalent of bien-être and bonheur slowly morphed into a broad idea of fairness, first expressed as social equality.

"All the histories of all peoples are symbolic," Octavio Paz wrote. "That is why we ask ourselves what the true meaning is of the Crusades, the discovery of America, the sack of Baghdad.... We live history as if it were a performance by masked actors who trace enigmatic figures on the stage."

Agar Adamson was an amusing Canadian colonial snob of the early twentieth century. He was also a talented regimental commanding officer, with a wonderful combination of courage, humour and concern for his men. He served throughout the First World War, much of it commanding the Princess Patricia's Canadian Light Infantry. Every day he wrote a letter to his wife, describing in detail the destruction of the world around him. At first he despaired of the accents of the other Canadian officers, their narrow interests, the poor cut of their uniforms, their incapacity to understand the superiority of the British. He was certain of the lowness of the lower ranks. But as the reality of the war descended upon him, he found himself bitterly complaining about the unjustified superiority of the replacement gentlemen officers. He began replacing his own killed and wounded officers with corporals and sergeants he would insist on having promoted. He remained a snob, but almost as a way to entertain himself and others. He commanded the regiment at Vimy. A week after the victory, he wrote to his wife, "I am since our last engagement, more convinced than ever that nothing but a mutual understanding and a mutual feeling of respect can keep a Regiment together and make it do its best in the face of death." There is nothing more hierarchical than an infantry regiment, and in most countries the disasters of the First World War made them even more hierarchical. There seemed no other way to deal with the new, easy delivery of mass death. The curious conclusion of the Canadians was to marry hierarchy with egalitarian openness. I've often seen this in its contemporary form when visiting our military operations in Bosnia, Kosovo and Afghanistan. It turned out to be the way our soldiers could do things best.

LaFontaine did not pick his concept of social equality out of the air. It was already deep within the Canadian mythology, awaiting a new conceptual language. Some of it was buried in the centuries of experience during which Aboriginal egalitarianism seeped its way into the life of the newcomers. Some of it had been laid out by others—by Louis-Joseph Papineau and Joseph Howe, for example, or through the anti-slavery movement of the late eighteenth century.

The story of slavery, like any ethical drama, reveals at once how our mythologies weigh against our reality. There were some four thousand slaves through the full history of New France; a good three-quarters were Aboriginal and 1032 were of African origin. Under the British regime, Aboriginal slavery continued. They were mainly held in small numbers by over a thousand francophones. Meanwhile, a few hundred richer Loyalists, who became large landowners, arrived with some two thousand black slaves. Thus slavery was very real, but not a broad phenomenon and not an economic policy, as it was in the Thirteen Colonies to the south. But these numbers also remind us that a large percentage of Black Loyalists lived in the same society as slaves who might well be relatives. It tells us something about racism, both habitual and legally organized.

Yet it would be a mistake to fall into a simple cynical view of that society. The colonial view is always that failures reveal a void at the core of society. The racism against and mistreatment of both Black Loyalists and slaves is clear. This *unfairness* was part of what caused twelve hundred of these Loyalists to leave for Sierra Leone in 1792. Yet that was also a story of triumph. Those twelve hundred Nova Scotians sailed off in January to found the first successful country of returning Africans. This was a treacherous business, but novelist Lawrence Hill is right—this was also a great story of courage and demonstrated a fundamental belief in fairness. We should be celebrating it as part of our story.

This does not wipe out all the rest—the mistreatment, for example, of returning Aboriginal and African-Canadian veterans after the World Wars. Nor does it justify myriad wrongs, including the destruction after 1964 of the Africville neighbourhood in Halifax. But it reminds us that these Canadians were not merely victims and should not be stereotyped as victims. They made their contributions as soldiers, writers, activists and farmers. There were many successes and many successful communities. I think of the Elgin Settlement in Ontario, made up of people who came to Canada via the Underground Railway. They knew that there was a fairness in the society and that that fairness, even if withheld, was theirs by right. That it was often withheld was a matter to be struggled over.

And the anti-slavery movement cut across most political lines. The 1793 Anti-Slavery Act of John Graves Simcoe was a half measure, blocked in part by those few large Ontario landowners who owned slaves. But Simcoe was supported by the other Loyalists. It was the first of its kind in the British Empire. And a range of senior judges—William Osgoode, James Monk, Pierre-Louis Panet, Pierre-Amable de Bonne, Thomas Andrew Strange, Sampson Silter Blowers—simply ignored the law in the late eighteenth and early nineteenth centuries. They clearly thought it didn't go far enough. Most of the time when slave owners claimed rights before the courts, they were turned away as if slavery were illegal. The story of slavery reminds us that Tories were not necessarily the problem in Canada. In many cases, as with the judges, they were among those most opposed to slavery. Perhaps the explanation was their non-utilitarian idea of human dignity. The effect of their actions was that by early in the nineteenth century the owners were bereft of the mechanisms of public support and the phenomenon of slavery was withering, long before Britain banned it in 1835 and, of course, longer still before the U.S. Civil War and the Thirteenth Amendment of 1865.

The story of slavery is central here because it illustrates the real dividing line in Canada. It was between the pro- and anti-democratic; those who believed in fairness versus the autocratic; what we might call the humanist versus the Family Compact. In other words, the real division pitched the school of *peace, welfare and good government* against those devoted to the idea of *order* as a central principle of power.

This same division can be seen in the drama of Joseph Howe. In 1835, the Nova Scotian Family Compact set out to destroy him financially and professionally with a formal accusation of libel. They attempted to use the law to undermine freedom of speech. It was the equivalent of what we have come to know in our own time as libel chill, in which people with money undertake expensive legal suits to frighten off criticism. Howe had to defend himself. Near the end of his four-and-a-quarter-hour speech, he said, "When I sit down in solitude to the labours of my profession, the only questions I ask myself are: what is right, what is just, what is for the public good." LaFontaine, Papineau, Mackenzie, Baldwin, leaders everywhere in the Canadas had read this speech before the uprisings of 1837. Howe's victory had been the first for a modern idea of free speech. It was an essential part of their belief that they had a right to fairness. He had also laid out a new vocabulary for considering Canadian society. In 1920, Fred Dixon, the imprisoned leader of the 1919 Winnipeg General Strike, modelled his own self-defence on that of Howe and won acquittal.

1841—The Concept of Harmony

On the evening of September 3, 1841, Robert Baldwin sat quietly in the new legislature of the unified Canadas in Kingston. It was the opening session. He was the leader of the majority, a coalition of anglophone and francophone democratic reformers. He was nevertheless the Leader of the Opposition, because the Governor General, Lord Sydenham, had chosen to keep his own Family Compact friends in power. And they had run on an anti–responsible government platform, as real democracy would cost them their jobs and their contracts. LaFontaine wasn't there. On election day a Governor General's Orange Order mob, one thousand strong, had descended from Montreal upon his constituency of Terrebonne with clubs and prevented his voters from getting through to the hustings—the voting platform.

Baldwin was waiting, looking for a strategic opportunity to demonstrate what the power of the majority meant. He needed to introduce the principles of *The Address to the Electors of Terrebonne* into the reality of political events. He had prepared four resolutions laying out the practical principles and implications of democracy. That night he suddenly saw the political opportunity, and he rose to introduce them in the House. The government was without a majority and loath to appear to be flagrantly anti-democratic. So they amended the four resolutions very slightly in order to make them their own. Baldwin accepted the amendments, and the resolutions were carried. In theory, democracy was now no longer a matter of partisan politics.

This was perhaps Baldwin's greatest moment. It would take another five and a half years of tough political slogging before the theory actually became reality, with the formation of LaFontaine's government on March 11, 1848.

His second resolution stated that only ministerial responsibility to Parliament, not to the Governor General—in other words, full democracy—could produce "that *harmony* which is essential to the *peace, welfare and good government*" of the state. The surprising element here is the idea of harmony. How did Baldwin come to introduce it? This was not a concept central to the Enlightenment.

Thomas Jefferson had used it, but not often, and usually to mean agreement. He meant "harmonized" rather than harmony and used the words interchangeably. "Union of opinion … gives to a nation the blessing of harmony.…" He argued that the United States would buy Louisiana because it was difficult "to live in harmony [with] strangers of another family [rather than] our own brethren and children." James Madison was the U.S. public figure who most often invoked harmony, but again he meant agreement—"internal harmony and subordination." At best he meant something like effective government. The great fear of the founders of the United States was that, having created their country out of a violence that papered over the country's fundamental internal contradictions—such as the interwoven arguments in favour of states' rights and slavery—it would break apart again. And it would do so violently. They were right to be afraid, as that was precisely what happened some seventy-five years later. That original fear of the founders still lies at the heart of nationalism in the United States and still drives the country's idea of citizenship expressed through loyalty.

Baldwin used harmony in quite a different way, influenced by its philosophical sense. The German philosopher Gottfried Leibniz personified this approach. He saw "the universe as a harmonious system in which there is at the same time unity and multiplicity, coordination and differentiation of parts." This sounds almost exactly like the non-monolithic idea of Canada. English philosopher Lord Shaftesbury in the early eighteenth century focused on "the Greek idea of balance and harmony." All of these ideas were part of the general knowledge of a well-read man such as Baldwin.

There was one other more intriguing factor. As I have pointed out several times, harmony was a concept central to the culture of Aboriginals. The architect Douglas Cardinal: "Cultures are based in harmony as a way of being." And the indigenous meaning was very close to that of the Greeks or of Leibniz or Shaftesbury. Harmony was a concept of the whole and of a balance that went far beyond mere humans. What's more, in their negotiations among themselves and with Europeans, Aboriginals invariably placed themselves and their argument within the concept of harmony. It was an all-inclusive view of the natural order of things, an order in which humans were merely a part. It related to their complex balancing of individualism and group and place, each existing at the same time apart, in complex relationships of co-operation and as nodes "in an interconnected web." There are myriad Aboriginal expressions for this. One well-known Cree concept is Witaskewin, or harmonious living, which means living together on the land, that is, an agreement to live together in peace. You could translate it today as democratic federalism or practical environmentalism.

Witaskewin relates to other Aboriginal ideas, such as that of the great circle that can grow to include outsiders. These are broad ideas of welfare or social equality set within an animist concept: of people, animals and place as one.

Does all of this explain Baldwin's use of the term? Not necessarily. One thing we know is that Baldwin's nationalism was built upon an idea of historic Aboriginal leadership. He was not alone, and there was a romantic side to this school, with its idealization of Tecumseh as the great martyr of the Canadian dream. Baldwin had written poems about Tecumseh. But none of that is a reason to dismiss his form of nationalism as irrelevant. At least it was an attempt to place his Canadian project within a concept of the Americas, instead of in the shadow of imported ideas.

13

Imagining a Fair Country

1848 and Immigration

On March 11, 1848, the first democratic government came to power, with LaFontaine as prime minister and Baldwin as his number two. They were young men—forty-one and forty-four, respectively—filled with energy.

The cabinet they formed was called the Great Ministry and it set about changing the face of the Canadas. Some one hundred and fifty laws passed over the next three years would constitute the legal foundations of modern Canada. The cabinet's first law, of March 23, aimed to improve the lot of poor immigrants. Cabinet was picking up on an earlier law and giving it real teeth. The law involved serious taxes or duties on shipping companies in order to create a fund to help the poorest get settled: *An Act to create a fund [to enable] Indigent Emigrants to proceed to their place of destination, and of supporting them until they can procure employment.* The law then set out taxes, fines and bonds to ensure ships were clean, immigrants kept healthy, that they were landed free of charge in the right spot. And if brought to Canada too late in the season, the immigrants were to be financially supported through the winter by the shipping company.

The point is obvious. A concept of aid to immigrants had been developed for the Loyalist refugees seventy years before. It had included land grants, farm implements, food and clothing for two years. This principle of welfare as an attempt at fairness became normal procedure. Military engineers laid out the roads. The land grants were precise. The aid was carefully defined. By the time of the opening of the prairies to Northern and Eastern European immigrants, federal settlement officers were choosing large sites and drawing up the town plans before meeting the groups of Poles or Swedes or Ukrainians when they arrived at the railway station. We know that none of this was sufficient, that much of the land was badly chosen, that many immigrants suffered. In some cases a generation was lost, with whole farming regions abandoned in the early twentieth century. We can imagine the despair those new Canadians must have felt, having risked all by leaving their countries. But the intent had been to help these people fare well. The immigrant settlement programs of today are also insufficient. But a great effort is made, and these programs are the direct inheritors of more than two centuries of intentional immigration aimed at creating new citizens and supported by intentional programs aimed at fairness. As in the 1780s with the war-shocked Loyalist refugees, most without even the proverbial suitcase holding all their belongings, so today with thirty thousand refugees a year and two hundred and seventy thousand immigrants coming from every condition imaginable. We forget that only a quarter of them are cherry-picked for their skills. Each one of these immigrants has every right, even though he may not believe it, to speak up whenever these support systems do not deliver fairness. Once they are citizens they have the obligation to make themselves heard. And whenever possible, established Canadians should be doing so on their behalf. The intent is fairer systems. That was and is the desire.

There is one other detail in the 1848 law worth thinking about. It talks of regulating ships coming from Great Britain but also from any port in Europe. The assumption already was that immigrants could arrive from anywhere.

Anywhere in the 1840s meant Europe. But Europeans were not thought of then as one social or cultural or even racial family. The British and French thought of Eastern or Northern Europeans as profoundly distant from them, in almost exactly the same way that early twentieth-century Westerners thought of Asians. The debate over opening the prairies to Scandinavians and Eastern Europeans had all the connotations we experienced a bit later over opening Canada to East and South

Asians. When the Ku Klux Klan set itself up on the Canadian prairies in the 1930s, its target, in the absence of a large African-Canadian community, was the immigrant in general and, in particular, the pacifist religious minorities, such as the Mennonites.

Over the last two and a half centuries each new group of immigrants—and therefore of citizens—has provoked some sort of debate. The outcome, given our non-monolithic idea and our triangular foundation of three broad cultural groups, has been to conclude the debate by widening the circle. Sometimes the process has been slow and laced with the stupidity of racism. Nevertheless, the outcome has been a continuation of the original idea of immigration and inclusion laid out in the Royal Proclamation and the Quebec Act, with the modern refocusing of LaFontaine's *Terrebonne* address.

LaFontaine had prefaced his praise of social equality and political liberty in his address with a call for immigration. It might have been written last week:

> Canada is the land of our ancestors. It is our country as it must be the adopted country of the different peoples who come from around the globe to make their way into its vast forests to build their homes and place their hopes. Like us, their paramount desire must be the welfare [bonheur in the original] and prosperity of Canada. This is the heritage which they should endeavour to transmit to their descendants in this young and hospitable country. Their children must be, like us, Canadians.

In the next sentence he began his praise of social equality. In other words, people from around the globe were to be linked by their social equality as a guarantee of shared political liberty. The key to a society built on more than one language and on multiple cultures was an idea of justice based in fairness or, to put it differently, an egalitarian approach based upon a constant striving for fairness. There would be different races and an unprecedented jostling of cultures, often leading to mixed races. But it was their welfare, happiness, bien-être, bonheur, it was the justness of their situation, the fairness of it, that would help them work out how to live together in one great circle or civilization.

We talk often and vaguely about our values, frequently slipping into romantic banality. Here surely is the hard core of whatever values we have. There is nothing romantic here, nothing definitively achieved. Here is an approach to society that requires constant effort and a balance of openness and firmness.

~

George-Étienne Cartier was much more the thinker behind Confederation than John A. Macdonald. Cartier used the parliamentary debates over Confederation to explain how races would be brought together by ideas. The result of this political union, he said, would be "a political nationality independent of the national or religious origin of every individual." He dismissed as utopian the idea that differences could be made to disappear. He was referring to the utopian idea of the eighteenth/nineteenth-century Euro-U.S. nation-state: "We are different races, not in order to go to war with each other but to work together for our *welfare*." This is what Harold Innis called "the lack of unity which has preserved Canadian unity" or the opposite of what Supreme Court Justice Rosalie Abella criticizes as "the civil libertarian concept of ... equality as sameness."

There is an assumption today that Canada's openness to the world really began in the 1960s and 1970s. What happened then was important. It saw the removal of most of our remaining institutionalized racism. The exclusion of most Aboriginals from voting rights and most Chinese Canadians from citizenship were among the most important. Yet barriers remain, for example, in the structures that Aboriginals must deal with.

But if you wonder why Canada is able to take more immigrants per capita than any other country and make them full citizens within four to five years with quite a bit of success, while other countries stumble over far smaller numbers, the answer is not that we are nicer, smarter or that we changed radically in the 1960s. The answer lies, first, in the culture of minorities common among Aboriginals and in their idea of society as an expanding and mutating circle. Second, it lies in an expanding and intentional program of immigration over two and a half centuries that from the beginning was developed as a way to build citizenship and society. The second was built out of the first. We have had time to recognize most of our earlier mistakes, injustices and failures for what they were—betrayals of our original idea of fairness.

What is unusual in this approach is that it has always taken for granted a multiple personality order. We have learned to accept that people are capable of sorting out how to be more than one thing at once, knowing that their children will be yet another mixture or blend. People are capable of staying the same and changing at the same time. And the roots of this acceptance go back to the building of our triangular foundation between the sixteenth and eighteenth centuries.

In 1905, Wilfrid Laurier, then at the height of his power as prime minister, spoke at the celebration in Edmonton welcoming Alberta into Confederation as a province. People were flooding onto the prairies from Northern, Central and Eastern Europe. At the front of the great crowd were the established elites of the province. But behind them were the newcomers—the Ukrainians, Mennonites, Poles, Russians. They would become the elite within a half-century. Partway through his speech, Laurier spoke over the heads of the elites and directly to them:

> We must also have the co-operation of the new citizens, who come from all parts of the world, to give to Canada and to Alberta, the benefit of their individuality, of their energy and their enterprise.... Canada is in one respect like the Kingdom of Heaven, those who come at the eleventh hour will receive the same treatment as those who have been in the field for a long time. [L]et them take their share in the life of this country, whether it be municipal, provincial or national. Let them be electors as well as citizens. We do not want nor wish that any individual should forget the land of his origin. Let them look to the past, but let them still more look to the future. Let them look to the land of their ancestors, but let them look also to the land of their children. Let them become Canadians ... and give their heart, their song, their energy and all their power to Canada....

Were these words overly optimistic, coming at the very moment when the full blast of twentieth-century racism was about to strike? Probably.

But one of the jobs of a leader is to remind citizens of their most decent intentions. A prime minister, minister or premier must never play upon people's fear of *the other*, as was done repeatedly, for example, in 2007 over the dress of Islamic women voters, in the hope of gaining support from other parts of the population. This is a dangerous and irresponsible game. A fair country is the result, yes, of happy accidents, fortunate circumstances and goodwill. But in the long run it is the outcome of a conscious and intentional approach to the public good.

In the Supreme Court case following the 1995 Quebec referendum, John Whyte spoke for Saskatchewan and summarized the idea of community and fairness: Our ability to live with difference is dependent on our capacity to keep on trying to imagine the other while weaving together the fabric of society. "A nation is built when the communities that comprise it make commitments to it, when they forgo choices and opportunities on behalf of a nation…when the communities that comprise it make compromises, when they offer each other guarantees, when they make transfers, and perhaps most pointedly, when they receive from others the benefits of national solidarity. The threads of a thousand acts of accommodation are the fabric of a nation …"

This is quite different from soft phrases such as *a community of communities* or even *multiculturalism*. There is something old-style European about these latter words, vaguely nineteenth-century, Austro-Hungarian, as if Canada were a bunch of watertight communities stitched together by a legal framework. They are one-dimensional, linear concepts.

What is interesting in the Canadian idea is just how multi-levelled and multi-faceted lives can be at the same time. That's what I mean by a multiple personality order. The philosopher Will Kymlicka is very good at explaining this complexity and the desire for fairness it contains.

Quebec has been developing an interesting concept—intercultural-isme—which of all the words in use comes closest to describing how Canada actually functions. It was originally developed in the 1970s and 1980s by provincial civil servants and a few academics eager to argue that Quebec had an approach to complex citizenship that was quite different from the pan-Canadian model of multiculturalism. Their argument required that Canadian multiculturalism be set up as a straw dog of unintegrated communities—indeed an Austro-Hungarian nightmare— while Quebec's concept was all about the intercultural dovetailing relationship among four groups: the francophone majority, the anglophone minority, the Aboriginal minority, and the *cultural communities*, that is, the newcomers, with French as the central convening language for all four. Of course, the straw dog—the official definition of multiculturalism from the 1970s—had never actually been applied to how Canada worked. Instead the whole country, including Quebec, had been slowly working out how to describe what we do and what to call it.

If you read the very fine report produced in 2008 for the Quebec government by the thinkers Gérard Bouchard and Charles Taylor, you discover that we have all come out in pretty well the same place. They were commissioned to ask all Quebecers, and to think themselves, about how newcomers were and should fit into Quebec. Bouchard and Taylor are both very smart as well as sensitive to the complexities of real lives. They are not ideologues. They are not interested in some people's fixed ideas of how lives *ought* to be lived.

They concluded that more should be made of interculturalisme. They describe it as "conciliating the new cultures with the continuity of the francophone core and the preservation of social ties." The one key difference with the pan-Canadian approach is their perfectly understandable concentration on French as the central convening language, as opposed to bilingualism. In any case, bilingualism has always been strong in large parts of Quebec. Bouchard and Taylor also insist on the importance of being "open to the rich and creative contributions of *the other*." And as everywhere in Canada, they insist on the need to deal with artificial blockages such as the confusion over credentials, the lack of long-term second-language education and the few mechanisms in place to help newcomers find places in smaller communities.

Interculturalisme is still not quite the right term to describe how we live together. But it is by far the best word we have, and I find myself using it more and more often.

There was a vigorous debate in Ontario in 2004 over whether Sharia courts could be created to permit Islamic family arbitration in the province. The Islamic community itself was divided. What struck me most was that each time I was in Europe at a meeting or giving a speech, people would bring it up, clearly upset. They said Sharia courts were going to be imposed in Canada, limiting women's rights. This, they said, was the failure of multiculturalism. It had come apart, just as they had always suspected it would. There was a certain self-satisfaction in their panic, as if they could now say everyone was doing as badly as they were. The perceived superiority of the Canadians on matters of immigration had been proved a bit simple-minded, just what they would expect from an ex-European colony.

I usually replied that first, the guarantees in the Charter of Rights overrode any other court. No arbitration tribunal could ignore that. Second, there was a public debate going on. Talking is good. No doubt this edgy conversation would take time. And that time was an essential part of working out a sensible answer to the question. My rather dispassionate reply seemed to create greater panic, even anger, as if they had always known there was something wrong with the way Canada put all those people together.

Eventually, the Ontario government decided that the problem was not Sharia courts of arbitration. Rather, the error lay in the broad decision some years before to permit any sort of religious family arbitration. The intention had been good—to keep families out of the bruising, expensive formal court system. But the fallout was worse than the advantage gained. So these arbitration courts were banned for all religions. It had been a decade-long experiment that was finally put aside.

Since then the provincial government has been re-elected. There were no signs, during the campaign or in the outcome, of cultural communities or ethnic minorities punishing the government for its decision. New Canadians don't tend to see themselves in such Manichean terms. They have multiple visions of themselves.

There are those in Canada who are as panicked as the Europeans about the country being so open. They talk a great deal about our values— usually in a vague but urgent manner—and worry about the presence of so many immigrants from extremely conservative religious and social backgrounds. They forget that that has almost always been the case.

Did the Northern Irish arrive in Canada in the nineteenth century open-minded and ready to learn French while reaching out to Catholics? Did the attitudes toward women's rights of many Portuguese men from the Azores match those of most established Canadians? What about the attitudes of Serb and Croat immigrants to each other? What about the Finnish communists who went to cut logs in northwestern Ontario? Or the Italians from small southern villages? The whole Canadian experience of immigration has been one of experimenting with adaptation. It's not about humiliating people by shutting them into preconceived models.

That is why the strength of the public school system has always been the key to new citizens finding their way. And that is why the desire of many in the established middle classes to withdraw their children from the public system is deeply irresponsible. To do so is a failure of citizenship; an unwillingness to take the time to help right whatever is wrong in the system; a failure to consciously accept that Canada works because of the mixes created in those schools. If the elite desert them, they betray their country. And that is why the actions of many provincial governments over the last few decades, with that of Mike Harris in the vanguard, to cut back on programs and services in public schools were—and these words are not often used in Canada—intentionally evil. The slowness with which many more recently elected provincial governments are undoing this damage and working out new ways to re-energize the public system represents a profound confusion as they fiddle with bookkeeping instead of investing in the core of the public welfare.

1849 and the Middle Way

On the evening of April 25, 1849, an angry Montreal mob burned down the Parliament, then located in Montreal. The Members were almost suffocated inside. The largest library in Canada, with its invaluable historic collection, went up in flames. LaFontaine's democratic government was only a year old.

The mob went off in search of both him and Baldwin. They looted the prime minister's new mansion and Baldwin's boarding house. It seems likely they would have killed both men had they found them. Over the next few days they twice attacked Lord Elgin, the Governor General, the second time stoning his coach as they chased it through the street.

They said they were outraged over the Rebellion Losses Bill. The Opposition claimed that francophone rebels from 1837 were going to be reimbursed for their property losses. This wasn't true. Their anger was more fundamentally about the rise of a new model of government—a relatively even-handed democracy that erased the control of the various Family Compacts and ensured that real power was open to the whole community.

The government used as little force as possible to re-establish order. This failed. On April 27, the cabinet, including Elgin, met quietly in the Château Ramezay to decide what to do. Outside, the mob was still in control.

The ministers were given a report on the situation, prepared by an anglophone minister. It was probably the work of consultations with LaFontaine and Baldwin. There are telltale terms within the text that were used elsewhere by the two politicians. The core of the report lies in two sentences.

> In an emergency of this kind the Committee of Council are of the opinion that the proper mode of preserving order is by strengthening the Civil Authorities.

> The Committee of Council depreciates the employment of the Military to suppress such disturbances as those which have disgraced the City of Montreal.

I've heard cynics argue that the government was afraid to send anglophone soldiers to fire on anglophone rioters. This is an ignorant reading of the time. From 1849 through 1851, the bourgeoisie throughout the Western world were caught up in a civil war, within both their own class and their own families. The pro-democracy and anti-democracy movements were busy killing each other in great numbers, often brother against brother. Lord Grey, the British minister of the colonies, was furious when he learned that the troops had not been used. He wrote Elgin about the need to follow Napoleon's dictum that professional soldiers should always be used against mobs because they don't miss when ordered to shoot. The dominant theme of the day throughout Britain, Europe and the United States was *order*.

Besides, if they were afraid to ask soldiers to fire on the anglophone mob, why did the council name a francophone cabinet minister, Colonel Étienne-Paschal Taché, to organize an armed special police force of citizens? Colonel Taché, with military experience, would have been the wrong man for the job if their central aim was to protect anglophone rioters.

LaFontaine and his government accepted the report and decided against using violence, even if a few more buildings burned and their own dignity was assaulted. Why? Because they didn't want a permanently divided society. They decided on restraint, put human lives ahead of property and sat tight.

They chose public welfare over public order. This restraint and calm was of a revolutionary sophistication for the nineteenth century, particularly between 1848 and 1851.

"The middle way is no way at all," John Adams had written to General Horatio Gates early in the American Revolution. "If we finally fail in this great and glorious contest, it will be by bewildering ourselves in groping for the middle way." It could be argued that this myth of the impossibility of a middle way lies deep within the U.S. psyche. The position in which Adams and Gates had put themselves certainly required courage. They were the underdogs. Yet the more powerful the United States has become, the more the idea of the middle way has come to suggest failure.

LaFontaine's government revealed something quite different—the possibility, when necessary, of a military middle way. A balance of firmness and restraint was often the best way to deal with complex problems. This was something the newcomers had slowly learned from the Aboriginals. And it had begun to emerge in Canada as a formal philosophical and mythological position with the Royal Proclamation. In 1837, this had disintegrated and everyone had seen the damage done on all sides. In fact, each time there has been a loss of restraint in Canadian internal crises, the damage has been lasting.

In the crisis of 1849, you can see some of the roots of what would emerge a hundred years later, as if from nowhere, as "peacekeeping." As

I have said, there were those who would see Lester Pearson's invention of the United Nations military force as a curious accident and a withdrawal of Canada from international realities, a cowardly refusal to engage, even a betrayal of our armed role in two World Wars.

The reality was quite different. Peacekeeping was not only a perfectly logical international outcome of developing a middle way over two and a half centuries as an approach to running such a complex society. It was also a perfectly logical outcome of our two World War experiences and our frustration with empires, ex-empires and future empires using Canadian armies as they wished, and confusing real ethical causes with their imperial interests. The very fact that Britain, France and the United States disliked the peacekeeping model and more or less stood aloof from it until the terrible civil war in Yugoslavia in the 1990s should have been enough to tell us that we were onto something interesting.

As so often in Canada, the real questions surrounding the middle way are not left wing–right wing. They are self-confidence versus a sort of colonial insecurity, fairness versus order. You can see this in the most surprising of places, for example in the Canadian Certificates handed out in the 1930s by the Imperial Order of the Daughters of Empire. These were given to immigrants of non-British origin who had to be naturalized as *Canadian citizens and British subjects*. It is generally said that there was no such thing as a Canadian citizen before 1947. This is untrue. We were both Canadian citizens and British subjects. As for the IODE certificates, they couldn't help but include some bits of imperial horn-blowing. But more surprisingly, they were dominated by a foreshadowing of the Charter of Rights, extolling Freedoms of Speech, Assembly, Religion and Democratic Government. And they laid out five great principles. The fifth was THE CASTING OFF OF OLD HATREDS— "Canada has set her feet upon the paths of peace, at home and among the nations of the world." This sounds more like a continuation of the middle way than standard empire worship.

Peacekeeping began to evolve the moment we invented it. And our soldiers were central to that evolution. Commanders are faced every day with the conundrum that LaFontaine's government had to wrestle with. It isn't all that hard to kill the enemy. But, as I pointed out earlier, each successful killing can cost you the support of a village or a tribal group. The strategic solution seems to require a very sophisticated middle way filled with firmness balanced by prudence.

1866 and the Role of Order

In September 1864, on one of those oppressively hot Canadian summer days, the future Fathers of Confederation met in Charlottetown in the beautiful, intimate P.E.I. legislature. On October 10, 1864, equally oppressed by cold, darkness and continuous rain, they finished their negotiations in Quebec City on a cliff overlooking the St. Lawrence, in a convent converted into the Parliament of the Canadas. In the Quebec Resolutions, *Peace, Welfare and Good Government* was present as in all earlier documents. On December 4, 1866, they began a discussion that would lead to the London Resolutions before the end of the year. They had crossed the Atlantic to tie down the details with the imperial government and *Welfare* was still in its place. Then came three drafts of the British North American Act. *Welfare* was in each of them, although separate mention of *Peace, Order and Good Government* abruptly appeared, along with the arrival of Lord Carnarvon, a Conservative, as the new colonial secretary.

In the next draft, *Welfare* was gone. And in the final Constitution only *Peace, Order and Good Government* remained. There was no public or written explanation. All we know for sure is that the change was intentional.

It is here that we first come across the now-standard story that this change was somehow an expression of Canada's Tory past, going back to the Loyalists. And John A. Macdonald was a Tory. We have already established that the vast majority of the Loyalists were not Tories. And they certainly weren't Tory in the sense suggested by this argument.

What's more, this explanation misrepresents, as Stephen Eggleston, one of the great experts on the *Peace, Order and Good Government* question rightly points out, the Canadians who went to London to negotiate Canadian independence. They were a mix of conservatives and liberals. The conservatives were descendants of the LaFontaine-Baldwin Liberal-Conservative movement, and therefore enemies of the old Tory, anti-democratic Family Compact crowd. The liberals were a divided group of those who were also descendants of the LaFontaine-Baldwin coalition, and the more extreme Grits, who were obsessed by such things as representation by population. One way or another, they all belonged to the democratic reform movement. They were all different sorts of enemies of the old Tories and the Compacts and the Cliques. From an ethical, emotional and conceptual point of view, although not necessarily political, they saw themselves as the inheritors of Howe, LaFontaine and Baldwin. At various times most of them said as much. The year 1864 was the great democratic breakthrough and the third attempt, after 1840 and 1848, at laying out a broad idea of the public good and how to serve it. Confederation was about creating a bigger political canvas on which the earlier marriages of democracy and the complex public good could be successfully played out. John A. Macdonald, George-Étienne Cartier, Charles Tupper and Robert Wilmot were all conservatives or liberal conservatives. They were also advocates of public education, to take just one example of a major policy that the old Tories or Compact members wanted no part of. Cartier had been a disciple of LaFontaine. And for both Cartier and Macdonald, the Canadian model of leadership and fairness was illustrated by LaFontaine and Baldwin. The Fathers of Confederation were the great reformers of their day, young and ambitious for the country they were creating.

As for the rumour that order replaced welfare because of a drafting error, or that it was done on the initiative of a junior British bureaucrat—both suggestions are ridiculous. These future Canadians had crossed the Atlantic to negotiate our independence. They were highly intelligent and they debated every word in the BNA Act among themselves and in detail. The outcome may have been a compromise, its long-term effect may have been unforeseen, but the choice of words was intentional.

It is worth remembering that only once before in Canada's political structuring had the word *Order* been used. In 1763, the first British governor, James Murray, received three legal documents. The Royal Proclamation and his public commission both spoke of *Welfare*. His private instructions spoke of *Order*.

Colonies then came under the power of the Board of Trade in London. Murray quickly discovered that he was serving two contradictory forces. One, outside the Board of Trade and made up of political reformers, was experienced in the Americas and had some idea of the public good. They wanted a fairly run colony. Murray represented this group. It was they who ensured that francophones received those citizens' rights that no Catholic could hold in Britain. They represented the *welfare* or bien-être approach. The other force was led by the Lords of the Board of Trade itself, and they saw colonies as mere economic opportunities. They considered it the governor's job to facilitate money-making for English or American English merchants and traders. The francophones were to be swept aside. This was the *order* school and those were the intentions of Murray's private instructions.

Murray chose to ignore the desires of the board and the traders. "Nothing," he wrote, "will satisfy the licentious fanatics trading here but the expulsion of the Canadiens, who are perhaps the bravest and best race upon the globe." Foolishly he sent this letter to the Board of Trade. The Lords of Trade and their American merchant allies would poison Murray's years as governor and eventually drive him out.

It was this Tory element within Canada that would evolve under more compliant governors into the Family Compact/Château Clique. The anger of the Boston and other American traders over being more or less shut out of the Canadian fur market would also grow. After 1774, they would unsuccessfully lobby for the revocation of the Quebec Act as a way of removing French-Canadian competition and getting control of both the northern trade and the Indian lands. After 1776, they would increasingly join the movement for a break with Britain as the best way to satisfy their ambitions.

These earlier struggles are highly relevant to the replacement of *welfare* by *order* in 1866. *Order* was generally used in the British Empire to describe the use of authority or power. *Welfare* was used to describe the nature of governmental policy, which implied the existence of a public weal.

In practical terms, power meant power over programming. As late as 1942, the Judicial Committee of the Privy Council—the equivalent of a Supreme Court in London for the Dominions and the colonies—had to interpret the meaning of *Peace, Order and Good Government* in the

India Act. They said it referred to the scope and not the merits of the legislation. In other words, *Order* referred to power over the extent of the law, not to the nature of the law, which would come under *Welfare*.

This rather dry differentiation relates directly to the two central explanations for the switch of 1866. Lord Carnarvon, a Conservative minister, took over on behalf of the British government partway through the Canadian negotiations. His central aim seemed to be to save the imperial government money by getting it out of spending obligations in Canada. And their major cost was the British military establishment in Canada, small though it was. *Power* in 1866 meant that the Canadians would assume power over programs, that is, pay for their own defence.

The second explanation relates to the Canadian negotiators and their desire to get real self-government. Again, this was the first time that a colony of a European empire had achieved independence without going to war. A clear sign that this independence was real was that Canadians would be in control of their own security. This sounds like an idea Cartier would have pushed. He had been one of the few successful rebels in 1837. After Confederation, he would go on to write Canada's Militia Act, create the Canadian Army and become its first minister.

If these British and Canadian explanations are accurate—and there is no other convincing argument—then the switching of words was all about short-term, instrumental ambitions. It had nothing to do with old-style Toryism. It had everything to do with a new-style nationalism embraced by conservatives and liberals alike. And it did not suggest a rejection of the long-developed sense of *welfare*. Neither Cartier nor Macdonald had a philosophical bent. They were highly intelligent and sophisticated individuals specialized in the business of governing, often for the right reasons. But they didn't tend to abstractions and theories when it came to government.

Societies are living bodies. They have bone structure and innards. But they must develop muscles to activate the body. And they must maintain these muscles, which may take the shape of ideals or nationalism in one form or another, or myths of race, or dreams of grandeur, or power in the form of *order* or fairness in the form of *welfare*.

There was no intent in the 1866 replacement of *welfare* by *order* to let the growing muscle of fairness waste away. Nor did it. Indeed, the Fathers of Confederation strengthened the official concept of welfare. They did this by transferring the idea, through a multiple use of Psalm 72, to our national motto and to the actual description of the country. I'll come back to this later.

But the disappearance of the concept of welfare from its historical place could only complicate public perceptions and change the way public debates were structured. Canada continued to work its way toward an idea of fairness but as if it had lost its overarching language, almost as if these improvements were ad hoc or accidental. The long-term effect of the short-term decision in London was to create a growing confusion as to the purpose of the state.

14

Order and Fear,
Fear and Order

The ideas of the *Terrebonne* address and the Great Ministry of LaFontaine and Baldwin from 1848 to 1851 were somehow misplaced along with much of our history. A new school of historians emerged from 1867 determined to treat Confederation as a brand-new beginning designed to make up for past failures. They represented in many ways the Tory school, and the past failures were theirs. But if Canada was a brand-new beginning, they could erase the memory of welfare or fairness, and its gradual evolution through our history. Now, by treating Macdonald as a pro-Empire, pro-British hero, they could revive the old theories of the Compacts and Cliques in the name of Victorian loyalty of the great and eternal empire and, of course, in the name of the virginal creation called Canada.

This school of thought seized upon *Peace, Order and Good Government* as its motto. It was at last a way to reject patriotically the ideas of complexity and of a non-monolithic society that had so long dominated. Clarity could be claimed to be acceptable for the first time in Canadian history. At first their loyalty and patriotism was all about Britishness. The francophone, Aboriginal, to say nothing of other minority elements, all existed but were swept to the margins of the country's image. This in turn dragged us into a series of internal crises in the last quarter of the nineteenth century and on through to the divisive moments of the First World War.

And then, as the eternal empire began to fade, the promoters of clarity simply switched their loyalty to another, so that today the equivalent obsession involves a special relationship with our closest and most powerful neighbour, the United States. This is framed as loyalty, not friendship. And anyone who asks questions is simply anti-American, just as anyone who once questioned contributions to the British Empire was simply anti-British.

How can you tell that this school is all about loyalty and not about friendship? For a start, major choices are not presented as choices. At best they are presented in a Manichean manner. There are no choices—only what is presented as the professional, orderly self-evident versus the emotional and incompetent. Instead of a choice there is administrative logic—the natural outcome of an orderly society, down to the tiniest detail.

In 2007, it was announced that Canadian border guards would have to be armed. The world's largest undefended border—a century-old boast—would have to be defended. It was simply a matter of dealing efficiently with international security risks, a simple matter of order. Since those on the border would be armed, therefore all employees exposed to the public must be protected against the expected shootouts. Passport officers deep inside airports receive passengers who have already been vetted in every possible way before getting onto planes. They must now be treated as potentially armed when they get off those same planes. Passport officers must therefore wear bulletproof vests. Observe as you come through after your next international flight. They sit there stiffly, uncomfortable, often sweating.

When has a border guard desperately needed a pistol? When was the last armed attack at a border post? How many border guards have been shot at? How many exactly? Two? One? Zero? Are they in any real danger? Is the danger greater than for a child crossing a street after school? If passport officers were in danger, surely it would be a job for the police, whose job it is to maintain peace. Even they seem to have difficulty doing the right thing in moments of crisis. What is a border guard to do with a pistol, a little training and no daily experience in armed crises? Wouldn't they be more of a danger to themselves and the public than to any potential terrorist?

Yet the arming and padding of these perfectly ordinary civil servants has taken place without debate, as if it were merely a matter of order. It is a great deal more than that. First, it creates an atmosphere of extreme distrust where nothing has happened to justify this.

Second, it reflects the inferiority complex of those who made such decisions. The old colonial tick—the sort of thing from which the Family Compacts and Cliques and Empire worshippers writhed—requires that you pump yourself up to Empire standards to compensate for your personal sense of inadequacy.

Wherever you look in the world you find that those obsessed by order require disorder to fulfill their inner fears. They live the Hobbesian nightmare. They fear *the other*, a profoundly anti-democratic characteristic. They desperately seek certainty and clarity, all the while asserting that clarity is a sign of toughness. Actually, the need for clarity reveals a childlike and romantic character. They don't have the self-confidence to live with complexity and uncertainty.

Crime statistics go down year after year, but those obsessed by order need to believe that there is a man around the corner waiting to murder you—you in particular. It is a personal threat. They themselves would be surprised not to find that man waiting for them. "Symmetry in any narrative always means that historical reality is being subordinated to mythical demands of design and form." Northrop Frye, the calmest of men, had a sharp eye for this kind of panicked *order*. Why are passport officers sweating in bulletproof vests while sitting in the safe inner sanctuaries of airports? Because their leaders—ours—are insecure men living a personal psychosis of fear. Leaders driven by fear are the source of populism. Their personal dread equips them to find and release the fear that lies within each of us. That is their skill.

A successful society is able to subdue the natural fear of men and women sufficiently to release our positive and creative characteristics. The power of populism is that it brings an atmosphere of insecurity to the fore and so causes even the most stable of societies to be consumed by that fear and so become obsessed by order.

British political theorist Sir Bernard Crick: "They know how to create a general climate so that the exceptional seems normal." Curiously enough, populism acts to install order against fear, yet never removes that sense of insecurity. Fear is what it lives off. Cicero: "As an instructor of good behaviour, fear lacks permanency."

Thousands die every year of suicide, more even than are killed by drunk drivers, which is more than those killed by homicides, a number that has been dropping yearly. Almost no one has died inside Canada from terrorism. Yet that thing that does not happen is the best source of fear. So public money flows toward what doesn't happen. And after that it flows toward a fear of homicide.

There is a curious assumption within this admiration of fear. Even in its extreme populist forms, respect for the orderly will make the citizen more passive. We may become more querulous but not deeply troublesome to an orderly system.

The Genius to Divide

The British, having got what they wanted out of Confederation—release from paying for someone else's defence—then set about undermining the Canadian half of the bargain. A series of cases were brought from Canada before the Judicial Committee of the Privy Council—our court of last appeal until 1949. The judges ruled in most cases against the power—that is, the *order*—of the central government. The legal concept at the centre of these decisions was indeed *Peace, Order and Good Government*. The British judges ruled, very precisely, to limit severely the power of the federal authority to establish *order*.

I'm not interested here in the old argument over British interference in Canadian affairs. Some of the judgments were probably right, many others were wrong. The more important point is that first the inserting of *order*, then the rulings to cripple it, deformed the Canadian debate over national policy. As with any federation, there will necessarily be constant bickering over the division of powers. There are no right answers about the division of powers, only a sense of the need for some reasonable but indefinable balance. So the battle for power would have swayed back and forth whatever the Constitution said. And indeed it has.

The strategic effect of the Judicial Committee lies elsewhere. It used the section on *Peace, Order and Good Government* to turn the decision of powers into the central question of Canada's existence, in fact, of Canadian public life. In the context of *order*, they made all debates seem to be about the "scope and not the merits of legislation." They made form, not content, the driving force of Canadian politics. Over the decades this has become increasingly the case. It matters less whether children are hungry than who writes or does not write the cheque. Nothing national in scope can be discussed except under the magic umbrella of form.

Whatever the merits of the Judicial Committee's power-sharing decisions, the damage these did to the public good is perfectly clear. Their rulings empowered provincial governments to limit or remove French-language minority education rights a century ago. It took a century to repair the damage and restore rights that had been in place since the eighteenth century. The committee presented the central question as one of provincial rights. In fact, it was the ignorance and indifference of a British court when faced by the real welfare of real Canadians living in a real minority situation. In 1903, again in defence of provincial rights, they ruled that British Columbia, and therefore any province, could disqualify voters on racial grounds. In another dispute, over which province should own what is now the northwest of Ontario, the Judicial Committee sided with Ontario against Manitoba and Ottawa. The ruling still makes no sense. The people of the region still treat Winnipeg as their national capital. Why? Because it is their geographical capital. Toronto and the rest of Ontario belong to a distant, different world. In 1922, they struck down anti-combines legislation on the basis that it was an unjustified use of the federal government's power under the *order* provisions. It is hard to think of a ruling more directly aimed at supporting the old Family Compact idea of limited government and severely limited citizen powers. In the mid-1930s, the Judicial Committee ruled R.B. Bennett's New Deal unconstitutional. The suffering on the prairies in the Great Depression was not, they ruled, dire enough to permit invoking the *Peace, Order and Good Government* clause. A London Law Lord's idea of prairie poverty would be interesting to consider. They also limited Ottawa's power over internal trade and commerce, leaving us to this day in many cases with more internal barriers than international. This is not a situation they would have permitted within Britain then or today within the European Union. The only case on which they were clearly right was the Persons Case in 1929, in which the Judicial Committee ruled that women were, after all, *persons*.

The Judicial Committee's decisions were mainly about *order* and *power*, but were they also about a concern for provincial rights? There are three possible answers. First, all empires automatically divide power inside their colonies. In Morocco, the French as quickly as possible gave military power to the Berber minority in order to undermine the Sultan of the country. The English moved Indian minority merchants into their Buddhist colonies to control the economy. Ask the leaders of any empire for organizational advice. They will tell you to turn minorities against majorities, and smaller minorities against larger minorities, then in the resulting chaos reap benefits for yourself. By the time the Judicial Committee got into the Canadian game, there were few benefits for them to reap. But the belief at the heart of empires that you can reap benefits from the disorder you cause others is instinctive. Empires believe in order because it allows them to use disorder.

Second, the man who shaped the Judicial Committee's attitudes toward Canada was Judah Benjamin, former Attorney General of the Confederate States during the U.S. Civil War. With the victory of the North and the freeing of the slaves, he fled to London and recycled himself as an influential lawyer. He pled regularly before the Judicial Committee and his constant theme, not surprisingly, was states' rights. Canada was one of his favourite subjects. Was his interest based on an idea of the public welfare of Canadians or was it a transferral of his failure as one of the leaders of a pro-slavery secession in the United States?

Third, Lord Haldane was the dominant Law Lord of the twentieth century and the happy inheritor of Benjamin's theories. Two things are fascinating about Haldane. First, in his mind Irish Home Rule was inextricably confused with the need to strip power from the central governments of the new Dominions. He rightly supported Irish Home Rule. He was ashamed of Britain's brutal and bloody role there, involving tens of thousands of dead each time there was a repression. This violence came in a context of extreme poverty maintained by English-based absentee landlords, in turn producing desperate emigration and constant depopulation. This was one of the worst tyrannies in modern Western Europe. For Haldane, all of this was part of the same legal situation as the powers of the central governments in the Dominions.

The political division in London over Irish Home Rule was a bit like the division in Washington over ending the Vietnam War, except the destruction of Ireland had gone on for centuries. Haldane made much of his belonging to the reform group supporting Irish rights. "But we felt not less the necessity of studying how the sense of liberty might be made to reach Canada, Australasia and even India."

Even India. I'm sure that Howe, LaFontaine and Baldwin—who installed democracy in Canada before Haldane was born—Cartier, Macdonald, Mercier, Tupper, all the Fathers of Confederation, had any of them still been alive, would have been relieved to know there was a British lord standing ready to teach them the meaning of liberty and to do so in the context of British policies in Ireland. These Irish policies and the accompanying violence would continue to our day. The English-Irish problem may only now be ending.

Haldane could be dismissed as a comic Empire figure in the Colonel Blimp tradition, operating in an ignorance so isolated as to be inconceivable in the real world. But he can't be dismissed, because with each ruling he was teaching us all about liberty—that is, he was trying to shape Canada in the model of the pre–Civil War United States.

The second mildly fascinating thing about Haldane was that he worked hard to protect the Judicial Committee's power over life in the Dominions. His job was "to make the part of the Empire from which the appeal comes have the sense of seeing that there had been a mistake, if one had been made.... The task is one which, I think, on the whole, suits well the genius of the British Empire." Providing, of course, that the judges were all British, sitting in London and not unnecessarily confused by the realities of other people's lives.

Again, what matters here is not the specific splits of federal-provincial power. Much more important is the direction in which this process of defining *order* took the expression of Canada's imagination. Our energies were deflected from the conceptualization of policy and toward arcane battles of ministerial and bureaucratic control at different levels. Nevertheless, Canada continued to grow as an intentional civilization producing unusual content. However, we could no longer sound like an intentional civilization. In our legal, public descriptions of ourselves, the concept of welfare, fairness, bien-être had been erased. We had to function almost without any language to make sense of what we were doing. It was as if we could only conceive content as form. But civilizations can survive only so long without an honest language to describe themselves. You cannot build for long if you must present your purpose as accidental.

15

The Eddy Line of Fairness

You know that this lugubrious atmosphere, of a country finding its way accidentally, has begun to matter when you have a large, well-trained elite that seems increasingly incapable of action, as if incapacitated by some unexplained force, as if they cannot conceive of Canada as an intentional civilization capable of undertaking unusual and original initiatives. And so they are reduced to arcane battles of short-term power and profit. They have difficulty imagining content as anything more than form. It then seems as if our own country is unable to do what should not be that difficult to do.

One day we learn that two years after the enactment of a 2004 federal program to send cheap drugs to poor countries, not one pill has been sent. The next day public and private technocrats offer a multitude of technical justifications. The subject is dropped.

Once a year we are told that Canada has among the lowest per capita number of doctors within the Organisation for Economic Development (OECD). The result is long waiting times and overwhelmed emergency wards. This has nothing to do with medicare. It has to do with the number of places in medical schools and the number of doctors brought into the country. It is a simple matter of money—not that much—and action. Complicated explanations are given. Progress is perhaps being made. But so slowly.

We had a steel industry. Quite a good one. Two years later we don't. Other countries, smaller and poorer than Canada, still do. Some of them now own ours. Technical explanations masquerading as market talk are given. Senior employees—not capitalists—walk away with hundreds of millions of dollars. They make vaguely capitalist sounds on their way toward the eternal golf course. The government announces an even vaguer inquiry.

I'm not suggesting that this and much more is the outcome of changing one word for another, *order* for *welfare*. What I am talking about is how we imagine ourselves and what effect that has on our ability to act. If we imagine ourselves as a place of order rather than one of fairness, we will have effectively prevented ourselves from acting as we wish.

Our politicians and other sorts of leaders from the public and private sectors seem unable to rise to their feet except to read some formulaic screed written by someone else. They resemble the mid-eighteenth-century aristocrats Voltaire wrote of—functionally illiterate. They don't need to be literate. They hire people to be literate on their behalf.

What could they say if they did think in public? The answer lies all around us. The ideas of welfare, bien-être, fairness, bonheur did not disappear in 1867. They merely disappeared from the Constitution. They carried on in our mythology, although now in competition with an almost-official mythology of Canada as a place built on Tory Loyalist and church-bound Catholic foundations. Canada was reinvented as a loyal offshoot of the Empire: loyal, Victorian, kicking at its cage from time to time, but oh so politely.

The idea of Canada as a fair place continued to find its way through our history after 1866, but almost as if we were stumbling through a maze in the dark, a curious maze designed in the name of order. Laurier, the early Mackenzie King, even Robert Borden did manage to speak clearly of fairness, all the while bowing, as they felt required, to the Tory myth, as if not to do so might bring them down.

When the mythology of welfare and fairness did emerge, it was not necessarily from where most people might have expected. Some of the early Methodist and Catholic business leaders—Timothy Eaton, Alfred Dubuc, Robert Simpson, Hart Massey—saw their business as having a purpose beyond profits. They saw them as tools to improve "the social and moral well-being of their communities." There in 1902 was the

Grand Master of Vancouver's Freemasons, after the laying of the corner-stone of the city's library, exhorting everyone to seek "the welfare and happiness of mankind." Nellie McClung, the strategic leader of the first wave of feminism, became one of the most convincing humanist voices in the country. There she was in 1915, arguing that Canada should be "the land of the fair deal" or of "the second chance." Striding back and forth on stages across Canada, she had people laughing and mad and worrying not just about votes for middle-class women but about the exploitation of immigrant women in sweatshops. In the first half of the twentieth century, she was one of the great voices spreading *fairness* as the mainstream meaning of Canada.

As the century advanced, the country did build up its mechanisms of *fairness*, many of them put in place by a particular province, some by Ottawa, some by conservatives or liberals or socialists. But the overriding mythology in this country of *order* was that these remarkable initiatives were mere programs. They weren't fundamentally important like *love of country* or *loyalty* to some superior international force. Often they were not sufficiently *respectful* of constitutional methodology to be embraced as truly meaningful. They were not expressions of our civilization. We did not have, and still do not have, a sense of self that expresses the intimate relationship between the practical structures of fairness and the reality of the mythological country.

Yet in 1961, introducing his medical assurance plan in the Saskatchewan legislature, Tommy Douglas argued that health care "is something to which people are entitled by virtue of belonging to a civilized community." The policy was not just a policy. It was an expression of the people. In fact, policy is the easy part. Once decent people can express the elements of fairness as if it were normal, they will more or less agree on what has to be done. What is important is our state of mind — how we imagine ourselves, whether we have the language to imagine ourselves. If we do, then what seemed difficult will now seem relatively natural. That's what doing something intentionally means. If we do not have a strong sense of how we built ourselves over the centuries around the concept of welfare, bien-être, fairness, bonheur, then we will always be hanging on to tolerance, openness, complexity, difference as if these were happy accidents we can't quite explain.

But if you think of civilizations as great rivers, then you see that the true line of a society can keep rising to the surface if you allow it to. It is a matter of riding the current of the collective unconscious. It is there, carrying us, even when we deny it and are caught on snags or sucked off into eddies. We may float along, half-consciously, lying to ourselves about our society—for example, that we are a slow and cautious people because we are the product of an anti-democratic Tory tradition devoted to order. But the stronger current of our real experience will still be there. "The land and the myths have grown together this way, from then until now."

The better we understand the current, the better we can move down the river like an experienced canoeist, with purpose, taking full advantage of the eddy line. Purpose is neither accidental nor willful. It emerges from the collective will, which feeds upon our shared experience. So our capacity to express that experience is of enormous importance.

That is the role of memory. And it tells us that we exist, as we have for a long time, on a positive tension between individual and group rights, but also between individual and group responsibilities. This is a reality that has its roots deep in the traditions of northern North America and its peoples, but also in imported European traditions and some in the mixing of both of those together, over a long period of time. Memory, if we make the effort to express it, tells us that this mixing of traditions works and can work better still if we understand ourselves as a country guided by *peace, welfare and good government*, a peaceful country that dreams of a fair society well governed.

PART III

THE CASTRATI

16

The Nature of an Elite

How long can a country survive with a deeply dysfunctional elite? History is filled with answers to that question. At a certain point, if there is no serious renewal or no re-emergence of a purpose that links those in positions of power to the sort of purpose felt by the citizenry, countries often crumble or collapse. Or they are dragged against their will into another sort of existence or are subjected to a rude, unexpected change of direction.

Canadians have a fairly solid sense of themselves. If you seek, among the complexities of our national life, the expressions of common themes, the often-repeated desires, the shared indications of intent or frustration, you can identify quite easily what sort of country we keep saying we want this to be. Whenever asked, whenever listened to, citizens express with some confidence what kind of education system they want, what kind of health care, what minimum standards of living, what approach to justice. These are contemporary manifestations of fundamental themes. If a people know how they want to treat social and physical well-being, and shared rules of behaviour, and responsibility versus authority, then they have a good handle on the way they want to live together.

Yet our structures of leadership seem unable to digest these expressions of fairness, inclusivity and effectiveness. Although entrusted with the mechanisms of power, those in charge seem to lack the self-confidence to listen. They seem paralyzed by the reality of their responsibility. Instead, they peevishly concentrate on disparate, short-term details. If they reveal any hint of grander themes, these usually involve trying to drag the country off in directions the citizenry have never expressed much interest in. These are usually focused on a narrow and again short-term idea of efficiency, order and whatever the latest imported fashion might be.

And so, when I look at how my country functions, what I first see is a largely failed elite—people given responsibility and power in a multitude of ways by the citizenry and yet somehow unable to act. There are all sorts of explanations for this lack of self-confidence and disturbing mediocrity. Some of them are proper to our times—what you might call the results of a bad quarter-century. Others are the modern expression of problems that have been with us for centuries. They are one part of our collective unconscious, the negative part of that long sweep of our history running underground, then unexpectedly resurfacing with seemingly inexplicable force. Periodically these short- and long-term forces combine, and the result is the kind of leadership that leaves the citizenry confused, uncertain of how to provoke sensible action. That is the story of the last quarter-century.

When this sort of situation drags on, we begin to wonder how long the country can survive. Over what is now a long democratic history of one hundred and sixty years, Canada has managed to hang on, in good part because its citizens want their country to exist. This desire for continuity includes even a large part of those who more recently have voted to break up the country. How else could you interpret their involvement in key national debates, in spite of two major obstacles? After all, Quebecers have been faced for a long time now by the incompetence of federalist leaders in representing the larger debate. Parallel with that has run the determination of sovereignists to carry out an intellectual cleansing of any interesting or positive shared memory, both within and beyond provincial limits. That includes any memory or understanding of the national structures and factors within which the province actually functions. The result is that most Quebecers can hardly tell their country exists.

But the Quebec debate is only one part of this dysfunctional problem. And so we limp along, badgered relentlessly by low-level boosterism from our leaders and eased on our way by wealth gushing out of the ground or dug out or cut down and pulped. None of these resources have put themselves where they are because of our intelligence. We have not imagined or created them. Natural resources are simply there. With gifts of fate such as these, civilizations are judged in history by how wisely or fecklessly they exploited the wealth that destiny handed them.

How, you might ask, can I assign such importance to our elites when I have been arguing through the first two parts of this book that we are an egalitarian society in search of fairness? The answer is that we often misunderstand the meaning of the word *elite*. All societies have political leaders, civil servants, people who risk their lives for the rest of us, creative voices, professional intellectuals, corporate risk takers and business managers. These are, by function, leaders. That leadership function makes them into an elite. But a quick glance around the world also shows that elites come in all shapes and sizes. Ours is of the relatively innocuous, penetrable sort. People rise into it and fall out of it with surprising ease. That ought to be a great strength. Few members manage to hold on to their influence, social position or even financial advantage much beyond two generations. There are a few exceptions, surprisingly few. This is very different from most other democracies, in which the elites are quite stable. But in our case, if there is a constant cleaning out and flowing in of new blood, it is all the more disturbing if they are failing in their role.

And it is their failure as a leadership group that I am arguing.

What is a successful elite? One that is able to think about the direction of its society and about its own role in helping society as a whole to think about itself. This is an elite that can explain itself to society, and is able to act in both the broadest and the narrowest sense upon the ideas that emerge from this thinking and explaining. These are people who want to build and to own, to be on the edge of creativity whether in business or the arts. They want to own things in order to shape events. To be a player. To create wealth. The more the actions of these public or private leaders are tied to a broad understanding of the situation at hand, the direction and the risks, the more successful the elite is. Pericles on statesmen: "To know what must be done and to be able to explain it; to love one's country and to be incorruptible." Moses Coady, the Nova Scotia priest who, from the 1920s on, did so much to break down the barriers of class and put power into the hands of marginalized fishermen, miners and loggers, had no difficulty saying to these poor and little-educated citizens: "In a free society we can recognize no other force but the force of ideas." And they loved him for the dignity and hope that he brought them, of course by his practical actions, but above all because he helped them build themselves up through their imaginations and their intellect. It is that force of ideas on which Pericles based his idea of the statesman.

What is a failed elite? One afraid of ideas, afraid to talk with the citizenry through ideas, afraid to encourage the wide discussion of ideas in order to find the basis for its actions, unable to act except in a veiled or populist manner, afraid of the idea of power except as an expression of interests. A failed elite would rather sell than buy, rather trade in wealth than create it. They would rather be employees than owners, managers than risk takers. Some people believe elites fail because of their particular ideology. But ideologies are usually the refuge of the fearful. It is fear or mediocrity or both that defines a failed elite. And the sign that this is what you are dealing with is its incapacity to solve problems.

17

Signs of Failure

To Be Sick

Since 1992, the medicare system has been rigorously undermined by federal and provincial governments. The formal starting point was the Barer and Stoddart Report of 1991, which recommended a 10 percent reduction in medical school enrolment, a 10 percent reduction in post-graduate medical training positions and a reduction in our use of foreign-trained doctors. Up to that point, the doctor-to-population ratio had been climbing. The next year, governments accepted the recommendations and froze that ratio at 2.1 doctors per 1000 Canadians, a level well below most other Western countries. In a second initiative, the same sort of policy was applied to nurses. The third piece of strategic brilliance was a cut or freeze in the number of hospital beds. In some places, a fourth initiative was undertaken. It used a reduction in funding to cut the number of operating rooms.

Health economists who supported these strategies explained that health care was a service business. Doctors wanted more patients in order to make more money. If you reduced the number of doctors, nurses, hospital beds and operating rooms, health-care costs would be brought under control. Presumably this would be because there would be fewer patients. These professional recommendations do sound like a darkly comic story by Jonathan Swift, his sequel to "A Modest Proposal." But the civil servants and politicians apparently had no sense of irony, let alone humour, and so took the recommendations at face value and implemented them.

Taken as a whole, this was a managerial concept to save money in four silos of health care. Nobody seems to have taken into consideration the damaging effect in a whole range of other silos inside health care and beyond. They didn't take into account the effect on the public's well-being.

These four initiatives—none of which were a function of public health care, let alone of single-tier public health care—are responsible in large part for the waiting-list crisis, the pressure on emergency wards, the burnout of doctors, the rise of private clinics. A decade of artificially underproducing elements essential to the health of citizens—doctors, nurses, beds and operating rooms—couldn't help but produce a crisis.

Professors Barer and Stoddart might protest that that wasn't what they had intended. If so, why have they not been on the front line of public debate protesting the misuse of their advice? And I do mean the front line. They should be ensuring that the Canadian people hear from them. After all, it is their advice that has been used to cause suffering to Canadians and to undermine a successful health-care system. Why haven't the mass of their fellow academics been on the front line with them?

The civil servants responsible for health care have not given to their ministers clear advice in which they lay out the source of the crisis and the simple mechanisms for repairing the situation. Politicians have huffed and puffed, proposing such silly bandage solutions as formal limits on waiting times. That is the equivalent of ordering there to be fewer traffic accidents without addressing driver skills, cellphone use, drinking and driving and road conditions. It has a King Canute air to it. Put your throne on the sand at low tide and order the tide not to rise.

The example of this broad elite failure, in the single area of health care and spread out over a fifteen-year period, is profoundly troubling. Worse still, it reveals an intellectual and emotional incapacity to look at the larger picture. For example, 1 percent of health-care expenditure goes to prevention! One percent! This ridiculous lack of forethought isn't even part of the standard health-care debate.

In a parallel move to save or make money in public schools, physical exercise was one of the student activities cut back and school boards signed exclusive contracts with junk-food corporations to make up for general budget shortfalls. The elites were then surprised at an explosion in child obesity, with all the short- and long-term social costs, a good part of which are medical. Only now are there the beginnings of a reversal of policy in a few provinces. But there is also a continuing failure of silo thought. One branch of experts—school boards, civil servants and politicians—worry about having to replace the income from the junk-food manufacturers that now finances some school programs, while another branch of experts—civil servants and politicians—has to pour out money to pay for the treatment of unhealthy children. The long-term medical implications for these children and its costs for the state and therefore the citizen are off the charts. But it's all the same pot of money. It's our money, not that of one silo unable to co-operate with another.

This is not a complicated problem. Most children could do the math that would demonstrate that school boards are not really making money by selling junk food. France simply banned the practice and a few years later, in 2008, their obesity levels levelled off.

Home care, an integral part of the health-care puzzle, particularly with an aging population, is treated as a side issue. Yet it is central to hospital capacity and to the chronic problems of older people, many of whom do not require the continual use of doctors and nurses and hospital visits unless, that is, no other services are available. Integrated thinking demonstrates that home care can be more humane and cheaper than using hospitals. Silo protectionism prevents society from thinking that way.

Dealing with the cost of pharmaceuticals strikes fear into the government elites. What do they fear? The large pharmaceutical corporations? Is it a matter of corruption? Or of corporate financial support for political parties? Under Brian Mulroney's government, special status was given to these companies via two pieces of legislation, passed in 1987 and 1993, in return for the creation and ongoing expansion of a research and development sector in Montreal. So far as I can make out, the corporations have not carried out their part of the bargain, yet the government has given them a free ride for almost two decades. This sort of unhealthy relationship is directly related to the slow decline in the part of the public budget spent on doctors and hospitals, while the part spent on pharmaceuticals has almost doubled. And the percentage going to bureaucratic management is up by some 40 percent. Other countries have built drugs into health care, thereby successfully cutting back on costs. The pharmaceutical corporations shout and threaten that they will withhold the best drugs if the public's drug costs are limited. They wave the red flag of their research and development costs. But at the end of the day, they want to sell their drugs. Besides, they know that they spend more on public relations and marketing than they do on research and development. Drug companies in the United States spend some $57.5 billion a year on promotion against $31.5 billion on research. In Canada, the numbers are far worse: $4.5 billion versus $1.5 billion, that is, 3 to 1. Even then you would have to examine what they actually meant by research. The point here is that our elites are too weak or confused or corrupt to deal with this financial sinkhole.

Ever so slowly over the last few years, governments have begun to invest in increasing the number of doctors. This is happening with no admission of their earlier and persistent failure and no explanation of causes. In this way they create the impression that the villain is single-tier health care, when the only problem has been a failure of political, bureaucratic and academic leadership. The new training spots are appearing at 3 percent to 5 percent a year—not nearly fast enough to catch up with the problem. Why are governments moving with such painful slowness? Because without any examination of what went wrong and of how we produce doctors, we can only go about facing the problem in the old, silo-based way, with its incremental and narrow envelope approach toward funding.

There are fifteen hundred Canadians going to medical school outside of Canada and the United States because of a shortage of spots at home. Most of them are enrolled in schools operating at Canadian standards in places such as Britain, Australia and Ireland. Most of them won't be able to return to Canada to work because there is no formalized system to recognize which schools meet our standards. And there aren't enough residency spots in Canada. The quantity of residency spots is the continuing almost-secret way in which the number of doctors is kept down. That bottleneck could be dealt with overnight; that is, it could be if there was any serious desire or capacity to solve the problem. Instead, you read that British Columbia is spending $1.6 million to increase residencies for foreign-trained doctors from six to eighteen spots. Or Ontario is investing $10 million to create 141 new family residency spots. And so on.

But we are short thousands of doctors, not 12 or 141. Four to five million Canadians are without a family doctor, not five hundred. The various competing managers and universities and provincial bureaucracies and medical associations are acting as if it were business as usual. If this were treated as the crisis it is, we could create an initial and medium-term leap in numbers. Besides, the costs involved—a million here, ten million there—are big in the life of most citizens, but peanuts in the budget structures of governments.

There is an even more fundamental miscalculation in this approach. It is not simply a matter of getting ourselves up to international doctor-citizen ratios of three or four. A majority of new doctors are women. A large percentage of them will also create and raise families. Many will work in their career for shorter hours than the traditional male doctor. Estimates put this anywhere from one-half to one-quarter of the hours of the traditional male doctor. This is perfectly normal. We also need mothers. What's more, a growing percentage of the new doctors—whether male or female—don't want the old medical life of seventy or eighty hours a week and little private life. What all of this means is that we need far higher doctor-citizen ratios than ever before in history. We need a new approach. We need to take the theory of health-care teams seriously, so that patients are not dependent in the old solitary manner on *their* doctor.

All of this has been known by our elite for years. Here and there things are being done, but again in an ad hoc manner, often by the doctors in spite of the system. Yet the broad policies seem unaffected. The elite are still imagining *the doctor* as the traditional solo male doing impossible hours. To get to these new ratios they are going to have to think about medicine in quite a different way. They don't seem to be capable of this.

To understand how dysfunctional our elite is, you have only to look at the explosion in tuition fees for medical schools. Government, faced by a crisis in the number of doctors, is instead trying to finance universities by making medical schools accessible only to richer families. In Ontario, the combined income of the parents of first-year medical students is now more than $100,000. In other words, the government and the universities are turning medical schools into a class system, not a meritocracy, unless the students are willing to go deeply into debt. The average medical student debt at graduation is more than $160,000. I'm told by medical schools that many of their poorer students are flipping hamburgers or doing other menial labour as an easy way to earn enough to stay in university. Do you, present or future patient, want your future doctors studying while in university or do you want them taking time off to work at McDonald's? Besides, there is a philosophical and ethical message behind these tuition hikes and the resulting heavy debt: Becoming a doctor, the message from our governments says, is about making money, not about public service. Yet that is not how young doctors want to be categorized.

Finally, this entire situation is increasingly confused by an irrelevant campaign for two-tier health care. There is no example in the world of health care becoming cheaper, better or more accessible because of a two-tier health-care system. The situation has been confused by the rise of a doctor, Brian Day, who managed to get himself elected president of the Canadian Medical Association in 2006. An advocate for private health care, he bases his arguments on international comparisons of costs that are simply wrong. He maintains that Canada spends more on health care than any country except the United States. This is simply untrue. For example, Germany, France, Switzerland, Norway and Iceland spend more as a percentage of their national economy. And yet most of these countries have formal two-tier systems. What is more, each of the European realities is quite different. Britain has a very powerful and effective private sector used by their elite. After a decade of reinvestment in the public sector, which had slipped badly, they are now still short of beds and doctors. They have serious wait times. They must send patients in large numbers to be treated in France, which has a surplus of doctors and beds. Why? Because the French government invested heavily in the public system. There is a small private system used by the elite for their softer needs. But France's success is based entirely upon the gargantuan effort made with tax dollars and government debt.

Perhaps Dr. Day is simply trying to provoke us, to get our attention because he is so outraged at the shortage of operating rooms. Or perhaps he is having fun being outrageous. The only difficulty is that Canadians who are sick or who have a sick relative or friend can't help but take him exactly at his word.

Dr. Day's underlying argument is that a private system takes pressure off the public system. No, it doesn't. His argument is dependent upon Canadians not paying attention to what actually happens in other countries. What does happen when there is a serious private tier? Precisely the same thing that happens when a critical mass of the elite send their children to private schools. The pressure from the top to make the public system work, effectively and at a high level, leaks away. Why? The elite are no longer participants. They are merely *noblesse oblige* managers.

It is often suggested that we already have two-tier health care because some members of the Canadian elite get faster medical treatment thanks to their contacts. That may be, and it should be dealt with. But that is a quite different situation from organizing your entire health-care system so that the elite automatically gets faster and better treatment than the rest of the citizenry. I can't help but feel that if someone like a Dr. Day is not laughed off the public stage, this is itself a comment on the failure of elites.

I'm not suggesting that the situation is easy. But what we do know is that we have a shortage of doctors and nurses, and a shortage of hospital beds and operating rooms carefully created by a decade of bad policies. These are not the only, but they are the central, causes for our health-care shortages. Neither have anything to do with single-tier health care. Both are now—very late in the day—being addressed in a painfully slow manner, without the benefit of any integrated strategy or any clear under-standing or public explanation of what went wrong. What has been an illustration of broad elite failure for fifteen years remains exactly that.

None of this answers the question as to why they fail. Why they find themselves unable to act. Why they are unable to act in order to solve real problems from which real citizens have been suffering for at least a decade.

Is it that they simply don't know what to do? Or they don't have the self-confidence? Or they don't have the intellectual capacity or training to see the shape of the problem? Or, to combine these questions, is it that they have only just enough self-confidence to follow slow and narrow managerial procedures—the sort taught in our business schools and rewarded in large organizations, whether public or private. Generations of deputy ministers in the 1950s, 1960s and 1970s had the intellectual self-confidence and the courage to recommend full policies to their political masters. What has gone wrong?

Are we dealing with ethical corruption? With people who don't understand ethics? People who cannot act because they don't know how to explain to themselves, let alone to the citizenry, what they believe must be done? Pericles would ask the question: Do they love their country? He would mean: Do they respect the citizenry?

To Be Poor

Take the level of poverty in Canada. Five million citizens try to survive below the poverty line; seven hundred and fifty thousand of them are dependent on food banks. Forty percent of those are children. There are six hundred and fifty food banks spread across the provinces and territories. Seventy thousand Torontonians are waiting for affordable housing, while hanging on the edge of personal disaster. Fourteen thousand Canadians live in homeless shelters. Over an eight-month period in 2007, homeless shelters in metropolitan Vancouver had to turn away forty thousand individuals for a lack of beds. Two hundred and fifty thousand Canadians live on the streets.

We walk by these people every day as if it were normal to see a fellow citizen living on a subway grate in winter. Why does it seem normal? Because the first food bank opened in 1981 in Edmonton to deal with a short-term crisis. Because a decade ago these temporary institutions were already supporting more than six hundred thousand Canadians. Because the number of children using them has steadily grown. And the number of children beneath the poverty line has grown 20 percent since

1989. Because the income of 40 percent of Ontarians has not grown in three decades.

So we have become used to all of this. We may talk about dealing with poverty, yet we act as if it were normal. Why? Because we have normalized poverty by agreeing to live with it in its modern form for a quarter-century.

Of course, there are people who are horrified and are trying to change things. There are thousands of volunteers, people donating food. The Ontario government is beginning to move some money toward affordable housing. The University of British Columbia has a wonderful program in Vancouver's downtown east side that involves dozens of professors offering courses to adults living in the hardest of conditions. The factor of dignity that this education is centred on has an effect on the other trials the poor are attempting to get through. The University of Toronto has followed suit in Regent Park with highly successful programs—aimed at high school students in this often difficult area. A program such as Pathways to Education in Regent Park has been so successful that it is spreading around the country. There are dozens of drop-in centres for youth in difficulty in almost every city. Calgary business people are looking for solutions. The majority of Calgary's food bank users have jobs. Forty to 60 percent of their homeless-shelter residents have jobs. These are the working poor, who cannot afford housing or enough food. Businesses are not paying them enough to live even a minimal life of dignity. But what provoked the city's corporate leaders to the promise of action was an unfavourable portrait of Calgary on U.S. television. Suddenly they saw their community through the eyes of the empire they so admire and imagine they are admired by.

The point is simple: More than a quarter-century has gone by. Good people have tried to improve the situation. But nothing strategic has been done. Some governments, like that of Mike Harris in Ontario, seemed eager to make matters worse. Others, like that of Ralph Klein in Alberta, were blithely indifferent. And in general all governments have been unwilling to assume their responsibilities, which involve taking tax money and investing it quickly and massively in housing and training. Over three decades, the percentage of those unemployed who receive benefits was shrunk by the federal government from 76 percent to 38 percent. Ottawa simply kept on changing the definition of *unemployment* until 62 percent of the unemployed had been categorized as not the kind of jobless who should be helped. Why did they do this? To encourage them to compete. And yes, the official unemployment level has come way down. But the poverty level is up. It has been little more than a statistical game aimed at moving people out of the politically sensitive unemployed category, where those in charge of the economy might seem to be to blame, and into the poverty category, where those who are poor can be abandoned as marginal and somehow hopeless. The situation is therefore no one else's fault.

In the 1980s, old-fashioned hospital mental-health wards were shut to save money, pouring their residents onto the streets. More than half of the homeless have mental-health problems. That doesn't mean they are not citizens or do not wish to work or to have dignified lives. Most of them could work, but they need a friendly, supportive sort of assisted housing. We know this. We see the people on the grates.

Now go to cities and towns elsewhere in the Western democracies. In the vast majority of them you will not see the equivalent poverty. The grates are not decorated with citizens. There are various explanations for this, but the most common is that action of some sort has been taken by those responsible for wealth distribution, mental-health services, housing, education and training.

The state of poverty in Canada is a failure of our civilization and it is an indictment of our political, bureaucratic, business and intellectual elite. It is a terrible failure because lives continue to be thrown away, as if it were normal that an executive should be paid $100 million for selling off a company he manages but doesn't own while hundreds of thousands of children are going to food banks. No amount of charitable donations by that lucky former chief employee justifies this situation.

Citizen-based organizations keep trying to push society's system into action. Some, such as the Community Foundations, a network of separate urban funds, also have national structures and are using them to try to draw the country into a conscious understanding of our reality. Yet there is still no elite-led discussion about how to define solutions and how to put them in place. Instead, we indulge ourselves with the sort of tax cuts that are meaningless to those who have a bit of money but have the effect of emptying the public coffers. Those in authority can then say with sincere hypocrisy that the times are tough, public money is hard to come by, and action on urgent social issues, although laudable, cannot be for today.

Why have our elites not taken action? The solutions are not complicated. Why do they seem paralyzed before this poverty? Why are they unwilling to engage in a public discussion about what this failure means? Why do they not have that simple respect for *the other*, their fellow citizens, who need the support of their society?

These are not mysterious, abstract, generic questions. Every child in a food bank is the direct result of specific actions or inactions by real individuals in positions of authority. Think specifically by name of all those prime ministers and premiers and ministers of finance, housing and social affairs who have chosen not to act since the 1980s. Or have limited their actions to small, uncoordinated initiatives. Think of those clever deputy ministers, assistant deputies, directors and economic advisers who averted their gaze while recommending to their political bosses that housing and other poverty-linked responsibilities be passed down the chain from Ottawa to the provinces and from the provinces to the cities, while each level held on to the cash sources that the next level down of government would need to fund the programs. Think of those ministers and senior civil servants and economists who invented and carried out the *across the board cuts* approach to debt reduction in the 1990s. There is nothing wrong with debt reduction, but this unsophisticated, even barbaric, approach paid no attention to the different situations and needs in different ministries. It allowed the cutting of *non-essential* programs rather than administrative jobs. Poverty-reduction programs are strangely enough always non-essential. Think of those business leaders who encouraged and continue to encourage the tax cuts that will ensure there isn't enough money in the public coffers to finance public housing, training or intense education. That is why we can understand where we are now only if we look coolly back over what very real people in real positions of authority have done through this long period of almost three decades.

Citizens have the right to judge the actions of those to whom they have given authority, directly or indirectly.

Among these thousands of leaders there are many admirable stories. People who have had wonderful ideas and fought hard for them—risked their careers, often sacrificed their careers. There are political and civil service success stories, federal, provincial and municipal. There are success stories around volunteers, non-governmental organizations (NGOs), private-sector initiatives. But there are no large patterns of success. No government can blame other governments with ease, which is the normal Canadian strategy for shifting blame. Only by judging the actions of their elites can Canadians judge themselves and measure what might be done. This idea of judging our leaders, except in the context of periodic elections, has a frightening Jacobin echo about it to the ears of those in authority. They find it unfairly personalized. But one of the central forces of history is that of judgment, leading to action, followed by the effect on those acted upon. The playwright René-Daniel Dubois calls it the Polonius syndrome: Inaction by real people in positions of power in a real time of need is a form of action. It is a choice. Each one of these individuals has a name, a family, a career, a pension. Increasingly over the last three decades the idea of professionalism and of managerial structure has meant that they do not have names, are not seen or heard as individuals, are not personally accountable. They are just temporary occupants of defined positions, hidden behind generic titles, abstract email addresses or answering machines or spokespeople.

Some members of these elites have become more socially conscious as they rise toward the top. They begin to notice the poverty in their communities and are horrified. They feel that government has failed. They lament that failure but aren't surprised. They conclude that the private sector, the volunteer sector or public-private partnerships will have to step in to do something about this suffering.

Of course, they must do something. Many of them are. There is a great deal more they can do. But what they can do and what most public programs can do don't fall into the same category. They are not interchangeable. Most public programs are large, national, regional, often costing hundreds of millions or billions. The initiatives that the private and volunteer sectors can undertake are often local and highly specific, requiring hundreds of thousands or a few million. I am not denigrating these efforts. Quite the contrary. They are essential. And they have a particular role to play, which can involve taking greater risks than big public programs. They can be on the cutting edge. Or they can be inserted into all those difficult corners that the big program can't be. They can often lead the way for bigger programs that can eventually be normalized within tax-based services.

What they cannot do is replace the democratic public effort—either in sheer financial commitment or in stable, long-term operations. To pretend that that kind of public commitment can be replaced by private initiatives is to advocate a return to Victorian *noblesse oblige* charity. It didn't work then and it hasn't worked over the last three decades.

In 2005, there was a sign of hope when a two-year, $1.6-billion federal program for affordable housing was announced. But the money was never allocated.

Again, what is the explanation for this failure before such poverty? One partial answer is the isolation of elites. They resemble the classic First World War staff officer who spent his time at headquarters poring over maps and memos. He didn't have time to see the trenches. Very few of our elites have ever gone to see the effect of their actions. They are too busy managing public and private affairs to go to homeless shelters to see how many working people sleep in these places because their jobs don't pay them enough to rent an apartment. Or to see how many single mothers must bring their children into food banks.

To Be Unable to Swim

Take a much simpler example of this disassociation from reality. The eulachon is a small smeltlike West Coast fish. At 20 percent oil content, it is probably the fish richest in oil anywhere in the world. You can light a dried eulachon like a candle. Over thousands of years, up and down the Pacific coast it has been a prized commodity—dietary and financial— because of its vitamin-rich oil. The annual runs of this fish used to involve thirteen West Coast rivers. Until the 1990s, the eulachon came so thick you could take them out of the rivers in buckets.

Then licences were given for shrimp trawler fisheries to operate at the mouths of the eulachon rivers. Hundreds of tonnes of these little fish were taken as a by-catch and thrown back dead. At the same time logging was slowly clogging the spawning rivers, as it had for salmon spawning rivers. The eulachon population plummeted, in many areas disappeared. Apart from the shrimp trawlers, the by-catch waste and the clogged spawning rivers, there may be other causes.

But the central cause is elite failure. It is a matter of specific errors made and not corrected. How can you correct mistakes if there is no capacity to admit them in the first place? How can you set policy when there is no integrated approach to public or private policy? You just stumble on at first as if the crisis were non-existent; then as if it were mysteriously free-standing; then, regretfully, as if those in positions of responsibility are limited in their power to act by competing political and economic interests.

Why can't the public and private leaders think about more than one thing at once? Why don't they understand what a child understands— that the thigh bone is connected to the hip bone? Why can't they organize how to look after logging, shrimps and eulachon at the same time? Laziness? Financial self-interest? Corruption? Ignorance? A sense of entitlement? A silo mentality? All of the above?

And why, the moment they learned that the eulachon population was collapsing, did they not suspend the new shrimp fisheries while they examined the situation? Why throughout the Canadian fisheries on both coasts will they not explain to the public that about half the fish caught—often more—are simply jettisoned dead back into the water because they are not the seasonal legal species. I can't think of any other industry that blithely continues with a 50 percent waste policy, as if this were normal, professional, just a management matter, something to consider one day, perhaps.

Again these are specific decisions made by real individuals with names, careers, lives. Their highly personal actions caused this disaster. From beginning to end, they have failed in their responsibilities. But they will go on to retire and play golf as if the decimation of the eulachon population were, well, just the sort of thing that happens. And they, after all, were just doing their job. They were, as the old Nuremberg war trials defence went, just obeying orders.

To Become Inconsequential

Lester Pearson did not just do his job. During his decade as foreign minister, he wasn't looking for orders to obey. Before that he had been the deputy minister and a long-time international player. He knew the issues and was part of shaping them

Foreign policy is all about digesting an impossible multitude of factors into a long-term sense of intent. That combination may permit countries to avoid destructive mistakes and meltdowns, to react intelligently to crises. Judging foreign policy is a bit like judging human actions that affect the natural environment. If you are naïve, cynical, egotistical, narrowly focused, the unintended consequences may be disastrous. Foreign policy can also be about being ready to move when those rare opportunities for change open up. A country that has enormous power can try to force change, but the sea of shifting factors then simply produces unintended consequences that wipe out or deform the original intent. That is President Bush's story. Those without power can force change by acting unilaterally. Sometimes they set out to release those unintended consequences. Osama bin Laden, for example. Sometimes they have no idea where it will all lead, such as the various ethnic nationalists of Yugoslavia.

Those who are intelligently focused can sometimes produce the sort of constructive change that their power doesn't warrant. When this works—and the effects aren't wiped out by unintended consequences—it is often because there was a broad ethical purpose that could absorb widely shared self-interest.

Canada has had twenty-three foreign ministers since Pearson. On average, a different one every 2.1 years. As prime minister, Pearson limited himself to one foreign minister. He understood the purpose of longevity. Over the last fifteen years, it has been one every 1.6 years.

In two years a minister can't even figure out how the Byzantine internal politics of Foreign Affairs headquarters works. Any kind of serious international experience could help a minister get off to a fast start. But over fifty-one years, only three of the twenty-three ministers had that experience on arrival in the job and only one of those—Mitchell Sharp—was left there long enough to do anything. Lots of good people have been given twenty-four to thirty-six months to make a brief bit-player appearance on the world stage. In a half-century, only five have been given any time to do the job properly—Howard Green, four years; Paul Martin Sr., five years; Sharp, six and a half years; Joe Clark, five and a half years; Lloyd Axworthy, four and a half years. In most cases, the longer they were there, the better they were at it. Therefore, the better Canada did in its international role.

As the habit of spinning inexperienced ministers through the job has accelerated, so the Byzantine nature of the department has become more Byzantine. Don't misunderstand me. I can't think of a ministry with a higher average quality of civil servants. Our embassies do the best they can in the absence of a real long-term foreign policy. The young recruits are remarkable. Our ambassadors are impressive.

But if we don't have a foreign policy, what are they to do? Of course, we do have a foreign policy. It simply has no continuity, no stability and no long-term reach. It is largely about fashions that come and go.

As the minister's role is shrunk ever more into something resembling that of a long-weekend houseguest in the Pearson Building, so a departmental culture has developed that might be called *please the minister*. When she arrives, it is as if there has been no minister before her. She is first worn out as she attempts to understand the department and the hundreds and hundreds of interrelated international issues. Then she is encouraged to think of one or two issues she might like to attach her name to for public profile and legacy purposes, as if she were a Princess Diana figure—honorific rather than consequential. She is to be pleased but not followed. If she falls for this, she can be kept out of everyone's way. On top of which she will be sent off to endless brief international meetings on a short leash with carefully prepared banal instructions that have little to do with real choices.

The Ottawa cynic will say that all of this has to do with the prime minister's desire to control foreign policy. That is only a very partial explanation. Prime ministers have many other jobs to do, and little hope of developing any solid sense of long-term foreign policy. Few of them have had serious international experience or have studied anything international or even travelled. For example, three prime ministers in a row were convinced of our need to be in Afghanistan without really understanding that Pakistan was a central problem and not, as Washington reassuringly insisted, our great ally. This could have been a deal-breaker. It certainly should have shaped our diplomatic and strategic approach, both of which are outside the responsibilities of our military on the ground. Whichever way the finger of blame points, the explanation is the same: Short-term, part-time enthusiasms do not work in foreign policy. This doesn't tell you whether we should or should not be in Afghanistan. It tells you that, right or wrong, we run our foreign policy as if enthusiasms could trump understanding and concentration.

To avoid taking their foreign ministers seriously, prime ministers give themselves a personal foreign policy adviser, usually a career profes-sional, who works out of the Privy Council Office, within shouting distance of the prime minister. He quickly becomes the foreign minister's immediate rival. There is usually another professional adviser—a Sherpa—to guide him through what he doesn't understand.

What is the result? Canada is an international amateur.

What is the sensible long-term view for a country such as Canada? A medium-sized country with a powerful neighbour must always create what amounts to a balanced position on the international terrain. If it is too far from the neighbour, it is in trouble; too close, it is in trouble. So it needs multiple, overlapping alternatives in order to survive. This can only be achieved if the country balances self-interest with the interests of others. This sort of shared policy is the most complicated kind of foreign policy and only works if it is long-term. And sharing self-interest can only get you so far before local interests start tripping you up. So you need to rise above mere self-interest to a level of ethics that others can accept, that they share. Done well, the flow of ethics will carry the various self-interests along in its slipstream. This doesn't mean ethics pays. It means that if you broaden the relationship to ethical drive, there will be room in it for the assorted self-interests.

Pearson understood this. So did St. Laurent. So did Diefenbaker. That was why St. Laurent began building a friendship with India and the other non-aligned countries. That was how Diefenbaker came to side with India against Britain to force South Africa out of the Commonwealth in 1961. In this way, they began the international campaign against apartheid, a campaign that much later Brian Mulroney would drive to completion by opposing his close British allies.

Yet once Nelson Mandela came to power and the critical building of democracy phase began in South Africa, Canada virtually disappeared from the process. Did we lose interest? Were we bored by the absence of drama? Like good boy scouts, were we troubled by the absence of a clear ethical battle? Had we convinced ourselves that we didn't have the money to be helpful at this stage? Did our leaders want to take trips to Washington, London, Paris, not to lesser places? These colonial travel habits of our prime ministers and ministers set much of our international concentration or lack of it.

Britain, which supported the apartheid regime for commercial reasons; France, which concentrated on selling weapons and nuclear reactors to the same racist regime; the United States, which didn't care one way or the other provided the regime was pro-Washington—all of them swept in from nowhere during the dying days of apartheid to present themselves as the close allies of democratic liberation. Individual Canadians, such as the great public servant Al Johnson, did go to work with the new regime. But there was nothing that could be called a phase-two Canadian policy. And today inside South Africa it is as if our thirty years of solid, loyal, and courageous leadership has evaporated from that nation's history.

This South Africa story is increasingly symptomatic of what happens in other areas. We took the lead on the negotiation of the anti-landmines treaty. The result was a great international triumph for Canada. Now no one seems to know we were ever involved. Why? The minister changed. Landmines were his legacy. The department moved on to new enthusiasms. And there was a new visitor/minister who would need a new project. The International Criminal Court (ICC) is tied to a broad idea of international justice. It is run by the Canadian who helped put it all together. It was another Canadian foreign policy triumph. Really? Who would have thought? That stuff, landmines and justice, that's old hat. Besides, it's mushy, sentimental, not real policy. Besides, Washington isn't on side. Who cares about those one hundred and forty or so other countries we convinced to stand with us on those two treaties if Washington has indicated disapproval? Anyway, we now have new enthusiasms. The Cultural Exception agreement is one of the most remarkable international breakthroughs of the last decades. It removes culture from the primary judgment of commercial trade organizations such as the World Trade Organization (WTO). Suddenly smaller and medium-sized countries such as Canada will be able to build their cultural structures without international punishment. Who cares anymore? The minister responsible, Sheila Copps, wasn't even at Foreign Affairs. She was at Heritage. Besides, we're on to other things now. Our northern foreign policy? We have a new one. The third or fourth in a decade. The Arctic Council? We drove that into creation through difficult negotiations. That's passé. Besides, Washington isn't enthusiastic. We don't want to lead in the North unless Washington cheers us on. Besides, how could we give a current minister or prime minister credit for something created by a predecessor? Let's just start over, ever young, ever virginal in worldly matters, ever changing, increasingly irrelevant.

What happens when foreign policy is not about foreign policy, but is instead about jockeying for position as the new enthusiasms roll by one after another? First, diplomats ask themselves where they ought to be. The answer is in Ottawa, caught up in the Byzantine activities of headquarters. Not surprisingly, there are more diplomats in the Pearson Building than there are abroad in our embassies. That is the classic measure of success versus failure, or purpose versus loss of purpose, in any organization with an international mandate. Imperial historians usually date the unstoppable decline of the British Empire to the year late in the nineteenth century when the number of naval officers in the Admiralty in London overtook the number of officers on ships. They had their reasons, just as our diplomats have theirs. History is indifferent to human explanations.

The effect of such imbalance is to undermine the potential of diplomacy and to humour the delusion that thinking comes from the top. To understand what this means, it is worth going back to the crisis days of the early twenty-first century when righteous enthusiasms from above caused everyone on the ground who understood the role of Pakistan to be ignored. A decade earlier, as Yugoslavia slipped toward civil war, it seemed impossible for those on the ground or anyone who understood the situation to communicate what was actually happening to those in authority. Instead, there was amateurish top-down leadership throughout the Western world and a resulting catastrophe that continues to unfold.

In the specific case of Canada, the central explanation for weakening on-the-ground diplomacy has been costs. It's too expensive to have too many people abroad. So we keep them at home and hire local employees, often of goodwill and talent but not part of the long-term experience and ambition of Canada. We could have developed a formalized system for engaging diplomats' spouses, who are there anyway, well educated and often sacrificing their careers at home. We still could. But an overwrought fear of conflict of interests so limits the little we have done in this area as to waste the talents we have available. We would rather hire a local who has never been to Canada and cannot really explain or sell who we are or what we have to offer.

What is the most valuable unpaid support system for our foreign policy? The foreign students who study in Canada and return home to join their national elite. Do we have any sort of exchange-student strategy? Our closest allies do. We think it more important to earn a few dollars for our universities by concentrating on those foreign students who can pay the most. That is not a strategy, nor is it concentrated on potential top students. What about Canadian students studying abroad? They will become the informed part of our population who are interested by and perhaps influential in key countries. Of course, Canadians can study where they want. But do we have a strategy to encourage a critical mass to go to areas that might produce long-term advantages to Canada? We're too passive for that.

What about culture? Here is the cheapest and single-most influential voice of Canada abroad. Not only that, it is a long-term influence on how the world thinks about Canada. We have actually had a highly successful long-term strategy that embraced culture as a pillar of foreign policy. This approach lasted several decades. But after 1988, a small group of trade utilitarians in the Pearson Building decided that culture was the enemy and should be eliminated from foreign policy, unless it could be reduced to the market equivalent of selling crude oil or widgets. The idea of influence or—as they put it—branding was good so long as it didn't come through culture, which failed as a scriptable method of *messaging*. In other words, culture isn't useful because it isn't *propaganda*. And an efficient use of public funds required controlled *messaging*.

An obscure and—as I've said—Byzantine battle stretched on for a decade until the recent passage of two ministers in quick succession, politicians who were unprepared for the job, allowed the anti-culture group to slip through a budget cut that destroyed the program. It was to be replaced by an old-fashioned propaganda approach, dressed up as utilitarian, profit-based programming. The sort of thing that can be nicely written out for auditorlike reports at home, while having no effect abroad. What happened wasn't either minister's fault. They couldn't possibly have understood the true nature of the manoeuvre. And what a brilliant victory for that small group of senior diplomats expert at playing the back corridors. What a success. They managed to destroy one of the few successful, long-term Canadian strategies for giving the country's international reputation some widespread weight—the sort of weight that is about Canada rather than a particular government's policy. The strategy was cheap, effective and supported by our best-known international figures, who co-operated while seeking no direct financial benefit. They enjoyed supporting their country. Oh well, who cares? It's only foreign policy.

The Fear of Living without Fear

Besides, our elites don't appear to want the citizenry at large thinking seriously about foreign policy. After all, they themselves don't take it seriously.

It is far easier to lead through fear and a constant atmosphere of crisis. This method has been a fallback strategy for leaders in trouble since the early nineteenth century. At the heart of it lies elite contempt for the citizenry as an intelligent, sensible population. Instead, they are seen as people who can be spooked by fear and crises. This is commonly described as populism.

Canadians have been pretty good at not reacting to this sort of strategy over the centuries. We have had our low moments—the fear of the Métis, of the yellow peril, the Japanese peril from within. Francophones and anglophones have had periodic explosions in which one fears the other—the conscription riots in 1917, the bilingual air-traffic controllers crisis in 1976. But compared to other countries we have been not too easily or too often seduced by these temptations. And as we have slowly eradicated much of our institutionalized racism, it has become much harder to get a fear campaign going. Yet as elites lose direction or as they find it hard to convince the population to buy into their ideology, so fear and crisis re-emerge as a solution to the problems of power. The fear of violence in our cities has been a favourite political tool for several decades.

It doesn't matter that murder and attempted-murder rates have been falling since 1990, violent crimes since 1993, and that total crime is at its lowest point since 1977. Public discourse is all about getting tough on crime. Our papers—all of them—leap to this subject of fear and crisis at every excuse. Whatever the politics of newspaper, radio or television, they all want people to pay attention to the ads they carry. And fear, they all believe, is the best way to attract attention to the programming that surrounds the ads.

This is also a common topic for those in the elites who can no longer express racism. Instead, they concentrate on crimes that may have been committed by people from the groups they used to be able to express racial ideas against.

Getting tough on crime requires the writing of get-tough-on-crime laws and the addition of police to the panels that recommend judges. Part of the strategy of fear is to blame the justice system for not doing its job. This takes us right back to the riots of 1849 against the Rebellion

Losses Bill. The rioters were really against the rise of democracy as a system of fairness. Today, fair judges means a loss of influence for populist leaders.

Is it unfair to assert that many of our governing elites have contempt for the citizenry? The answer to such a question must always be anchored in the reality we all live. The specific answer can be found in the rise of state-run gambling. To gamble is every citizen's right. To have your democratically elected government use the citizen's money in order to organize campaigns to push people to gamble is quite a different matter.

In 2007, $15.3 billion was drawn out of the citizens by their governments at various gambling institutions or machines. Of the $11 billion profit, almost $8 billion went to provincial governments.

Our provincial governments run constant campaigns to encourage gambling. These are aimed at the poorest, oldest, most marginalized part of society. The money they raise from these non-taxpayers replaces that which would otherwise have to come from the richer end of society. It is difficult to think of a clearer illustration of elite contempt for the citizenry. For that matter, it is difficult to think of a clearer illustration of elite self-contempt. We have thousands of years of history that tell us about elites who turn to gambling for state revenues. Without exception, history identifies those leaders as degenerates who are responsible for dragging down their civilization. How far down? Each case carries a particular lesson.

Let me take this a step further. The richest province—Alberta—is, as the writer Andrew Nikiforuk puts it, the mecca of gambling. With 10 percent of the population, it takes 20 percent of the profits. Oil prices have only recently gone through the roof. Until then, video lotto terminals (VLTs) earned more for the government in some years than the oil sands. In other words, the royalties paid on this oil have been so low that the petroleum corporations have been literally subsidized by the gambling poor.

The Catholic bishop of Calgary condemned all of this strongly in 2006, and in particular the $2 million revenue raised annually from various sorts of gambling by the Catholic school board. The president of the local Catholic teachers union replied that "what the bishop has raised is an excellent moral question.... Are we going to be the sacrificial lambs for proving that the moral high ground must be taken by Catholics over all others? We would do so to our own detriment." This could be described as the Pontius Pilate argument.

Racism is also an excellent moral question, as is homelessness, as is a fair justice system, as is active citizenship, as is freedom of speech. Even the encouragement of obesity by school boards is an excellent moral question. You cannot choose among these and other excellent moral questions to suit your budget. The other difficulty relates to all of these excellent moral questions and the respect that schools and principals and teachers may receive from their students. What message does a student maturing toward her rights and obligations receive from trustees and principals who cut the school's ethics to suit their budget.

The situation is the same for leaders throughout our society. What about the theatre companies, dance companies, museums, publishers who happily take a small percentage of these gambling profits? They who are meant to be our ethical voice lose it, or so they seem to feel, in order to stay in business. The truth is that money for schools or theatre can be found elsewhere so long as our ethics remain solid.

Besides, these are not real net profits the governments are distributing. Their calculations of the costs of gambling do not include social costs or costs to medicare or employment or unemployment or bankruptcy or suicide or crime or the justice system. Those costs certainly account for more than the amount handed out to charities and arts organizations in order to silence them.

Leaders who set out to undermine their poorer citizens in order to save the rest of society small amounts of taxes are dysfunctional. How else could they encourage a fear of public debt in order to justify child poverty? The constant harping on each problem in medicare to force the country toward two-tier health care, rather than setting about solving the problems, is another example of encouraging fear. Fixating on the problems of public education, as if to encourage or justify any move toward private education, rather than fixing those problems, again, is all about government by fear. What more effective way to frighten citizens than to suggest their children may fail to learn or even be unsafe in public schools?

These are examples that combine encouraging fear with constantly insisting we are in a crisis—a crisis of crime, of health care, of education.

Another example of leadership by constant crisis is the more insecure side of the nationalist movement in Quebec. Of course there are constant difficulties attached to the existence of a linguistic minority. But that isn't the same thing as a constant crisis. And whenever the movement begins to lose traction, it searches for any trigger to cause an explosive sense of crisis. The historian Jocelyn Létourneau puts it this way: "In order for Québec society to get on with life, we must first stop conceiving of it as being in crisis, on the edge of collapse, in the process of being absorbed, slipping down a slippery slope, on the verge of disappearing...."

The disturbing element is that this strategy of fear and crisis is often attached to a class system. Quebec's elite is wonderfully bilingual, often trilingual and lives at the expected national and international level. The deep unilingualism of a large part of the population is presented in a patriotic context, but in Canada and North America this locks them into some of the lowest incomes in the country. The equivalent elsewhere in Canada is the argument for two-tier health care. Those who have been made afraid that they will receive bad medical treatment gradually make possible elite treatment for those who can afford it.

The Fear of Getting Along with Others

That citizens have difficulty digesting how this sort of class system works has a lot to do with provincial divisions. Only a fool would argue against Canada's existence as a country divided among a multitude of powers. But that is quite different from the use of those divisions by local leaders to misrepresent what they are doing.

Roy Romanow, the former premier of Saskatchewan, describes the Council of the Federation, set up by the provincial and territorial governments in 2003, as "a bizarre redefinition of Canadian federalism." He says it takes us "from one based on greater co-operation to one of greater compartmentalization." The council's founding document makes this very clear. Its only muscular statements are about joining forces to oppose the federal government. There is hardly a hint that the provincial governments should work together to remove the arcane barriers among them in areas of their jurisdiction. The protectionism of provincial professional and trades organizations gets in the way of Canadians who want to move to another part of the country. The provincial trade protectionism and desire to tax some goods that cross their territory from one province to another stand in the way of our internal economy. We all know that in some ways it's easier to do business across international borders than within Canada.

If anything, our increasingly humourless and acidic struggles over federal/provincial powers are really about administrative elites fighting over administrative territories. Much of what is presented as a desperate struggle to protect French culture, by one level or another, is really about administrative elites squabbling over those same administrative territories. It is about power, not culture. Much of what is presented as constitutional powers is only marginally about constitutional principles. It's about the minutia of control.

In Sioux Lookout, Ontario, there were two hospitals. One fell under federal jurisdiction and served the First Nations reserve. The other was provincially run for the town. Neither of them was adequate. For years the two communities stood together calling for one new hospital that they would both use and that would share the two budgets. After much bureaucratic grief—neither civil service wanted to lose control over an administrative service—the decision was finally made to go ahead with one hospital. I ran into a senior figure involved in pulling them together, and congratulated him on setting such a valuable precedent. There are dozens of smaller communities that could benefit from such a concentration of health services. He laughed bitterly. He had won this one exception to the rule, but the deal made it clear that this could not be treated as a precedent.

In 2007, the provinces began discussing a national power grid. Some provinces have energy to sell. Others are desperate to buy. Yet they couldn't agree out of fear that an effective system, by definition, would lessen provincial control. As with oil and gas, if the United States wants our energy there is no problem. But if some of us would like to buy it from others of us, well, that verges on a threat. Quebec premier Jean Charest reassured everyone: "There won't be a single east-west line. There will be several lines in several places." And indeed, in 2008, a regional Quebec-Ontario agreement was put in place.

This approach will probably waste a good part of both the money made and the energy shipped. The lines will be awkward and expensive to manage. But the provincial civil services will have given themselves lots of extra work to justify their lives. They will call these *constitutional jurisdictions*. And the citizenry will have to pay higher taxes to finance this self-indulgence.

The same intentional ineffectiveness has us exporting Western hydrocarbons to the United States in conditions that amount to an unbreakable contract in quantity and price, locked in by the North American Free Trade Agreement (NAFTA). Meanwhile, the eastern half of the country is dependent on unsecured imports from wherever. Neither quantity nor price is secured. And were we to lose our foreign sources we would not be able to compensate with Canadian energy from the West.

There are dozens of brilliant examples of this sort. It is very difficult to move quality Canadian wine across provincial borders, which explains why it is hard to find them in most of Canada. In other words, our provincial systems are organized to prevent the sale of quality Canadian products. And indeed, they are organized to discourage the sale of quality products by smaller producers, even within their own province. The sale of Australian, French or Californian wine, on the other hand, is encouraged by the provincial liquor systems.

Why not? If you fiddle around long enough with this sort of ineffective planning you will have created systems so complicated that no one will be able to run them without your support. Civilizations are normally judged by that central philosophical tenet—the ability of citizens to imagine *the other*. Over the last quarter-century, Canada's leaders have reimagined this idea: Don't imagine each other. Civilization is not about *the other*. It's about process and administrative control, which is the opposite of imagining *the other*. We have every reason to be proud of how cleverly we have institutionalized mediocrity.

Fear of Flying

Think about the self-satisfaction with which the CEO of Air Canada, Robert Milton, let it be known in early 2008 that he and his fellow managers had worked out how to structure the company in order to get around Canadian ownership rules. Now, with great pride in their cleverness, they were ready to sell off Air Canada to a U.S. airline.

Beyond this delight in low-level Machiavellianism—which was treated as just a matter of business by public commentators—there was a more revealing aspect to what was said. You could sense his pride at having got the company to the point where it could be sold off. There was no suggestion that he could have led Air Canada in a campaign of international acquisitions. Why become a powerful industry leader when you can become an employee? Why lead when you can follow? Why take risks when there are people who will pay you handsomely to walk away? "[A]nybody that actually ties up with Air Canada gets a unique piece of geography...."

What is troubling here is the pleasure, enthusiasm and self-satisfaction expressed over the possibility of ridding oneself of the responsibility for ownership, that is, of responsibility. The justificatory argument is that airline companies everywhere are being bought out or are merging. Of course they are. That is the direct outcome over several decades of a deregulation that didn't work because it wasn't designed to fit the realities of air-travel economies.

But that doesn't explain Milton's view of life. The central point is that some people are indeed selling, but others are buying. Some people and some cities or countries are becoming more powerful at national and international levels. France, for example, has not for a long time been a great aeronautics centre. Nor has Air France been a particularly successful company. Yet through ambition and drive France is turning itself into a power centre of aeronautics and air travel.

France's strategy is simple. Both the government and the business elite treat their leadership of the European Aeronautics Development consortium as a centrepiece of France's foreign policy and its international economic strategy. And they treat the Airbus business as a wealth-creating, technology-driving, city-building mechanism. A visitor to

Toulouse, headquarters of Airbus, quickly sees how successful this strategy is. Meanwhile, Air France has been encouraged to take control of other companies, such as KLM, the Dutch airline. Now France is both the leader of a Europewide consortium that includes the Germans and the British, making it one of the two largest airplane manufacturers in the world, and it controls an expanding consortium of airlines.

In Canada we have the same pieces of the puzzle and therefore the same potential to create a powerful centre. Bombardier, one of the four top airplane manufacturers in the world, is in Montreal, as is Air Canada. Yet the general discourse in our business community involves complaining that Bombardier leans too heavily on the public purse—as if Boeing and Airbus and Brazil's Varig were not far more dependent on both public money and an international strategy led by their governments, as if the airplane business were not dependent everywhere on public support. More important, there is no sense in Ottawa or among Canadian economic strategists—if there are any who could honestly be called thinkers and strategists—that the existence of a manufacturer and a decent airline company in the same city could be the basis for an international economic policy. This is the sort of strategic policy that could give a broad spectrum of Canadian businesses and Canada's foreign policy real clout around the world. Instead, all that our strategists talk mainly about is whether they could betray free market principles through government intervention in the market or, alternately, how many people are employed in that particular business. And indeed, from time to time, the federal and provincial governments do financially support Bombardier. As they should. But this is never done in the context of a long-term, integrated aeronautics strategy. Instead, these interventions are mainly seen through the prism of jobs. Of course, we all want the economy to produce jobs. But to view the economy simply from that point of view produces the classic passivity of colonial societies. After all, long-term jobs and a range of them from top to bottom are the product of an equally long-term commitment to key industries by investors. In the absence of very particular circumstances such as the Auto Pact, this long-term commitment usually requires a critical mass of local ownership, which in turn produces wealth creation, research, downstream development and so on. These are the meat and potatoes of a full economy. These are the mechanisms of leadership, the sources of power.

In Canada the commentary is more likely to suggest how lucky we are—we, a small and powerless people in the global economy—to have so many jobs. Besides, how could the creation of deep and complex economic structures with the attached creation of new, multi-layered wealth be allowed to stand in the way of Air Canada's managers' essential need—perhaps it is a right—to sell off the company in order to fund the golf games of their retirement in Palm Springs.

Of course, managers don't always have a choice. Disastrous circumstances may turn owners into sellers. But that isn't the Air Canada case. It's just that they see themselves as sellers because they don't see themselves as the managers of real owners. Worse still, they see themselves as mediocre leaders, incapable of organizing and carrying out an expansion drive, too frightened to shape events. They see themselves as employees, not employers. If I look at them in the context of the history of the free market, they appear to me to be failures as capitalists, as the managers of capitalists and as offensive strategists.

Fear of Owning

When you look at how Canada came to lose its entire complex and successful steel industry through a series of takeovers squeezed into little more than two years, ending in 2007, you conclude with the same answer. The industry leaders, financial market potential investors, regulators, civil service leaders and politicians all saw themselves as followers, as temporary holders of wealth. And since others wanted control of our industry in order to shape it to their own interests, it was our duty to hand it over as rapidly as possible. Why? In order that the new owners should derive the downstream, complex, long-term benefits. Our reward for such passivity? Some handsome payouts to short-term, first-tier managers. And with luck the new owners would allow the second-tier and below employees to continue as their employees.

Nothing about the marketplace prevented the Canadian companies from banding together to create a strategic force. After all, that is what the companies that acquired them were doing. That is what is happening in sector after sector, as the world's economy moves away from capitalist ideas of competition toward mercantilist ideas of market control. There was some talk of banding together by a few of the most interesting leaders. Too few. Too late. Too slow. Not coordinated. Not thought through. And they were dealing with a country—ours—in which the elite consensus is that national economic strategies are passé or impossible or theoretically wrong. We are virtually the only country with a developed economy in which the elites have come to such a pessimistic consensus.

Nothing prevented our owners and managers from turning their corporations into much more sophisticated "medium-sized players with profitable regional niches." That is precisely what the Finnish steel maker Rautaruukki has done with great success. Finland: population 5,238,460. Rautaruukki: revenues of £3.7 billion and a profit of half a billion euros. You don't have to be a giant to do well. You just have to understand that there are several options, that being in the private sector doesn't lead you down a single path of singular options to a single, predefined conclusion. And you have to want to be an owner. You must have the self-confidence, drive and imagination it takes to be an owner.

Why have our companies been incapable of creating either the strategy of niche leaders or of industry giants? There are certainly technical flaws in our takeover rules. But if this were really the problem, why did our corporations wait until 2008—in other words, until it was too late for many strategic industries—to begin calling for those takeover rules to be changed? What really happened was that the economic elite of Canada waited for night to fall, then went out looking for a highway to stand on. And when the traffic of international markets came barrelling down upon them, the Canadians were pleased to find themselves blinded by the headlights and grateful to be recuperated as roadkill.

Being saddled with such a depressive self-image, they didn't even think that it might be a good idea to have an aggressive strategy bringing together the key players. Other countries—the United States, Brazil, Britain, China, India, France, Germany, Australia—have such strategies. Sometimes these strategies are easily understood as national policies.

These can be both aggressively offensive and stubbornly defensive. Often the offensive strategies are half-invisible, obscured in tax rules. Or they may be buried deep inside an unspoken elite consensus that unites public and private leaders. As for the defensive, protectionist rules, they are usually buried in state, provincial or even municipal regulations. In the United States, a few states have become corporate domicile centres because their purely technical rules make a hostile takeover almost impossible. And again, there is usually public-private elite consensus, which can erect mazelike barriers as if out of nowhere.

The OECD charts our restrictions on foreign investments as either the most restrictive regime or one of the most restrictive out of thirty countries. But then you begin to look at the list. France, Spain, Germany, the United States, Japan, and on and on are all listed as open economies. In reality, they are all far more restrictive than Canada. Unfortunately, our elites act like unsophisticated, earnest little boys. On paper, these other countries are indeed much more open than Canada to takeovers. And the OECD bases its analyses on these declared national public regulations. In reality, the economic structures of these other countries are much more difficult to penetrate than ours. Some of them—Japan, for example—are virtually closed. Their official, written rules for foreign takeovers are mere form. What matters is that their elites—public and private—have the self-confidence to believe that they are capable of organizing economic strategies that put them in control and keep them in control. The key is, they keep their eyes on ownership and the power it gives them.

The OECD doesn't compare which written rules are enforced, which are not; which unwritten rules exist and in what form; which countries hide their rules at lower levels. And it certainly doesn't examine national elite consensus. The reality is that if a Canadian business leader doesn't know how Germany functions, hasn't studied France's web of laws and regulations, its business culture, doesn't speak Italian, doesn't have good advisers, he or she simply won't understand how these countries work, let alone be able to penetrate their ownership structures in a strategic and successful manner. Some of the time, the key rules are not only local or regional but are disguised under superficially unrelated categories—

that is particularly true of the United States. Finally, it is part of the rather pedantic approach of Canadian administrators that we have lots of rules on the books. We like to be clear in such matters. Our unwritten culture is that we simply don't enforce our rules. We have panels and so on. There is a process. But the conclusion is predetermined. Then we turn around and say of ourselves that we have strict rules and are therefore protectionist. This is a form of self-loathing that I will deal with later. Besides, in the real world, our foreign ownership levels are far higher than those of the officially unprotective countries. How could that be if we are so closed and they are so open?

What I am describing here has nothing to do with such romantic notions as defending iconic companies or such defensive mentalities as protectionism. What I am describing is a lack of self-confidence, a lack of ambition, the absence of a sense of risk, the lack of a deep desire to create wealth and to build on that to create more wealth. What I am describing is people who don't want to be in charge. Meanwhile smaller countries, smaller companies, smaller pools of capital push themselves forward and grab control of our power.

At the core of our problem lies a mediocre managerial class. This is odd, because our myriad business schools have gone to a lot of trouble to create these managers. Our problem, therefore, is neither the result of inattention nor of unexpected events. It must be the result of some more profound set of errors. It isn't simply that our managers have neither the taste nor the talent for risk. They like to see themselves as modern leaders. They vaunt their dedication to shareholders. But what they mean is short-term holders of shares, not owners who want to build wealth. It isn't surprising that they identify with this sort of speculation, mistaking it for ownership. Their own reward lies not in building wealth but in selling off the company. The CEO of one of the largest companies recently sold, when asked off the record by a real capitalist how he could have let something of such essential value to the Canadian economy escape, replied, "You don't understand. I made a hundred million dollars." In other words, the manager earned $100 million for losing the company he was in charge of. The selling-off of Alcan, which has major implications for Montreal as a business centre, earned its CEO

$42 million. The central group of managers will receive $800 million. In 2006, Stelco brought in a CEO from the United States who took eighteen months to engineer a sell-off of the company and walked away himself with $67 million.

There are constant attempts by economists and business school professors cut off from the real world to convince us that Canadians buy more companies abroad than are bought by foreigners here. These numbers can be played with on all sides. But the strategic element is perfectly clear: Canadians tend to buy lots of bits and pieces around the world. In the process they rarely gain any strategic power on world or foreign national markets. So even when they do go abroad, they do so in a non-strategic way, leaving themselves highly exposed in those markets in those countries. Foreigners, on the other hand, have been buying large strategic pieces of the Canadian economy. They take control of whole industries, such as steel or pulp and paper, or critical parts of them. And these moves are often tied to getting control or at least a strategic position in related or downstream industries. Once in control, they begin playing these big pieces according to their own rules based on their own interests. You can hardly blame them. It is rare in the world where herds of deer obligingly gather on highways at night in the hope of being hit. And then thank you for knocking them down.

In February 2008, a study prepared for the Federal Competition Policy Review Panel was leaked, revealing that Canada was the country with the easiest foreign takeover rules in the world—I repeat, *in the world*. Not simply NAFTA or the OECD. For twenty years, people who confuse trade and ownership, as if these are inseparable parts of opening up to the world and becoming more competitive, have insisted that Canada was closed, protectionist and therefore soft compared to others. And besides, they have insisted, why should we worry about opening up? Everyone else is happily buying and selling. Borders no longer matter when it comes to ownership.

The 2008 study shows that only three countries are running a deficit in this sort of buying and selling—the United States, Britain and Canada—but that the United States has sold off only 2.1 percent of its market capitalization while Canada had sold off 12 percent in a mere seven years. Canada's buying and selling stands at an $80-billion deficit. It showed that the Netherlands, Spain, Germany, France and Australia were net buyers. That Canada's takeover rules favoured foreign buyers over domestic buyers. That the United States and Europe had far more effective barriers to foreign ownership.

None of this is new. It was as true in the 1980s as it is today. But our politicians, civil servants, business leaders, economists, management experts and the quasi-totality of our economic journalists have been happily lying to themselves and therefore to us about how the world works. Anyone who suggested we were functioning at a self-imposed disadvantage was mocked as a naïve nationalist left behind by global realities. In reality, it was this frightened elite that was naïve and provincial, incapable of standing up and fighting for a leadership place in the world's markets.

The results in Canada are incidents that are sometimes comic, sometimes so Machiavellian as to be painful to watch. The detailed cleverness with which the Ontario Teachers' Pension Plan worked in 2008 to exploit loopholes in the rules in order to sell off BCE/Bell to three U.S. investors was terrifyingly fascinating. They were promising the maintenance of the legally required Canadian control through having a majority of Canadians on the board. Everyone could see what was really happening: The energy of ownership was being shipped abroad. Technical voting ownership was remaining here. Konrad von Finkenstein, chair of the Canadian Radio-Television and Telecom-munications Commission (CRTC), who was obliged to rule on the communications issues, expressed astonishment at how this could be managed. He felt himself hamstrung by a peculiar Family Compact–type ruling from one of our ever-weak, pliant and unsuitable-for-a-developed-country financial regulators. He couldn't help exclaiming, "I'm astounded ... The interpretation that the Financial Services Commission of Ontario put on these things is not one that I as a lawyer and a former judge would put on that legislation in the regulation." Von Finkenstein is the former head of the Competition Bureau of Canada and could sense that something was profoundly wrong. He managed to toughen up some requirements, but felt himself to be trapped by the financial commission ruling. The central point here is that real power lies where lies the real control over the money. All the rest is theatre. As for the politicians, they kept their heads down. This is one of those cases "where $500 million in collateral benefits" would go "to managers and directors (or their firms)," which perhaps explains why such efforts were being made by the management, but, as far as I can see, with no consideration of the company's interests. After all, the buyers were financing their operation in part with BCE's own money, as well as saddling the company with debt. But this sort of unethical behaviour has been administratively normalized around the world over the last quarter-century. What is particularly strange here is that these complex efforts to rid Canadians of real ownership were being masterminded by a fund that has a theoretically ethical ownership—teachers. Yet they also were silent.

At least the selling-off of our beer industry had a comic side to it. One of the two leading Canadian beer brands was relentlessly marketed to the public as an expression of pure patriotism. Then in 2005 one of them, Molson, was taken over by Coors, a U.S. company known for its own political patriotism of a particularly neo-conservative and inward-looking sort. Molson pretended that it hadn't been bought out. Instead, the deal was presented as a partnership—a North American success story. The way it was presented, you might have imagined that this was a two-way deal. Coors would sell Molson beers in the United States. Molson would sell Coors beers in Canada. Molson would soon be a favourite beer south of the border. But in 2007, Miller, a larger U.S. brewer, was merged with Coors to produce MillerCoors in an attempt to split the U.S. market with Anheuser-Busch. Suddenly it seemed that Molson was not slated to become a big player in the U.S. market. MillerCoors would struggle for the U.S. market while the remnant of Molson would try to hold its own here.

And yet the two leading Canadian beers, Labatt Blue and Molson Canadian, had been losing their public at home. The explanation in good part was that the new owners were taking the Canadian public-relations budget and using it to sell their U.S. beers—Coors and Budweiser—in Canada. Why not? That's what ownership is for—the power to set strategy. Only Canadians think ownership doesn't matter.

Our economic leaders tell themselves, and then us, that the marketplace and open trade decide the shape of the economy. Everyone else in the world thinks ownership is about getting as much control of the market as you can in order to get what you want.

At the same time the real owners of our beer sector have cut back on developing new beers in Canada. Invention happens elsewhere. Where? Where the owners live. For beer drinkers, that is what we might call the loss of the research and development function. When you lose ownership, you lose the creativity function.

In 2005, I found myself at a dinner in New Delhi with the head of a very large, family-owned Indian firm that buys and sells a wide range of commodities and products all over the world. He had had a half-century of experience with the Canadian market, coming here dozens of times. Abruptly he leaned across the table so the others wouldn't hear. "What is the matter with Canadians? Your business leaders haven't got any guts. They can't hold on to their companies. It doesn't last." A few months later I was at a similar sort of gathering in France and the head of a large private investment fund suddenly blurted out not so discreetly—"What's going on in your country? What precisely is making it go wrong? You're abandoning your sophisticated economy in order to become dependent on raw commodities." He went on to talk about the instability of commodity-based economies, how the money slips away and doesn't generate real wealth. How he was selling his clients' interests in Canada because the commodities had pushed our dollar too high. "Isn't there a debate over this?" A real debate about economic strategies, policies, choices. Not the sterile, immature categorizing of free-traders versus protectionists that we have been reduced to over the last quarter-century.

Instead of seeing themselves the way foreign markets see them, our corporate leaders live a life of denial. There was a great deal of huffing and puffing, after Alcan was sold to BHP, about how the Canadians would be a real factor in the Australian mining giant's empire. Only a few months later BHP and other foreign corporations on the offensive in the same sector were talking about recutting the international pie, with Alcan reduced to various passive assets, to be broken up and tossed about as suited the real players. All of this was of course unrelated to any concrete interests of any aspect of the Canadian branch plant company or the Canadian economy or Canadian strategic interests, let alone to those of regions such as Quebec. In other words, the result of such sales of strategic elements of our economy is that those elements are transferred from the active to the passive part of the national, continental and international board game.

What is our problem? It has nothing to do with global economic forces. It has everything to do with weak managers frightened of the real market. And beside them are public officials who seem to understand nothing about economics as power. And hovering over these two groups is an eerie sense of emptiness—the artificial stillness brought on by a fundamental absence of ideas. An absence of concepts, of strategy. A curious provincial calm bred of the lack of sophistication necessary to deal with world forces. These people tread the waters of management while those elsewhere in the world swim about in them with self-confidence and ideas the way a shark glides around defenceless prey.

In the case of Alcan, there was much hand-wringing offstage by various Canadian business and governmental leaders. But they didn't dare protest in public. And neither the Canadian nor the federalist Quebec government seemed to understand fully how their capacity to govern was being interfered with. The Quebec-sovereignist parties, fixated on romantic concepts of political power and on their devotion to free trade as a force to help separate their province from Canada, seemed unable to focus on the reality of how economic power actually functions, as it slid away before their eyes. They are convinced of the particularity of their political position, yet they seemed as intellectually deprived as other Canadian leaders when it came to understanding that strategic takeovers have absolutely nothing to do with theories of free trade or with the international rules of the marketplace. From the point of view of economic theory and reality, these are two separate issues.

18

What Does All of This Mean?

Donald Macdonald, the former minister of finance whose 1984 royal commission on Canada's economic prospects led to the 1988 free trade deal with the United States, told me recently that he still felt the deal was the right decision for Canada. But when it came to the evolution of foreign ownership—"I have come full circle."

Like so many others, he had become troubled years ago by the slowness, lack of focus, the bureaucratic torture that were all part of the old Foreign Investment Review Agency (FIRA) system. The private sector will adjust to almost any system providing the rules are clear, leave room for profit and can be dealt with fast. FIRA certainly failed on the first and last points. It was another version of Canadian economic policy as boy-scoutism, cut off from international realities, all eager and ineffective.

FIRA disappeared and was replaced by our current system. This time it was all about heroic clarity, promising toughness and delivering nothing.

Macdonald has therefore reacted to what he can see—a strategic selling-off of the national sectors that matter. He has sensible ideas for rules and strategies. So do Peter Munk, the chair and founder of Barrick Gold; Dominic D'Alessandro, the CEO of Manufacturers Life; Gordon Nixon, the president of the Royal Bank of Canada, Canada's largest bank; and the Beaudoin family, who control Bombardier. They have all made public statements suggesting various changes in Canada's passive approach to takeovers. Thomas Caldwell, one of our leading investment advisers, writes of "mediocre corporate management" and a system that discourages risk-taking. What is happening "is one of the great corporate tragedies of our time." He describes the options and bonuses managers give themselves as theft. He says many corporate leaders agree with him privately but don't want to speak publicly. That fear of public debate is central to our elite failure. And it is characteristic of a colonial business class in which loyalty to the Compact is considered a sign of professionalism. Scott Hand was on the losing side in the 2006 Inco buyout—although he personally did very well out of the disaster. The world's second-largest nickel producer is now a subsidiary of Vale, a Brazilian mining company. Hand says, "Canada's takeover rules are perfect—for a boy scout economy."

All of them would agree that the statistics showing our legal corporate headquarters to be growing in number are nonsense. "A head office of a subsidiary is not a head office." Why? Because it is missing the leadership jobs, the key service jobs, the research and development jobs.

These five men represent some of the most powerful business leaders in contemporary Canada. Yet Conference Board of Canada economists, who do not earn their living in the marketplace, accuse these most successful of our corporate leaders of "sentiment and emotion," of being "commercially xenophobic." These protected employees, who rarely leave their cloistered offices in Ottawa, hide behind the Conference Board to accuse the few Canadian business leaders who do well around the world of suffering from "fear of foreigners." They argue with a certain glee that foreign owners are better for Canada than Canadian owners.

Every page of their 2008 report on foreign ownership reveals a deep self-loathing, a contempt for the country that expects guidance from them, and an amateur sort of analysis that represents clear professional failure.

The economists in the Ministry of Finance use almost the same numbers and make reassuring sounds about head offices, without analyzing the type of head office and what they do or do not contain. They reveal no understanding of economic strategy—the sort of strategies used by other countries. They use the old concept of *foreign direct investment*, which does not differentiate between real investment—that which works to create wealth—versus buying out fully developed corporations—or entire sectors—in which the purchase implies no invest-ment in wealth creation. In fact, the buyer usually uses the wealth of the company bought out to finance his taking control. Often the buyers then treat the company like a car in a wrecking yard—they cut it up and sell off the pieces that can make them quick money. When you read the assertions of the finance ministry thinkers over foreign investment or corporate headquarters growth, it is as if you are dealing with the brain dead. Strong words? Not at all. The strong words are those of economists in positions of influence who refuse to think. For example, although the figures are available, they make nothing of the difference between takeovers and new investment. Approximately 97 percent of what they call foreign investment is for takeovers; approximately 3 percent is for real new investment.

What is frightening is that Canada's economic policies are largely shaped from the ideas and advice of Ministry of Finance economists. When you look at their analyses, you find a provincial mindset with little understanding of how policies are set elsewhere in the world. It is as if they feel comfortable in their mediocrity because their predeces-sors made up their mind about what correct international economic thought involved in the 1980s. And no attempt has been made since to think about those assumptions. Not even the clear obsession of other countries with, first, ownership of their own strategic sectors as a key to economic strategy, and second, with ownership of specific Canadian sectors as a smart strategic move, has awakened them. Even our slide backward into growing dependence on the export of raw materials doesn't seem to trouble the department's economists. You would think that this regression toward the economic structure of our deep colonial past would have already produced some reaction. But no, they are happily ensconced in old convictions shared by no other ministry of finance in the Western world.

So here we are, almost all living in cities, pretending to be post-modern, sophisticated wealth creators, while our dependence on raw commodities grows and grows and ownership over those particular sectors slips away. We're just too sophisticated and modern to bother about it. Other countries are apparently not as sophisticated. And through all of this, the Ministry of Finance economists drone on, repeating their time-worn clichés. As the philosopher Hannah Arendt put it: "Clichés, stock phrases, adherence to conventional, standardized codes of expression have the socially recognized function of protecting us against reality, that is, against the claim on our thinking attention which all events and facts arouse by virtue of their existence."

If much of the managerial business leadership is insecure, frightened of risk and uninterested in building up wealth, their closest allies are the official policy advisers of the federal government. Here you see the direct effects of the dismantling of the Economic Council of Canada by Brian Mulroney. It had been created under Lester Pearson to give us an independent body of interesting thinkers. But that was no longer what was wanted. Since then the entire government structure has been subjected to a single, old-fashioned school of economics, which is ideological, narrow and doesn't take into consideration the Canadian situation.

Actually, it's worse than that. The government economists are so determined to present a picture of their relative powerlessness faced by international integration, and in particular North American integration, that they and their friends intentionally misrepresent our trade figures. For example, there is a constant assertion by government economists and the mainstream of Canadian economists that exports account for anywhere from 40 to 50 percent of our economy. In large part, this represents exports to the United States. Their conclusion is that we, therefore, can do little on issues such as specific policies for specific sectors or ownership rules without risking our export advantage. In other words, to want to own is to endanger exports. This argument is then used to suggest the inevitability of further North American economic integration.

Here is an area in which Statistics Canada does excellent work. And using those very public numbers, a young economist named Erin Weir, has laid out clearly what the real situation looks like. The trade numbers we constantly hear and read are actually gross figures. They include Canadian imports that are then assembled into Canadian exports. So while the accurate gross figure is around 41 or 42 percent, the real figure for Canadian exports is around 25 or 26 percent of our economy. There is an enormous strategic difference between a half and a quarter. As a result, the real growth in the part of our economy devoted to exports has only been about 7 percent since the 1988 treaty, not the 15 percent you get with gross figures. Of course, one of the other purposes in using these gross figures is to exaggerate the growth effects of the trade deals. What's more, the disproportionate growth in imports as part of our gross exports tells you how much downstream, sophisticated activity was leaving the country even before the recent rise in commodity prices.

To understand what has been happening, you need only look at the Statistics Canada charts of our trade balance. There are seven categories. Since 1988, the Consumer Products balance and that for Machinery and Equipment has continued to plummet ever deeper into deficit. The Auto sector was marginally in surplus in 1988, rose for several years, then began to drop and is now back where it was, although it is probably on its way into deficit. The Industrial sector is about where it was in 1988, but is probably heading toward a deficit balance. That leaves three sectors in surplus — all raw materials: Agriculture, Forestry and Energy. The last one now supports the whole trade system.

We have always been a trading nation. In the 1980s, we engaged in an economic system centred on accelerated growth in trade with the expectation of a sharp growth in more sophisticated economic activity. Over twenty years there has been growth, but the relative and therefore fundamental effect has been to undermine sophisticated activity, except in a few exceptional areas—think of corporations such as Research In Motion (RIM) or Softimage—and to return us to dependence on those old raw materials. There are many possible ways to interpret what is happening. One of the most obvious is that the more we integrate as a smaller player into the large and complex U.S. economy, the more we are assigned a specific role not by market theory but by the U.S. market. Given the shape and needs of the U.S. economy and the highly integrated role of regional political influences, it isn't surprising that our assigned role should be that of source of raw materials for U.S. industry and U.S. consumers. That's what peripheral and colonial societies are for. The history of every empire is perfectly clear about this pattern of organization. And given that the U.S. economy will want to do with those commodities exactly what it wants, when it wants, at the price it wants, it is not surprising that control—that is to say, ownership—over those sectors is now a priority for U.S. corporations or their competitors elsewhere. The sign of the deeply colonial nature of our business and economic leadership is their passivity and even pleasure at being despoiled. At least important people are paying attention to their bodies, that is, to their corporations. In a colonial situation, a mind is an encumbrance.

Finally, today's unassembled parts move back and forth across the continent and the oceans in search of assemblage. This is usually presented as rationalization, a modern sign of continental and international integration. It could equally be argued that this is an antiquated outcropping of nineteenth-century theory, wasteful, involving expensive fuels for unnecessary transportation, polluting and contributing to global warming. It may be, in the era of expensive commodities, marked by one particularly expensive commodity—oil—that the appropriate market structure is one that concentrates natural resources and more sophisticated downstream production in a severely limited geographic area. Perhaps it would be worth at least talking about this and doing some calculations that integrate all of the costs and effects of different systems. If we do inclusive economic cost calculations, it may turn out that long-distance-assembly options are too expensive. The long-distance transporting of low-value goods may also be too expensive. For example, the difference between Chinese production costs and ours is in good part that their economic analysis includes even fewer real economic factors than ours. Their analysis includes few social costs, few work condition costs, even fewer environmental impact costs. There is little enough discussion of alternate approaches elsewhere in the world. In the Canadian elite, there is no discussion. To discuss is to think. To think of alternate economic possibilities is to question the conventional codes of expression and so to raise the frightening spectre of reality.

This fear of debate then throws control over public ideas into very few hands and rarely amplifies the most interesting voices. If you look at the public discussion of Canadian business over the last two decades, you will find that a remarkably large space has been occupied by Conrad Black's opinions, adventures and, more recently, travails. Yet he has never been a capitalist. That is, he has never assumed the capitalist's role as owner for the purposes of wealth creation. He has only created one thing—one newspaper—and even that he couldn't hold on to for more than three years. Apart from that, his career has been largely about stripping corporations. Destroying them. As the most visible voice for Canadian capitalism, he has had a negative effect on how most Canadians imagine the marketplace. In fact, I can't think of anyone who has had a more negative effect on how Canadians think of the market. As one of the most active exploiters of libel chill, he has spread the impression that business leaders don't want freedom of speech. As someone who over decades denounced his own country for being inferior to the United States and Britain, he promoted the old Family Compact colonial idea of how business relates to Canada. In the end, he made the ultimate colonial gesture by throwing away his citizenship in order to join an arcane, powerless British institution. And when real capitalists or business leaders, such as the five I mentioned earlier in this chapter, have raised their voices to express varying opinions on our economy, who shouts them down and denigrates them? In part it is the columnists who owe the launching of their careers to Lord Black.

Meanwhile, *The New York Times* and its writers have no trouble looking at Canada and seeing a crisis. "Canada's vast mineral resources once made it the world's leading mining nation. Many international banks based their mining experts in Toronto and students from around the world came to study mining at its universities. Major miners, like Inco ... were respected for their innovation and operational efficiency." *The Times* describes how it all went wrong in steel, mining, forestry and breweries, and then the loss of real head offices, the loss of potential investments in the stock market, underwriting, accounting, legal work, the loss of charity donors. "Canada became the hunted not the hunter."

This crisis represents a failure in private-sector ownership and management. But it is also a failure of the establishment economists and the political leaders. None of them seem to understand the power that comes with ownership. If there is no power, then why do U.S. companies, Swiss, Brazilian and others want to own ours? If there is no power, then why is our economy so much more in foreign hands than those of any of our allies? For example, more than half of our manufacturing is in foreign hands, while the United States, Japan, Germany, the United Kingdom, France, Italy, the Netherlands, Norway, Finland and Sweden have kept the outsiders down to 4 percent. Our elites seem to be suggesting that by acting in this way we show how much more clever we are than all of our friends. There is nothing more fascinating than delusionary behaviour by public figures.

In the first half of 2008, it seemed as if something was changing. The Canadian corporation MacDonald Dettwiler tried to sell its space division to a U.S. corporation. This included the Radarsat-2 satellite, which had been developed in part for security and sovereignty reasons to allow Canada an all-pervasive eye over the Arctic. It also included the Canadarm robotic limb, which was our contribution to international space initiatives. The sellers said they had no choice because the U.S. space sector was closed to them for security reasons. In other words, this is one of those sophisticated faces of protectionism that the OECD doesn't see.

There was a relatively apolitical outcry, and the minister responsible decided to use the available regulations to prevent the sale. Apart from the usual suspects—making up the vast majority of economic columnists—people on all sides applauded this decision.

On the other hand, such a decision only makes sense if there is a national consensus—public and private—on how to build the sector. That means a long-term strategy—including financial arrangements—to ensure there is enough real investment.

What was fascinating was that this decision, taken in a rapid, clear, efficient, transparent manner, with no whinging and no apologies, produced no international protests. For two decades, we have been repeatedly told by politicians, civil servants, economists and business managers that any Canadian interference in the buying and selling of corporations across borders would cause a terrible fuss and damage Canada's international position, and in particular our ability to export our products. There would be swift and terrifying retaliation. Yet no foreign government or international body or important economic commentator criticized the act—because it was a perfectly natural decision of the sort taken regularly by other countries. This is an illustration of international ownership realities. All our friends and allies have a strategy. They have been amazed at our weakness and confusion in this area.

Equally fascinating has been the silence among our own business leadership. They have been so passive for so long that they don't know what to make of the decision. They daren't oppose it, but they seem to be treating it as an exceptional act, which it may be. There are no public discussions and no discernible private discussions, now that we have discovered we are capable of ownership initiatives, over what a responsible integrated strategy would look like.

An isolated initiative, even by a powerful minister, will age badly unless there is a sense among public and private leaders that the old ideologies need to be given a rest so that we can talk together about national economic strategies.

19

How Did They Come
to Be This Way?

How widespread is the sense of passivity or inertia among our elites?

A simple case answers this question. A federal program was created in 2004 to send expensive drugs for fatal diseases such as AIDS to crisis areas in poorer parts of the world at reasonable prices. The Access to Medicines Regime was to involve co-operation between manufacturers and government. Two years later, it was inadvertently revealed that no drugs had yet been sent. Public officials and private-sector executives immediately went into a public-relations defence mode, blaming the complexity of the program for their failure to embrace it or, to put this in ethical terms, for their failure to obey the intent of the law. But if the only problem was administrative complexity, they could have spoken up at any time in order to ensure these problems were straightened out. No doubt they would protest that they had been working on the problem, quietly, slowly, out of public sight. When the failure of the program was revealed, the minister responsible reassured everyone that the problem was being studied. In other words, the constituted elite in all its forms sat on the situation and let people die.

What does this particular example illustrate? An incapacity to act in order to solve problems by reimagining situations. What does reimagining mean? Engaging in the full sense of ideas. Real ideas are filled with uncertainty. To keep them alive you must constantly question them. Reimagining is important because ideas are the driving force of the most powerful and longest-lived actions. This means looking beyond the reactive world of managers managing situations with narrow, utilitarian thoughts.

The people I have been describing from health care through social well-being to business do not believe themselves capable of filling the role with which they have been entrusted. Their lives are a form of sedated despair. And so they downsize their role into one that is more passive and reactive. This is presented as a curious sort of sophistication, in which success is the wisdom to see mediocrity as managerial competence, problems as intractable, and forces as inevitable and uncontrollable—particularly when described as global. In other words, success is failure. All of this can be summarized as a fear of power, a fear of the reality of power, a reality that can be avoided through the comfort of passivity.

Is this an inescapable description of Canada's elites? Not at all. Our history can be seen as successive waves of self-confident leadership—people eager to get their hands on real power, ambitious to shape events through interesting, sophisticated, deeply thought-through strategies and programs, national and international. Read the pro-democracy leaders of the first half of the nineteenth century. Look at the ambitions of their business partners or those of Cartier and Macdonald. Read Laurier and his friends at the height of their powers. Mackenzie King is always an oddity, but look at his cabinet and the dollar-a-year men during the Second World War. In all these cases you get a clear sense of what self-confidence, sophistication and ambition sound like. You see them creating, building, risking, owning. You can identify their sense of purpose and its relationship to their actions. But between these eras it is as though we slip back into troughs of self-loathing, into what could most succinctly be described as a colonial inferiority complex.

Tom Kent immigrated to this country after the Second World War and began his remarkable career working with many of those who built modern Canada, in particular Lester Pearson. What had drawn him was "the self-confidence, the sense of purpose, the idea of where they were going." For these people, the size of Canada's population or its economy were secondary, and certainly not a barrier to thought or action. They saw themselves making up for size with intelligence, originality and courage in action. Out of that self-confidence came waves of broad initiatives that in turn led to myriad small reforms that have gradually made Canada in many ways a far better place now than it was then. You can see this in St. Laurent's attempts to build a *middleway* foreign policy; Diefenbaker's continuation of that, his returning of the suffrage to Aboriginals and his attempts at a Northern strategy; Pearson's massive social reforms; Trudeau's social and constitutional reforms.

But our most recent slow decline in leadership self-confidence, sense of purpose and direction has led to myriad passive actions or inactions that are undoing our capacity to build our society. Increasingly our elites attempt to slip into the vacuum behind other people's actions. Worse still, they attempt to imitate the surface appearance, not the reality, of other people's actions. What has caused this loss of confidence? Perhaps a more accurate question would be, what was it that changed the type of people who become our leaders?

A long-term answer might be that that negative side to our four-century-long experience has somehow, yet again, swept back to the surface, with all its colonial characteristics, its Family Compact belief in entitlement, its incapacity to believe that this is a real place. No country escapes the tensions set in place with its creation. The negative forces do come sweeping back from time to time. To deal with them you must be able to identify them as such.

Certainly the incapacity to recognize the Aboriginal core of our civilization is a factor that facilitated the resurgence of the old, insecure, colonial Family Compact mentality. And the belief in *order* not *welfare* is another key factor. Both of these misrepresentations of our long evolution deny us the language and the sense of self that we need in order to understand and explain ourselves.

A medium-term view might be that the remarkable and self-confident reform movement, born out of the Great Depression and then emboldened by the way we handled ourselves abroad and at home during the Second World War, blossomed in the late 1950s through to the early 1980s and then ran out of steam. No new wave of ideas has appeared to carry us on. Instead came a utilitarian economic ideology, mainly imported, not terribly interesting, apparently designed for industrialized economies, but not reimagined, thought through or adapted to our delicate balance between commodities and industry. It is not that this ideology was entirely wrong, but it was devoid of any intellectual weight, humanist or societal direction.

That this approach seemed strategically paper-thin and devoid of self-doubt shouldn't have surprised anyone. Remember, in Canada it was driven by trade specialists, hardly a profession known for its sense of economic or social complexity. Handing your economy over to trade negotiators is a bit like handing your transportation systems over to car salesmen because they are into transportation, they have a simple view of it and they are optimistic deal doers. And this was a period, after all, when two long-time finance ministers, Michael Wilson and Paul Martin, were thought to be heavyweight economic strategists. Whatever the successes of this utilitarian economic ideology, it could not deliver or encourage the sort of rounded approach that societies require in order to improve themselves.

It could be that the free trade policy argued in the 1988 election was right or wrong. But in the end it certainly wasn't about free trade, which we largely had already, and the last elements of which were being put into place through already existing mechanisms. It was about whether our elite should have the sort of self-confidence that builds a spirit of independence. This is not a protectionist or isolationist spirit, but one that makes leaders feel they can be at the origin of new ideas, or at least speak up for new ideas, and therefore lead the way in unusual developments. They can develop strategies that will help society shape itself. They can deal with the needs of the public good. They can be at the centre of ownership empires. This is the spirit that builds wealth, as opposed to simply pouring unrefined energy down pipelines to others who have the necessary self-confidence to do all the rest.

Quite simply, in the aftermath of 1988 this elite no longer seemed to have the emotional solidity needed to initiate actions. They became increasingly passive. Everything important enough to shape society was either presented as impossible given global inevitabilities, or just not the sort of thing sophisticated globalists would engage in. As they found action more difficult, so they seemed incapable of noticing that in other countries this sort of passivity was taken as a sign of weakness and naïveté. At the core of their loss of self-confidence was a definition of *opening up to the world* that actually meant *integrating as a bit player* into U.S. markets. They lost that strategic sense of economic critical mass that you will find in most other countries. And so an argument that suggested we were taking down borders gave birth to a new provincialism, in which small economic groups in Vancouver, Calgary, Toronto and Montreal turned away from one another toward their specific silos to the south. In Montreal, which in many ways has experienced a remarkable recovery, the actual loss of economic clout accelerated. With the loss of Alcan, the city and the province have been reduced to perhaps three major players. Vancouver has almost none. The situation is close to surreal, because these two cities in particular are having to make their way without the economic clout of solid corporate sectors. This may force the invention of new kinds of economies. But it may also mean that their well-being is floating on a fragile economic cloud.

Another medium-term explanation might be that the elite has never recovered from the arrival in power in 1977 of the Parti Québécois. I include in this group national and provincial leaders, including those of the separatist-indépendantiste-souvereignist movement. On all sides it was as if a sense of purpose were no longer possible. Instead they were all drawn into the details of what seemed to be endless constitutional imperatives and terribly important financial power struggles and the highly professional details of administration. None of this was an expression of the necessary righting of real wrongs in Quebec. Those wrongs had been on the road to rectification from the 1960s on, at both the federal and the provincial levels. Besides, much of what was wrong was actually a matter of internal Quebec structures and policies, and these were put on the road toward rectification by the Lesage government and then incrementally by successive governments. By 1980, the issues around fairness, justice, language and culture had been largely dealt with by all parties at all levels. There were lots of other things to argue about, but none that carried the weight of those that had driven society in the

1960s and 1970s. And none that rose above the sort of standard political differences that might be found in any country.

By the mid-1980s, the elites—federalist, anti-federalist, even Western—had become so obsessed by those details of dividing up financial and administrative power that they could hardly imagine the idea of advancing the shared public good. Their failure to deal with the poverty of a million and a half citizens across the country was as complete among rich Albertans, sovereignist Quebecers and federalists in Ottawa, on the left as on the right. In fact, of all the governments in Canada, among the weakest when it came to dealing with poverty were those run by the Alberta nationalists and the Quebec nationalists.

Whether the cause of the elite's loss of self-confidence is one or more of the possibilities I have given or something quite different, the most common sign of it has been their frightening incapacity to engage in any sort of conversation with the citizenry. They read us speeches they have rarely themselves read in advance, let alone written. They present issues in an insultingly simplistic manner, whether it is to do with conflict in Afghanistan, economic policy or health care. They seem terrified of the sort of intelligent debate the citizenry long for. They have no words because they know no words.

20

The Colonial Mind

Perhaps this intellectual vacuum in public policy is also an echo of the colonial undercurrent I keep coming back to. Leaders in colonies can rarely absorb local culture—their own culture—into the way they think. At some profound, unconscious level they think and act as if they find themselves accidentally in the colony. Accidentally or temporarily. Their citizenship is an inexplicable emotional accident. Their real culture is that of the empire. Or, in the words of economist and philosopher Amartya Sen, "The colonized mind is parasitically obsessed with the extraneous relation with the colonial powers." It is their responsibility to echo the empire's culture in order to keep standards up in this provincial place. How do you keep up standards? By ensuring that your models for thought come from there not here. By educating yourself and your children in their manner, if at all possible in their schools and universities, and failing that, by reforming your universities to reflect their idea of standards, by imitating their policies, invoking their heroes, holidaying where they holiday, following their fashions, drinking their wine. Does this sound silly? Of course. Almost nothing is sillier than a colonial mind at work.

But how else can we explain the fortunes being made by consultants peddling tired old imported ideas slightly reformatted for the local market or the growing number of speaking series delivering pre-digested clichés from people who used to be famous in the United States or the abrupt arrival in Quebec of century-old Parisian arguments insisting on pure secular education. Quebecers are rightly proud of such things as the high television viewership of locally produced programs and films. But turn to the way society is actually run—the concepts, whether social, political or economic—and you will find it is as imported, insecure, unoriginal and passive as in Ontario or Ottawa. All three proceed as if in fear of originality.

You can measure this disassociation between power and culture simply by examining what quality of politicians are generally named to run the federal and provincial ministries of culture. Or look at something even more basic. Who our public figures choose to quote in their speeches. Or analyze the sources from which they develop their policies. A 2007 Ontario government ad encouraging people to eat local produce stated: "Good thing they take the Road Less Travelled." Were they trying to get Canadians to travel to Robert Frost's beautiful state of Vermont? Or had they bought their public-relations programs from a Canadian subsidiary of a U.S. company that had standard pop-up models for tourism campaigns in North America? Or was the division between power and culture so great in their emotional interior that they simply couldn't notice? Or were they simply ignorant in the manner of colonial officials at sea as to how they might imagine themselves? And so it simply never struck them that if they wanted to sell Ontario produce, perhaps they should not use one of the quintessential lines from the poet of rival producers in Vermont. Perhaps they might use a line from a local poet. Atwood. Ondaatje. Pauline Johnson. How about *the edible province*? Just a thought.

Fear and Self-Loathing

Canada's leaders hate to hear any suggestion that they still suffer from colonial reflexes. They are convinced of their sophisticated worldliness. After all, only a sophisticated, worldly person could understand that the destiny of a smaller country is to have its interests defined by the empire of the day, indeed by outside influences in general.

Studies in a variety of situations around the world all produce roughly the same analysis of the nature of the colonial mind.

At its core is a personal insecurity that cannot be intellectually explained or dealt with. This may as easily involve a physically strong, well-educated, rich person as the opposite. In fact, the insecurity is more likely to blossom in successful persons because they quickly run up against the elite's confusion over its own purpose.

Such uncontrollable insecurity in turn produces a profound self-loathing. The sufferers can rarely identify or express their emotional state as either insecurity or self-loathing. And so it must be expressed in a compensatory manner. Sometimes this takes the form of aggressive cynicism, as in, nothing basic to their own origins could be worth struggling for. Sometimes the sufferers search for an individual or a cause they feel comfortable treating as greater than themselves—something they can adore and so emotionally attach themselves to. This must almost inevitably involve an important foreign element. In the shadow cast by what they accept to be a greater force, their insecurity is assuaged.

At a more profoundly confused level, this insecurity or self-loathing weakens the individual's desire to live. It is often said that in a deeply unconscious way, the colonial mind harbours a love of death. Humans are normally driven by a basic desire to exist. This gets us through life's complex circumstances. That desire is reinforced by our belief that life must be deserved. And there lies our motivation—accomplishment, creation, family, reward, admiration from others. But colonial insecurity makes it hard to believe that you are deserving, in part because your accomplishments do not carry the emotional weight of those who belong to a real place.

In practical terms, insecure people living in smaller societies find emotional security through the acceptance of their inferiority before another civilization. Their sense of belonging then takes on a happy, contented form of passivity. If you don't deserve life at its fullest, then you can accept all sorts of mediocre situations as normal, indeed as proof of your sophistication. For example, the idea that you could own, shape or build seems pretentious when you can make yourself feel secure by following, imitating and becoming dependent.

This is not simply a matter of politics or economics. Even the way we represent our literature tells us something about the colonial mindset. Roy MacGregor laid this out with perfect intellectual clarity in *Canadians*. Why is John Richardson's less than mediocre nineteenth-century novel *Wacousta* so relentlessly pushed forward as the founding statement of our sensibility? What is its message? That the nature and climate of Canada makes it a place to be feared. That the First Nations are violent and to be feared. That settlers must dominate in every way in order to assuage their fears. This deeply European view—steeped in the discomfort of the outsider—helped to set the pattern for a colonial interpretation of Canada. Ours was to be a place in which white Christians must be constantly ill at ease, uncomfortable, living far from their true civilizational inspirations. At the same time, they must also imagine themselves as cut off from the gigantic, uncontrolled nature all around them. They must struggle to survive, dependent on the originality of those fortunate enough to live at the centre of great civilizations. They must marginalize, weaken, if possible destroy, the local *Indian* civilization. Christianity, in its various forms, would be a safe, rigid structure to protect these Europeans from this uncontrollable, frightening place. Theirs was to be what Northrop Frye called a garrison mentality—"a closely knit and beleaguered society" existing with a "deep terror in regard to nature."

None of this is actually true about the Canadian experience of the preceding centuries, except in the mind of the colonial elites. True, the society was poor and isolated. And a civilization built on immigration has endless stories of difficulty. But this is not the way in which the new Canadians have emotionally settled in. They found their sense of comfort and place and belonging, and did so with astonishing speed, already in the seventeenth century.

To know that the space in which you live is uncontrollable and, in that sense, dangerous does not mean you live in fear. To know this means that you see yourself as part of the place and therefore neither as conqueror of it nor as locked up and frightened in a mental garrison. That was the Aboriginal message, embraced and digested by a good two centuries of early immigration.

Yet from *Wacousta* on, the elite interpretation of our literature, and therefore of our character, has been shoehorned into a British or French colonial mould. After all, French Canada went down a roughly equivalent road, pushed by the division between the pastoral settlements and the uncontrolled land beyond. And the French-Canadian *official* intellectual myth of pastoral settlements versus the dangerous, uncontrolled land beyond was almost effortlessly transformed into today's *official* nationalist definition of culture and loyalty. That is one of the peculiarities of the garrison mentality. To the extent that it exists, it does so among anglophones and francophones alike. And it involves freezing our idea of the past in an oppressive, nineteenth-century, Victorian cuteness, treacly in its portrait of rural or small-town European colonials.

All of this eliminated—and continues to eliminate —the reality of the lengthy, stable Aboriginal role in the shaping of Canada's fundamental mindset. Frye rightly pointed out that the garrison mentality was a phenomenon of the officer class and so eventually of the elites. But perhaps because he saw culture as an elite phenomenon, he then slipped into treating this colonial emotion as that of the whole civilization. "[T]here must be a period of a certain magnitude ... in which a social imagination can take root and establish a tradition ... Canada has never had it." Instead, he says, we rushed from wilderness to empire to world. He discounts the Aboriginal role as oral mythology, as "nineteenth-century literary conventions." And indeed that was how the colonial elites saw things. That is the *Wacousta* view of Canada.

And you can certainly see it in our view of our culture today. Our anthologies are largely narrow, linguistically defined collections, as if we can't digest the complexity in which we have lived and continue to live. The remarkable Aboriginal sagas and myths are absent, even though they account for many of our greatest texts, our most important poetry, our only original creation myths. The West Coast First Nations poems are often thousands of lines each and contain some of the best poetry written in Canada. They were reinvented by each generation of poets, storytellers, fire-keepers. We have those of a remarkable generation from the late nineteenth century, including Charles Edenshaw, Skaay and Gandl.

The greatest Canadian war poetry or in his case anti-war poetry was written by an Alberta farmer from Markerville, near Red Deer. For forty years, Stephan G. Stephansson worked his farm and wrote his poetry in Icelandic. His language explains why he wasn't arrested by the RCMP during the First World War and why he is absent from our conscious cultural memory. And yet what he wrote, like the sagas of the West Coast, are somehow recognizable as the voice of our collective unconscious.

Why do we not include these and other poems in our culture? Because they weren't written in French or English? That certainly never stopped anyone in Britain and France. They happily include work written in Anglo-Saxon, Latin, Celtic—known as Old Irish and Old Welsh— Langue d'Oc and Provençal. In fact, much of the most important litera- ture of both countries has been incomprehensible for many centuries and exists in the conscious public imagination only through translation.

The acceptance of such an inclusive view of cultural history in Canada would involve us pulling together our creative roots—that which was created here in Aboriginal languages, French, English, Icelandic, Chinese and so on. These can exist for us at a national level at least in our two national languages. And indeed we are perhaps climbing out of this false past by creating a new literature written by Canadians who carry roots from all over the world. For example, I would say that the most remark- able Canadian novel of the last few decades is *A Fine Balance* by Rohinton Mistry. Even so, none of us can escape from the confines of a false past simply by moving forward.

Take the influence of French and English on each other. This is central to our four centuries of shared culture. And yet our literature is treated quite separately, depending on the language in which it was written.

Even if anglophone and francophone poets or novelists lived in houses side by side, whether of Canadien or Loyalist or Ukrainian or Haitian or Jamaican or South Asian stock, whether they made love, learned from each other, ate together every day for fifty years, they are carefully pried apart, separated and passed on as representatives of closed-language cultures, either English or French. The result is that they are almost never read together or taught together. The possibility of a shared imagination across languages is structurally eliminated.

The result is that we reduce our cultures to mere colonial arms of the old empires, which have been transformed today into language empires — virtual empires with language as the army by which they function and influence. We act as if it is normal for our languages to have complex roots at their imperial source. But out here in the colonies our languages must be pure of source.

And so, I believe, Frye was wrong. We have had lots of time for our "social imagination [to] take root." The result is there in the way Canadians actually function. It is there in much of our literature. But the elites are in denial of this. They are frightened by the complexity with which it reaches back into our history. If the great and timeless West Coast epic poem *Raven Travelling* or one of the creation myths from the same area is central to Canadian culture, then that culture is not simply derivative of great foreign empires. If our elites could admit that that was so, they would have to deal with what it means to think of themselves as actually being from here.

The strategic touchstone is Aboriginal languages and whether they will continue to disappear. I have mentioned that we still have some sixty, from twelve language families. Whether non-Aboriginals speak them or not is beside the point. Each time one disappears, the First Nation in question loses access to its culture. More precisely, each time one of these languages disappears, I lose access to part of my culture. So do you. A door closes forever on our possible understanding of this place. Yet there are virtually no programs and scarcely a budget for rebuilding these languages. Do such programs work? The answer lies in the remarkable growth of French outside of Quebec over the last thirty years, both through French first-language programs and French immersion. Or in the revival of Welsh in Britain. Or in the growth of Mandarin—the northern dialect—in China. Or in the revival of Hebrew in Israel. Why are there no serious programs in Canada? Because our elites would rather follow the narrow track of their one imperial language back to its source across the water to where its sources lie.

There is one other way of looking at this denial of the Aboriginal role in shaping our shared mindset. The garrison mentality marginalized the idea of our comfort in the land, which is essential to the idea of belonging here. Of course, most of us now live in cities. We enjoy them. They are the showplaces of our continuing and successful immigrant/new citizen society. And that is good.

But there is also a certain triumphalism attached to our urban discourse, as if the elites see themselves principally in relationship to what are described as other *world* cities. This somehow justifies their discomfort with Canada as a massive non-urban, non-weekend house, non-rural place—a place most of them know little about.

And so the colonialism of the nineteenth-century elite can be linked to that of today. It has always meant vaunting the virtues of somewhere else, somewhere thought to be grand and superior. Emily Carr described the English-born middle class in Victoria as being taught at local private schools "how not to become Canadian, to believe that all niceness and goodness came from ancestors and could have nothing to do with the wonderful new land." They were taught "how not to acquire Colonial deportment which was looked upon as crude, almost wicked." This now sounds ridiculous. But look at the growing desire of the Canadian upper-middle class to send their children to private schools. Then look at the deportment those schools teach. Where does it come from? What does it imitate? One clear hint is that on the anglophone side, most of these schools rate well below the national average in learning French. Or for that matter other languages. Why? Because their model comes from places where bilingualism or multilingualism or multiple personalities are neither necessary nor admired nor admitted as a national possibility. Now look at the growing desire of that same upper-middle class to send their children to U.S. private schools, then U.S. universities for undergraduate education. How is this different from our colonial elites in the late-nineteenth and early-twentieth centuries sending their children to be educated in England? Note the astonishing levels of U.S. professors being hired by our universities. All of this is presented as merely a matter of meritocratic standards. But then the colonial mind, in its desire to present itself as sophisticated by someone else's standards, has always insisted that its choices are based on merit. It has always asserted that the problem with the place in which their body has placed them is that it isn't good enough for them. And it certainly isn't good enough for the minds of their children. That was the argument a century and more ago for filling our universities with mediocre professors from Britain and marginal clerics from France.

What are our elites seeking today if not to avoid "colonial deportment"? Each generation redefines colonial crudeness in a different way. But the underlying insecurity remains the same.

In 1888, a surreal and troubling novel by James De Mille was published posthumously. We don't know how much earlier he had written *A Strange Manuscript Found in a Copper Cylinder*. In it he viciously attacked the colonial mindset and its effects by creating a world that worships death. There, a young couple is singled out to be condemned to life. They are placed in what amounts to a golden prison in which they will have no choice but to live out their lives in splendour as virtual monarchs or Christ figures who must carry that burden of fear of life from which everyone else suffers. The female explains to the still-confused male: "You do not understand these people. Their ruling passion is the hatred of self, and therefore they are eager to confer benefits on others.... They value us most highly because we take everything that is given us." This sharp mocking of the colonial mindset would be a far better base than *Wacousta* from which to interpret our literature. Besides, it's a far better novel. It would help us to understand why our politicians are so uncomfortable with the possibility that we could be a source of ideas and why they are so comfortable with giving away our sovereignty to people who won't give away theirs, why our business leaders are so uncomfortable with the idea of ownership and so enthusiastic about concentrating on management.

Insecurity in Action

What does the colonial mindset look like in everyday life today?

The U.S. embassy in Ottawa sits on two major streets in the city's core—Rideau and Sussex, key both for traffic movement and as showpieces of the national capital. Immediately after September 11, 2001, the traffic lanes on either side of the embassy were closed. They are still closed, thanks to large, ugly cement blocks. Twice-daily traffic jams are now installed in one of the few beautiful, formal areas of the capital.

In the immediate atmosphere of uncertainty after the attacks, taking extra precautions around the embassy was a prudent initiative. But with time and reflection anyone could see that the precaution of blocking the two lanes carried no security advantage. To be blunt, it had no relationship to security needs. In fact, the embassy had only just been designed and opened with all the very latest bells and whistles of security built in. Nothing that happened on or after September 11, 2001, changed the technical nature of the security risk. All the experiences of recent attacks on U.S. embassies elsewhere in the world had been taken into account in its design. I thought about this as I drove by the U.S. embassy in Oslo in 2007. It is in a similar location to that in Ottawa. In Norway, suitable precautions have been taken, but no traffic was shut off. Oslo was not defaced.

The only difference between the two cities was the weakness of the Canadian authorities at all levels—political, administrative and security. It was part of their fear that any non-compliance with a Washington wish might be anti-Americanism. I'm not simply saying that they fear being perceived as anti-American. Much more important, they seem to fear that any action, however sensible, which is not actively pro-American, must be anti-American. That is a classic colonial mindset. You must anticipate the empire's feelings and needs. They should never have to ask. It is demeaning for a prince to be reduced to making requests of such minor people. Besides, what if by some fluke there were an attack? Removal would mean taking responsibility. In other words, any sensible identification of a Canadian point of view, however minor, is anti-Americanism.

This is not a matter of real political weakness. Nor does it have anything to do with a pro-American strategy. This is merely character weakness—a desire to be coddled and loved.

It is that character weakness that got us into trouble over Maher Arar; that which caused our refugee rules to be changed to suit Washington; that which causes our serious newspapers to give more coverage to the Academy Awards than do serious U.S. papers; that which discouraged our elites from leading an interesting public debate on Iraq and anti-terrorism; that which causes Toronto business people to think that bringing a National Football League team to Toronto from a declining U.S. city is a sign that Toronto is becoming an important place. The possible effect on the Canadian Football League is of no concern to them. What they want is their fingers on the hem of imperial reality. And entertainment is the most visible manifestation of the imperial robe.

In the early days of our engagement with Afghanistan, what struck me most was how little our leaders seemed to know about the place or the region. I'm not referring to our military officers, weaned on one trouble spot after another, who seemed to have done their reading and looked carefully at the history and the region. But, as I mentioned earlier, three prime ministers in a row seemed to have only the vaguest understanding of the long-established regional drama. And only the tiniest group of our diplomats seemed to understand the history of the area and the full implications of engagement. The security forces seemed to know only what was fed to them from Washington. Hardly more than one or two cabinet ministers seemed to have any sense of the region. The disastrous state of Pakistan and its equally disastrous role—self-evident to anyone who knew anything about the region—seemed to have escaped the attention of prime ministers, cabinets, the Prime Minister's Office and the Privy Council Office. And it went on escaping them until that country went into full meltdown. It's hard to know what is worse: that they hadn't been properly briefed or that they hadn't bothered to try to understand the region. That would require reading a great deal more than the standard Ottawa briefing notes and the misrepresentations coming out of Washington, where Pakistan had long been considered, treated and represented as a close ally. That Washington had chosen for decades to pretend that their Pakistan fiction could be the basis for policies in the region should have been neither here nor there for Ottawa. None of our other allies were taken in. If people in Ottawa did understand about Pakistan's real role, why did they choose not to let the Canadian citizenry in on the situation?

One of the things that constantly strikes me in Ottawa is how few people with any kind of power read anything beyond a briefing note. Only a scattering of ministers, ministerial advisers or senior civil servants actually seem to read real information—books, major independent analyses, even important magazines. The rest live off briefings. Most briefings I've read or heard wouldn't stand the test of a standard editor in a mainstream newspaper. Indeed, there is usually more information and more accurate information in these newspapers than in the secret briefings our leaders are addicted to. What's more, the sloppy use of information hiding behind confidentiality and secrecy is usually deflated when subjected to the minimum use of public critical standards.

In most other Western countries, there is not such functional illiteracy at senior levels. In most key countries, a good percentage of the leadership read, educate themselves, attempt not to slip into dependency on mere briefings, which shift power to those who wrote them. What then is the explanation for the Canadian situation except that those in power do not have the self-confidence to attempt to think, to think independently and to do the reading and discussing that would prepare them to think independently. They act like colonial politicians, afraid to shape events by acting as if they could be at the centre of new ideas.

When the then leader of the Parti Québécois, André Boisclair, took part in a television spoof of the film *Brokeback Mountain*, with Harper and Bush substituted for the two cowboys, there was a terrible scandal. It may have been the turning point in his leadership. Yet Canadian politicians regularly take part in far tougher political comedy routines. And there was no public upset about the representation of Prime Minister Harper. The scandal among Quebec journalists and political figures was that the U.S. president should be mocked by a Quebec leader. Radio Canada reported that the PQ was upset that Boisclair hadn't consulted his shadow cabinet before taking part. This was one of the most delightful illustrations of the colonial mindset in years. A Canadian politician can attack anyone in any way, just so long as they are not an important imperial figure. Underneath this fear lies the almost-delusionary belief that these important personages would actually notice. This is part of the desperate colonial need to believe that we have a special relationship—or could have—with Rome, perhaps with the Emperor himself.

LaFontaine in 1840 in *The Address to the Electors of Terrebonne* was already describing this sort of delusion: "It is a far too widespread mistake of colonial political parties that they believe they can expect sympathetic support from an Imperial ministry."

In other words, we have a long history of leaders who are afraid to think and lead. We also have a long history of strong leaders who think it natural to think and to lead. But they always have to fight off the accusations from much of the elite that they are betraying the Rome of the day and so endangering our dependence on their kindness. From the 1840s on—when the British repeal of the Corn Laws destroyed the purpose of the Canadian Corn Act and plunged our farmers into poverty—Canada had to deal with a long series of betrayals by London. The British move toward free trade was structured in such a way as to consistently favour the U.S. economy over the Canadian. The principal cause of the Montreal merchants' Annexation Manifesto in 1849 was the economic disaster caused by London. And then in 1871, London sided with Washington against Ottawa and we lost part of the Atlantic fisheries. Our history from that point on has been consistent. Given a choice between the United States and Canada, Britain chooses the United States. "English hav[e] little or no interest in Canada," was how John A. Macdonald put it. At the turn of the century, the Governor General, Lord Minto, a not very bright soldier, broke the rules of responsible government by using his position to publicly agitate for Joseph Chamberlain's Imperial Preference system and then to agitate for more Canadian involvement in the Boer War. Britain was tight for soldiers. This was the sort of inappropriate behaviour that the U.S. ambassador took up after September 11. Paul Cellucci regularly spoke in public to berate Canadians for not being enthusiastic about U.S. policies in Iraq, as if he were a pro-consul. In private, many Canadian leaders were disturbed, but the government did nothing to bring him into line. In 1903, we lost most of the Pacific coast because on a tripartite commission the British voted against us and with the United States, admitting that it was a matter of British self-interest. The Canadian judges on the commission called the decision "a grotesque travesty of justice" and refused to sign. This important loss for Canada ran parallel to the British campaign for Canadian troops in South Africa. That campaign included the Canadian colonial elite, provoked by London and its vice-regal representative, berating anyone who was not loyal enough to the Queen and to the homeland. Thus, over the same short period Britain permanently undermined our position on the Pacific while accusing us of weak provincialism for not wanting to fully engage in their colonial war against the Boers.

The point of this litany is that the more than justifiable anger in Canada against Britain had taken us very close to the point of either a clean break or at least the removal of any British role in our foreign policy. Yet this would take another three decades to complete. Why? Because at precisely that moment of accumulating humiliations by the British ministries, a good part of the Canadian elite became increasingly fanatical supporters of imperial grandeur. Was it knighthoods for railway barons and haberdashers? Was it the London tailors? Was it those little moments of glory during their visits *home* for the season?

Whatever it was, the pattern was perfectly clear. With every slap in the face, every political and economic humiliation, every jerking about and wasteful sacrifice of our soldiers' lives during the First World War, the majority of our elite responded with increasing devotion to the monarchy and the superficial signs of British superiority. This is what they call a colonial mindset—a marriage of self-loathing, humiliation and adoration.

21

Two Colonial Tales

How Ottawa Became a Capital

If you were to ask most Canadians how Ottawa came to be our capital, they would reply that Queen Victoria chose it. The fact that she didn't seems to be irrelevant. That her role was no more than that of any constitutional monarch or Governor General, who follows the advice of their ministers, is brushed aside.

Why? Because part of our sense of ourselves is wrapped up in this falsehood. We seem to want to believe that neither we nor our ministers were up to the task. But if we were not up to such a choice, what could we be up to, then or now, without important people elsewhere holding our hand?

Why would we want to insist that such an important choice had to be made by a woman who had never been here, in fact, hadn't even thought of coming or had chosen never to come? Whenever it pleased her, she travelled great distances by ship or train to the Mediterranean. Her navy controlled the oceans. They had very large and comfortable battleships. Hundred-metre long, screw-propelled, double-bottomed, iron-hulled transatlantic passenger ships had been plying the Atlantic since the early 1840s. There was no impediment to her coming except interest. Or rather, lack of interest.

In any case, would two brilliant and tough statesmen such as Macdonald and Cartier really have put such a delicate political matter as the choice of our capital in the hands of a marginally interested monarch with no local experience or direct knowledge? After all, this is a particularly complicated place, where geography, religion, language and regional interests formed and still form a multi-layered puzzle. The placing of the capital would be central to how the country functioned. Would they really—would we really—have allowed the principles of responsible government, in place for less than a decade, to be undermined in this way? Would they really have allowed her to indulge her fantasy by choosing "a remote little city," as Ottawa's one hundred and fiftieth anniversary celebrations quaintly put it in 2007?

If we believe any of that, then what we are saying is that we wish to celebrate our own incompetence and the weakness of our leaders. We wish to make much of what can only be seen as a humiliating colonial failure. And if it didn't happen that way at all, then our determination to pretend that it did can only be interpreted as a succinct illustration of the colonial mentality.

What did happen was certainly complicated, like Canada. But it didn't involve Queen Victoria choosing Ottawa. By 1856, Macdonald, Cartier and the Governor General, Sir Edmund Head, had pretty well settled on Ottawa. They had very good reasons. It was the only choice safe from the dangerous U.S. border. It was on the geographic line between francophone and anglophone Canada. It was at an historic juncture on the great water highway to the heart of the continent. That liquid highway had been central to the fur trade and was now central to the lumber industry. And until the Canadian Pacific Railway was built, which did not happen until three decades later, it would remain our original Trans-Canada Highway. Finally, with the Rideau Canal in place since 1832, Ottawa sat at the top of a trade and communications triangle. Militarily, economically and politically it was the right choice.

There was, of course, a political problem of regional rivalries. That had to be dealt with. But in Canada there are always such rivalries. And on every subject. Nothing has changed. Macdonald and Cartier needed to keep their heads down until the choice could be sufficiently sold to the public. And so the Governor General took the lead in organizing a rigged competition of five cities. This could not have been done without the full involvement and support of the government.

From these five, the Queen was to choose. Except that in reality she was given no choice. Kingston, Protestant and Orange Order to its heels, wasn't really in the running. LaFontaine and Baldwin had already rejected it in 1841 and forced the Governor General to move the capital to Montreal in 1844. And that was even before responsible government. Montreal, the natural capital, had disqualified itself with the 1849 riots. Again, LaFontaine and Baldwin had advised Lord Elgin to move the capital, this time to Toronto. He had wanted to stay, but the government advised and had to be obeyed. Toronto and Quebec City effectively eliminated each other: too Protestant, anglophone and geographically extraneous on the one hand; too Catholic, francophone and geographically extraneous on the other.

Ottawa was the only choice. The competition documents were organized to make this clear. And the Governor General wrote a confidential memorandum to make this perfectly clear: "Ottawa is the only place which will be accepted by the majority of Upper Canada and Lower Canada as a fair compromise." He went on to explain that it was the only choice because it was not really in either Upper or Lower Canada, but on the river between the two; that its population already represented the Canadian complexity; that being to the north got the capital off the border and would encourage more northerly development.

From a constitutional point of view, he was conveying the advice of his ministers, which he had accepted and in fact agreed with. He went to London on one of those fast, safe ships—which carried thousands of important people, who wished to come to Canada, back and forth across the Atlantic—in order to be on the spot at the right moment to make sure the monarch understood this was *advice from her ministers*, not a request for a choice. To be more precise, the Governor General presented his position—which was that of his ministers—to the Colonial Office. They accepted the Canadian recommendation and put it to the British cabinet. The cabinet accepted the Canadian government/Governor General/Colonial Office recommendation and sent it to the Queen on October 16, 1857, indicating to her "the decision of which has been submitted to Your Majesty." She received that decision, not an invitation to choose. By the end of the month she had formally accepted the position of the Canadian cabinet. After waiting for a delicate election in Canada to pass, the choice of Ottawa was announced.

A few years later, in 1860, the editor of *The Times* (London)—the closest thing there was then to an official voice of the British elite structure—wrote an editorial confirming that the Queen's choice was the one she "has been advised to take." *Advised* in responsible government parlance means *instructed*.

Interestingly enough, even with all of this preparation, it was the Canadian Parliament that then rejected Ottawa and so defeated Macdonald's government. After some fast manoeuvring, Cartier formed a new government and used the next few months for some complex and very local politicking. He managed to neutralize key regional interests by offering them immediate benefit. When he had the parliamentary votes in place, he re-presented the motion to Parliament. Ottawa was chosen—and chosen through the classic supremacy of the elected assembly.

The whole process certainly put Parliament to the test. It was an important part of Members learning how to rethink their loyalties. They had been used to voting and working mainly on behalf of their constituencies and their cities or regions. All new political structures pass through a difficult interim phase in which everyone must reorganize their sense of loyalty. They must recut the pie so as to transfer some of their sense of belonging. In the United States, that process included a murderous civil war. In France, it involved a series of civil wars.

Most of what happened around the choice of Ottawa was already in the public domain at the time. Witness *The Times* (London) editorial. The rest came out relatively fast. More recently, every detail has been worked through by David Knight, today's leading expert on the subject. And he brought it all together in a clear and fascinating book, *Choosing Canada's Capital*. It is about "conflict resolution in a parliamentary system." It isn't about distant, willful queens.

Knight's analysis was published in 1991. Yet fifteen years later—surely long enough for someone in the National Capital Commission to have digested the implications of the book—this public body entrusted with the physical and mythological well-being of official Ottawa, used the one hundred and fiftieth anniversary of its choosing to launch a major celebration built around the distant and willful queen. Why would they, with the compliance of the city of Ottawa, devote themselves to selling a falsehood? All their documentation begins with such phrases as "the Queen had chosen a remote little city." Buried somewhere in each text there are phrases that suggest the truth lies elsewhere. But their effort is concentrated on celebrating once again the humiliating falsehood.

Why? On the most obvious level, it's because they think a distant, willful queen is better for tourism than the story of democracy. Why put forward the story of Canada when you can focus on the Empire and its Queen—something important, *world-class* and foreign? Why explain the national capital when you can grovel in colonial gratitude? Besides, they are not in the business of explaining Canada. They're in the business of tourism dollars. It seems never to have occurred to them that how a people understands its history has an effect on how their country can act. The immediate point is obvious. To misuse your institutional obligation by spending millions of public dollars to knit and then wrap a false, kitschy and highly colonial myth around the neck of a serious country is a betrayal of your responsibilities. More important, it is a betrayal of the reality of Canada and its citizens.

In *The Unfinished Canadian*, Andrew Cohen asked straightforward questions about Ottawa, the sort of practical questions that actually reveal something fundamental about the state of mind of our elites. The city's site is not only historic but remarkably beautiful. How then did the architecture and planning of the non-official part of the city come to suffer "the desecration" of a generation? How in the ceremonial core did properties come to be sold for inappropriate use—inappropriate symbolically, politically and architecturally? Two ugly embassies of dictatorships and one ugly condo, apparently a favourite of lobbyists, now stand side by side on Sussex Drive with Rideau Hall, 24 Sussex, the National Gallery, Foreign Affairs and the embassies of our closest democratic allies. The condo overlooks the War Memorial, a sacred site in the capital. One of the dictatorships is a particularly fine model of repression when it comes to free speech and women's rights. Over the years I have continually asked myself, How did this happen? Who decided? What were the full financial arrangements in all three cases?

Why, it seems to me, mention these embarrassing little events? They matter because they highlight the sort of atmosphere that is acceptable around the belief that Ottawa isn't a real capital. It's just a place willfully chosen by someone who knew no better. Of course, the country is run out of there. But that doesn't make it a capital in the full sense.

If you believe that its choice was tawdry and willful, the rules surrounding its existence can be just as tawdry and willful. In this context, having power over the meaning and appearance of the city can be reduced to a conviction of local entitlement, local contracts and tourism. And tourism here is focused not on introducing people to their capital as a symbol of their country, but on tourism as a source of income.

Do I exaggerate? Why is Ottawa still limping slowly, after decades of painful debate, toward some sort of bilingualism? Why has it never embraced fully, joyfully and with respect for its obligations as national capital this central element of Canada, its Constitution and Charter of Rights?

Language policy has been treated at the municipal level as if it were a mere municipal matter. Nothing more. A matter of local choice and local budgets. A matter for local merchants to consider. The Canadian government has had to insert bilingualism as best it could into the national capital, as if it were a barely tolerated interloper and not the explanation for the city's size and wealth and purpose.

Yet Ottawa is the capital of a country with two official languages. It is the place chosen by the people's representatives to be the centre of our government, but also to become a place that illustrates the national character in its full complexity.

Why does anyone imagine there are a million citizens in Ottawa paying taxes? What are all those people doing there? What is the principal activity of the city? Responsibility comes with such an activity. And everyone has had one hundred and fifty years to get used to this simple reality: Ottawa is the capital of the people of Canada. This represents an opportunity and a responsibility. Above all, it is a privilege. And that means showing respect for the people of Canada. Not simply those who live there, although a good percentage of them are francophone. That privilege means showing respect for the whole country and its two national languages.

In other words, the link between the false colonial myth of how Ottawa became our capital and the reality of how it functions today is direct and important. In colonies or places with an elite bound by their colonial mindset, leadership is all about power without authority.

How Ottawa came to be chosen is the classic colonial myth. The message in this false story is that Parliament, government and therefore Ottawa are merely about power, to do with what they can. But authority is mysteriously elusive. No one quite knows where it is, except that it isn't here. That unhappy differentiation, between power as self-interest and authority as an elusive quality, is central to the elite's constant confusion over whether it exists to think for itself, to lead, to decide about owner-ship. In the tiny, delusional story over the choice of Ottawa lies a kernel of the almost-lunatic idea that real authority must be floating elsewhere, not anywhere in particular, but here or there depending on the circum-stances and, above all, in the hands of people who know little of this place and don't have its interests first in their hearts, if it is there at all.

How the Dominion Ceased to Be

At the core of the colonial mindset is its self-destructive logic. It is unconscious nihilism. Insecurity often drives an elite to believe itself incapable of taking the lead in its country's own affairs. For reassurance it seeks out and clings to some outside force, thus hoping for special consideration. Consideration for what purpose? To provide a direction and, as if by association, a certain importance. Typically this is called a *special relationship* by the insecure party. As for the outside force, it rarely bothers to call such a relationship anything at all, except when poked by the weaker party seeking more reassurance.

And when the much-hoped-for special consideration does not materialize, the insecure party is confirmed in its fears. The false hope for security becomes the mechanism for turning these inner fears into a reality.

The story of Canada as the *Dominion of Canada* is a perfect illustra-tion of this phenomenon.

During the 1866–67 negotiations in London, the soon-to-be Fathers of Confederation proposed that the new country be called the Kingdom of Canada. The subsequent legions of John A. Macdonald worshippers continue to present this as his personal initiative. In reality, the delegation functioned in a way that made such initiatives impossible. As for the insecure colonial-minded, they revelled then and continue to revel in the British refusal of this name as *premature and pretentious*. They are, as they were, pleased to have been put down.

What actually happened was far more interesting. First, the Fathers of Confederation in London were constantly in session. They discussed everything. This was an open, smart and egalitarian-minded group. Macdonald may have been chair and an expert at consensus, but that was how they worked—by consensus. It was as a group that they decided to put the name Kingdom of Canada into one of their written constitutional drafts.

Second, the British refusal was based principally on their fear of the reaction from Washington.

The United States didn't want a large, independent country on its northern border. That was what the name Kingdom suggested Canada would be. They rushed to get through their purchase of the Alaska panhandle just as the new country was being declared. Whatever Canada hoped to be, Washington wanted to hem it in and make it as weak as possible. Their leaders were very open about this desire in multiple speeches, documents and messages.

As always, London sided with the ambitions of Washington over those of Ottawa. These sorts of relationships are never *special*. They are about interests, which is something those with a colonial mindset just cannot accept. They want, they need love. No matter how many times they are rejected, they will bring it all back to love.

Third, the officials in Westminster didn't like the idea of Canada sounding like an equal of Britain. But that tells you more about them than it does about the Fathers of Confederation or Canada. That reminds you of why the Thirteen Colonies had broken off relations ninety years earlier. It also tells you why the Fathers of Confederation—who included Macdonald—constantly spoke in their private letters, then and later, about how little they trusted the British leadership, whether political or administrative.

Fourth, this was a group of men that did not suffer from insecurity and didn't take imperial stroking all that seriously. They were all clear in their own minds that they were there to create a large, powerful new country. Read their speeches and letters. They had no trouble expressing their loyalty to Britain. But that loyalty was not about obedience or colonial subservience. It had nothing to do with how they would run Canada.

Fifth, Canadians today find this idea of becoming a kingdom very peculiar. But put aside the question of the monarchy. The point about a kingdom was that it was independent and had authority. That's what the Canadians wanted. That is why the United States was upset. The existence of Canada as a nation-state was the first serious limitation to Washington's idea of American exceptionalism. Part of that exceptionalism was what would come to be called in the 1840s their *manifest destiny*. This was, as the inventor of the phrase, John L. O'Sullivan, put it, "[T]he right of our manifest destiny to spread and to possess the whole of the continent which Providence has given us...."

Sixth, this was the first time that a colony of any of the European empires had managed to extricate itself from the grip of the empire through negotiations, not war. Confederation was thus a cutting-edge initiative. Down this same path, cleared and laid out by Canada, more than a hundred colonies would follow over the next century. This new non-violent approach was and remains a remarkable tribute to the intelligence and the sophistication of the Fathers of Confederation. It was the first international illustration of the tough Canadian *middle way*, with its Aboriginal origins.

There is, however, an awkward side to negotiating your independence. It means that the language of national authority lags behind the reality. With revolutions, language precedes the reality. For example, the reality of U.S. society did not even begin to catch up with the brilliant language of the American Revolution, with its evocations of liberty and of equality among citizens, until after the Civil War. Even then, not a great deal could happen until the 1960s and the assault on segregation. The reaction of pleased astonishment to Barak Obama's race speech in March 2008 was a reminder that the United States had still not dealt with the disconnect between its original words of promise and the reality of its existence.

As for the Canadians, they found themselves blocked over their choice of names by the lag of language. They reacted by putting forward a more subtle proposal—the Dominion of Canada. The word has colonial origins—the Dominion of Virginia under Charles II, for example. But this suggestion, initiated by Leonard Tilley of New Brunswick, was what we would now call a typically Canadian manoeuvre. The British could be mollified by being allowed to understand the word as they wished. They would see it as part of their imperial history. The Canadians had a quite different understanding. And once Confederation was a fait accompli, they would be in a position to assert that understanding as they wished.

In the minds of the Canadian delegation, the word carried no colonial implications. Tilley had taken it from Psalm 72 and from Zachariah 9:10. In both, the word *dominion* was used to express power. Power "from sea to sea, and from the river unto the ends of the earth." The type of the country—the meaning of dominion—was to be tied to the country's motto, ensuring that its non-colonial sense would be clear. To make it perfectly clear you had only to read the official French translation: La Puissance du Canada.

The colonial-minded at home—which included francophone translators who didn't have the courage of their predecessors—complained that this was a political translation—"a domesticating translation"—forced through by George-Étienne Cartier. By a "domesticating translation" is meant a translation that has a particular local meaning, as opposed to one that conforms to the imperial use of language. The colonial-minded insisted that this was a false translation because the word *puissance* doesn't appear in Psalm 72; that the real meaning was the British colonial interpretation; that therefore there was no translation possible. The English word should therefore be used in both languages. Besides, as a still indignant and insecure contemporary translator puts it, with an attempt at sarcasm—"How puissant was the Dominion of Canada during the days, the months and the years following Confederation. The Dominion of Canada, was it a military, economic or political puissance."

First, this sort of argument is like the misrepresentation of Macdonald's power by his worshippers. If the translation was Puissance, that was the intent of the Fathers of Confederation. This was the word used in the official French version of the Constitution they put together. Macdonald read French without any difficulty. His favourite reading was the French novels passed to him by Cartier. Macdonald's new wife was fully bilingual. Neither Cartier nor Macdonald made decisions on their own. What's more, they were constantly talking to each other. In Ottawa, in the East Block of the Parliament Buildings, their offices can still be seen, virtually next to each other.

Second, none of the people who insisted that Puissance was the wrong translation, in fact a translation that didn't exist in the Bible, seemed to have bothered to read Zachariah 9:10:

–And his *dominion* shall be from sea even to sea, and from the river even to the ends of the earth.

–Et *potestas* eius a mari usque ad mare et a fluminibus usque ad fines terrae.

–Et sa *puissance* s'étendra depuis une mer jusqu'à l'autre mer, et depuis le fleuve jusqu'aux extérmités du monde.

Third, of course, in addition to being accurate it was also a political translation. Happily it was indeed a "domesticating translation." It was meant to be. All of the Fathers of Confederation would have been aware, understood and approved. None of them spoke up in disapproval, and some certainly did on other subjects. The role of language and therefore of translation is to find the true meaning for the place of use. Why on earth would Canada have wanted a colonial interpretation imposed by an empire from which we had just negotiated a polite distancing? The whole history of language in Canada has been about developing meaning that makes sense here. That is the story of the translations of Peace, Welfare and Good Government.

And to the extent that Cartier took the lead on developing this consensus, it should be added that he was particularly worldly, a writer, sophisticated, close to the religious Order of St. Sulpiciens, who would have been available for all advice on the translation of biblical texts, and even if they didn't like each other, he was the brother-in-law of one of the most influential rising clerics. Cartier knew exactly what he was doing.

Finally, was Canada worth calling a Puissance with Dominion over its lands? Its population was about the same as the Thirteen Colonies' when they declared their independence. And as we know, their population size didn't stop them making grand statements about themselves. As for Canada, it was already geographically large, not small, by international standards. It was already the third commercial maritime power in the world, and would eventually rise to be the first, before most of our shipping was sold off after the Second World War.

And within four years of Confederation, Cartier had led Canada into its reality as a continental power. He negotiated the entry of both Manitoba and British Columbia. Although Washington managed to buy the Alaska Panhandle from the Russians just as Confederation was being declared, Cartier pushed hard and was able to buy the Hudson's Bay Company lands, representing perhaps 80 percent of modern Canada. He created the concept of the transcontinental railway and put through the CPR Bill, which would result a mere decade later in the largest railway in the world. And with his Militia Act he created the Canadian Army, leading to the rapid departure of British troops.

When the Fathers of Confederation translated Dominion as Puissance, they meant it. They were ambitious, self-confident men. If you want to understand the meaning of Dominion, read the French. Canada was born as La Puissance.

As for Psalm 72, it is about a great deal more than power from sea to sea. It is, as the biblical scholar Walter Deller puts it: "one of the great visional psalms about the power of the ruler and his obligation to create a more equitable society, which means a particular obligation to the poor." Or as Father Yves Abran puts it, this psalm is about rulers devoting their power to the service of the poor. Or as Michael Peers, former primate of the Anglican Church points out: "Dominion has the same roots in Greek as The Lord. It means *what is expected of lordship*—authority on the one hand and responsibility for the welfare of the ruled on the other." Throughout the psalm there is an interwoven link between helping the poor and successful agriculture. "It is the just ruler's role to make nature fertile for the people."

Leonard Tilley was an evangelical low-church Anglican. He was focused on biblical texts and on the idea that the application of your social conscience was a demonstration of your faith. Tilley's intent by introducing Psalm 72 into the heart of Confederation would have been no mystery to these men. They all knew their Bibles. Among the Protestants they were mainly Presbyterians and Methodists, for whom Scripture was a matter of daily life. Many were fervent believers. The Catholics were not Bible readers, but the Psalms were a different matter. They were essential to the church services that made up a central part of their lives. Psalm 72 speaks for itself. It is all about the poor having the right to fair judgment, the saving of the children of the needy, and if to accomplish this, the oppressor must be broken into pieces, so be it. He who has dominion "shall deliver the needy when he crieth; the poor also, and him that hath no helper. He shall spare the poor and needy, and shall have the soul of the needy ... And in his days shall the righteous flourish; and abundance of peace so long as the moon endureth." Deller wonders if the heavy emphasis on Psalm 72 was not an ironic comment by the Canadians on the British class system, of which they disapproved. For many of them, it must have been an evocation of their dream that Canada should be a more egalitarian, a more just place, a harking back to the principles of Howe, LaFontaine and Baldwin.

The entire psalm is about the responsibility of those with dominion to look after the poor, protect peace and ensure prosperity. To pretend that the Fathers of Confederation didn't notice or didn't understand the sense of the psalm around which they built the core idea of Canada is to refuse to deal with them as intelligent, sophisticated men caught up in a great creative project. I can't think of a more conscious group in our four centuries of history.

How then did they come to allow the *Welfare* of Peace, Welfare and Good Government to be superseded by *Order* in a late draft of the British North America Act? Perhaps the answer lies in their ostentatious use of Psalm 72, one of the most moving and forthright biblical statements of egalitarianism, inclusion and justice. This is the psalm of welfare.

They all realized that with the introduction of *Order* they were in effect getting financial responsibility for Canadian security. With the cost came the power. This was a real compensation for not becoming so visibly independent as a kingdom.

Perhaps just as important was the other aspect of Psalm 72. To have Dominion from sea to sea—which in French also becomes to reign from sea to sea—meant to have responsibility from sea to sea: responsibility as rulers to ensure the welfare of the people. That is the meaning of the psalm. So while they lost the mention of welfare in the great old invocation of Peace, Welfare and Good Government, this phrase was now buried deep in the Constitution in a new way. They had lost the word, but gained a far broader invocation of that welfare in the name of the country and in its new motto.

What then went wrong? How did *Dominion* decline into a meaning that led it to be denigrated as a colonial term so that it finally had to be dropped? And how did our motto become no more than a simple celebration of political power over nature from sea to sea?

The most obvious answer is that those leaders most devoted to the idea of welfare disappeared in the first few years. D'Arcy McGee was assassinated in 1868. Cartier was dead in 1873. Joseph Howe came into the federal cabinet too old and too late in his career. He did a good job for a few years, then went back to Nova Scotia and died. Charles Tupper was sent off to do international work in London. And although Tilley stayed, he was marginalized as minister of customs until 1873.

Meanwhile the return of the colonial elites came as if from nowhere. Around the world empire worship was rising, whether in the British Empire, the French, the German or the Italian. The United States was busy inventing a new sort of empire. In Canada, our insecure elites leapt onto this wave. They saw the Dominion in the light of Britain. Something called the Canada First Movement was created, but they understood Canada First to mean Britain First. That is, Canada was to be Anglo-Saxon and English-speaking and Protestant. On the French-Canadian side, nationalism was increasingly about a retrograde church.

Honoré Mercier, the nationalist premier and hero of provincial rights, made his way on the rise of the Ultramontane movement—profoundly anti-democratic, anti–public education and anti-egalitarian.

With such an atmosphere on all sides, the original ideas of Psalm 72 and clear independence were obscured. Puissance remained in the Constitution but was dropped in all public use. And the British, in their increasing imperial glory, took to describing the independent former British colonies as the Dominions, as if to minimize any particularity of Canada and to make light of their independence.

And so the colonial mindset won control over the interpretation of what a dominion was. It was no longer about welfare and power and independence. It was about the British Empire. With this victory of their inferiority complex, the Canadian colonial elite condemned the term to eventual disappearance. Their victory was an act of nihilism.

With the turn of the century, Westminster began trying to interfere in the lives of the Dominions because they wanted troops for their failing effort in South Africa. Then they tried—unsuccessfully—to bolster their failing international economic position with an Empire Trade Policy and an Empire Foreign Policy. Then they pushed countries such as Canada on the question of troops for the First World War. With each attempt at interference, the confident part of the Canadian elite became, like the citizenry, more confident.

After the Statute of Westminster in 1931, Ottawa stopped using the word *Dominion*. In 1935, it was dropped from all treaties. In the same year the British accepted that the game had been altered definitively and so changed the name of the cabinet position in charge of *Dominion Affairs* to one dealing with *Commonwealth Relations*. In 1947, with the Letters Patent—in which the powers of the Canadian head of state were fully and formally transferred from the monarch to the Governor General—the term *Dominion* was dropped. And in 1951, Prime Minister Louis St. Laurent rose to tell Parliament that *Dominion* would be dropped from all new official documents and in general phased out. It was over.

If you read the arguments made in the House of Commons in 1951 by the Conservative Opposition in reply to St. Laurent, what is fascinating is that they don't know what to say. Even Davie Fulton, one of the most brilliant parliamentarians of his generation, is reduced to mouthing vague, romantic notions, while St. Laurent is cool and precise. Fulton doesn't know what to say because the term had been slowly devalued by those who did not have the self-confidence to embrace the full Confederation process.

Dominion began as a fine description of a national project for an independent country, as did *Puissance*. It reflected the now two-hundred-and-fifty-year-old idea of welfare. But in their desperate need for reassurance, for special consideration, for a special relationship, the colonial elite destroyed the word. It was, as I said earlier, a nihilist act.

22

The Roots of Failure

And yet this entire pattern I am describing does seem improbable. The insecurity, the self-loathing, the incapacity to act, the fear of owning, the resurgent colonialism. What is all of this doing in the oldest continuous democratic federation in the world, a G8 country, rich, peaceful, comfortable? How could its elite slip so effortlessly back into old colonial habits? Perhaps the examples I have been giving are random, not representative.

If that were so, certain things would not happen. There have been two break points over the last few years that simply would not have been possible in a normally led society.

In December 2005, at a key moment in a federal election, the Royal Canadian Mounted Police told the New Democratic Party that the minister of finance was under investigation for the possibility of leaks around his decision on income trusts. If a minister of finance were to leak, or somehow be related to a leak of, information on a major money reform, that minister would be guilty of a criminal act worth hundreds of millions of dollars. Perhaps more. The simple hint by the national police force that the senior financial authority of the land might be engaged in dishonest activity was enough to swing the election from a probable Liberal minority to a Conservative minority.

In other words, the RCMP interfered in the national democratic process at a strategic moment. Every citizen has the right to ask whether or not they intended through this interference to throw the election. Whether the government thrown out deserved its fate is beside the point.

Why the RCMP did what they did is a secondary question. Who in particular caused this to happen is of even less importance. No individual in the RCMP would have caused such an intervention to happen if the general atmosphere in the Canadian elite structure were not open to such interference. Was it a miscalculation for the RCMP? Yes. But did it happen? Yes. And, whatever the intent, was an election thrown by the security forces? Yes.

This is the sort of thing that happens in unstable states where undemocratic forces, domestic or foreign, feel free to interfere. You expect this in ex-colonies where the elites see themselves as not fully responsible. Or in deeply corrupt or militarily unstable countries. More specifically, this was one of several reminders that there have not been any serious attempts at control over the RCMP by civil authorities since the mid-1980s. Some attempts are now being made, and we will have to judge carefully whether these are about reform or about further politicization. But that is only one part of the problem. I can't think of a more basic test of elites and their structures—whether political, legal, journalistic or security—than their reaction to the throwing of an election by a police force.

The election was indeed thrown and virtually no voice was raised in protest. It was difficult for any politician to react in the middle of an election campaign. And yet it was essential that they do so, whatever their party. The opposition justice critic. Someone from the NDP, the party that had received this inappropriate message. The leaders of all parties. The Speakers. The clerk of the Privy Council. The deputy minister of justice. Anyone. All of them. There was silence. Only one journalist—James Travers of the *Toronto Star*—immediately saw the issue as a matter of enormous consequence for the country and its democracy. And he has repeatedly come back to it. "Canada is too cold, rich and stable to be easily mistaken for a banana republic." And yet the police interfered in the most important event of national politics and got away with it, leaving the air "heavy with the spoiled odours of banana republics." *The Globe and Mail*'s Jeffrey Simpson came back to it several times, at first almost more in confusion at this "injection of the police into an election campaign." By 2007, he had concluded that "an election turned on that letter, more than on any other event during the campaign." Apart from that, there were a few press comments here and there, but little more. Such calm in the face of the sort of police interference in the democratic process that would have caused a widespread scandal in most countries is in and of itself an eloquent statement of elite failure.

The second break point was the revelation in 2003 that a former prime minister, Brian Mulroney, had taken $300,000 in cash from businessman and lobbyist Karlheinz Schreiber. Mulroney neither sued nor denied the story. The story matters not because Schreiber is a dubious figure, nor because Brian Mulroney was a remarkable or incompetent prime minister. It matters because a recent ex–prime minister took a large cash payment from anyone for anything. Mulroney later insisted the correct amount was $225,000.

Yet for several years after the initial revelation, the Canadian elite structure sat silent. The police. The civil service. The government. Parliament. Finally, the work of the Canadian Broadcasting Corporation (CBC) and *The Globe and Mail* forced the story out. Again, the details were those of a banana republic. There have been similar incidents in other Western democracies, but very few in which the political leader was proved to have taken cash. Not even Jacques Chirac. Not even Silvio Berlusconi. Yet the general mood of our elite was that perhaps no more should be said or done. Or as little as possible.

All Canadians were understandably embarrassed for their country. Part of the press felt that these revelations undermined the good work they considered Mulroney had done as prime minister. None of them pointed out that the man had taken cash as if it were normal, natural or habitual in a situation that most public figures would have suspected might involve a sting operation. None that I could find pointed out that such a situation produced a far broader public obligation for the state to review any government decisions in which Mulroney was involved that benefited a single corporation or a small group of corporations. This has nothing to do with specific suspicions or accusations. In such circumstances, it would be a straightforward matter of due diligence. Given what has been revealed so far, the citizenry have the right to know what level of due diligence was applied to the administration of the public good in contract-related or corporate-status situations during that period.

On the question of taking large cash payments, the only attempt Mulroney made at an explanation of his actions when he was first questioned by a parliamentary committee was that he had hesitated at first on being offered it in an envelope in a hotel room. Schreiber then said, or so Mulroney explained, "I'm an international businessman and I only deal in cash." The former prime minister, apparently convinced by this argument, took the envelope. That the man responsible for leading Canada in some of its most important international business negotiations could offer such an explanation throws the seriousness of his leadership role into question. Was he really suggesting that he believed that that is the way international business is done?

The important point is not how this saga will finally end. What matters is neither our sympathy for nor our dislike of the man. There are those who revel in the suffering of any powerful figure brought low. Most people feel a certain sympathy for such a leader dragged down in full public view. Those are the contradictions of Shakespearean drama. But much more important are the central principles of public trust regarding public administration.

None of us want to think of these two incidents—the RCMP throwing a federal election and a prime minister, two months after leaving office, taking cash payments in an envelope in a hotel room from someone with whom he had had a long relationship—as representative of something fundamental about our country. We would prefer these to be one-off oddities. But first, these are events that strike at the core of our state. And second, in their aftermath they have been surrounded by widespread elite failure over a prolonged period of time. At the very least they are symptomatic of our elites' acceptance of an unacceptable level of behaviour. How else are we to interpret our elites' attempt to get away with acting as if nothing had happened, until that was no longer possible, and then attempting to minimize their understanding, and therefore the public's, of these events. This is the opposite of a country governed by constitutional convention and the rule of law.

Their reactions have been typical of an elite that sees itself as cut off from the citizenry, as if it has entitlements that free it from national responsibility, as if those entitlements are drawn from some source of legitimacy that lies elsewhere. This is a classic characteristic of the colonial mindset.

When historians explain the Family Compact or the Château Clique, the central concept is one of entitlement based on off-shore legitimacy. That original Compact believed, and its contemporary manifestation believes, itself entitled to run matters as best suits its narrow interests.

The selling-off of public companies by their managers for their own short-term profit and for that of short-term shareholders has nothing to do with the marketplace or with capitalism. After all, capitalism rates short-term profit well below the creation of wealth. Such actions have to do with a managerial sense of entitlement. In this, marketplace managers resemble many groups of professionals and their professional organizations. They use their administration of themselves through their professional bodies as a way to limit membership in their group. They do this in a way designed to keep their incomes up. And all of that has to do with a sense of entitlement. That they leave immigrant engineers driving taxis is not their affair. That the public is underserved in sickness and that the lives of excluded professionals are wasted are not their affairs. Their entitlement gives them ownership of a space.

You can see this in their attitudes toward the financing of the public space. We have had tough controls on private donations to political parties for several years now. Yet politicians and government continue to act as if they are beholden to the Compacts. Tom Kent calls it "the old friendship club." And in many ways it is nothing more than that—the old entitled groups continuing to function as they have for two centuries.

But this has been accentuated by the attempt of government over the last quarter-century to remodel itself in the image of the private-sector compacts. It isn't simply the superficial silliness of using private-sector efficiency models that, in order to work, would require competition and profit, neither of which are possible. Or giving everyone private-sector titles, from CEOs to citizens being called clients. The citizenry own the government. How can they be its client? Or adopting its financial methods—for example, funding by *envelopes*—which were supposed to bring responsible administrative spending. Each department, and within it each directorate or section, is allocated an envelope of funding. This is clear. And it is clear they must account for it in detail. And in a large private corporation producing soup or cellphones this might make good sense. Unfortunately, the actual effect in government has been to reward narrow, defensive behaviour, with individuals or groups defending their envelope. The best way to do this is to thicken the walls of their silos. To keep everyone out of their little world. So the best way to defend your envelope is to work against broad policy initiatives. It isn't surprising, therefore, that no attempt at broader policy is rewarded. Inclusive thinking is a threat to envelope financing.

This sort of corporatization of government has happened in many countries. But in Canada there was a specific effect when the new managers and their corporate manager language were folded into the old Compacts. The result has been a strengthening of their sense of entitlement.

To use a single example, the Canadian Food Inspection Agency (CFIA) was constituted from other public agencies as a *cost recovery agency*. It is now supposed to charge Canadians for the food safety inspections it does. When mad cow disease decimated the Canadian beef industry, the CFIA upped the number of inspections and insisted that an inspector be on site for each slaughtering, with the cost of that presence falling to the slaughterhouse. This was the tipping point that drove many of the smaller, high-quality operations out of business. These costs were the last straw. But mad cow disease was a product of the large, industrialized, non-specialty operators in the beef industry. So the corporatist approach strengthened the role of those responsible for the problems and weakened the quality producers. In the process, they also undermined the sort of value-added approach to beef that mad cow demonstrated we needed.

No official seemed to think that this mattered. They aren't particularly interested in ownership or local ownership or ownership devoted to value added. They don't seem to be interested in Canadian owners doing well. Rather, they are in the process business, and they were recovering their costs. Beyond that, it was as if shoulders were being shrugged.

⁓

The one saving grace in this general atmosphere has been the growth of a fresh and almost-parallel corporate community dominated by immigrants and new Canadians. In many ways, they resemble the self-confident business leaders of the past who helped to build this country. They don't carry a lazy sense of entitlement. Their businesses tend to be family-owned and they like that. They want to own. They want to compete. They believe in building wealth. They are the real inheritors of those earlier periods of wealth creating Canadian business leadership.

Leonard Tilley, the New Brunswick Father of Confederation who brought forward the idea of Canada as a dominion, meaning as a place of power, went on to invent the National Policy. It was he as minister of finance under Macdonald who developed the economic strategy that would create our industrial power. It is that power that has been slowly taken apart over the last two decades in favour of a return to a dependence on raw materials. And these are increasingly exported unrefined, as well as increasingly coming from sectors owned abroad.

Tilley argued in the 1870s that Canada was being used as a "slaughter-market by U.S. interests." In 1878, he launched his new policy—the National Policy—by inventing a quintessential Canadian argument: "The time has arrived when we are to decide whether we will be simply hewers of wood and drawers of water … or will rise to the position, which I believe Providence has destined us to occupy."

What we have seen elsewhere in our society is a growing celebration of the manager—the one who is entitled but not responsible. If you look at our universities, you see that the first line of investment and of strategy is the business school. Why? First, because this is a way to draw the corporations onto the campus. Second, because there is a belief that managerial skills are the first need of a modern society.

In general, this is untrue. It is particularly untrue for countries with smaller populations. Yes, we need a certain amount of managers. But above all we need owners, builders, risk takers. If you take a broader look, we need people who want to function outside of safe insider situations, people who put imagination ahead of management. Even the best management school can't do that. In whatever way they attempt to dress up their offerings, the underlying assumptions are that people become either employees or they become corporate service agents, such as consultants and lawyers. This is how a society of entitled groups likes to function.

In Canada, we have financial and other enforcement agencies so weak as to be an embarrassment at the international level. We have bureaucratized the structures of every profession, the theory being that we won't need to enforce anything if the industries and professions manage themselves. In this way, we have discouraged real leaders by blunting their place on entrepreneurial boards. These places instead fall into the hands of *independent* board members who are not independent by any real meaning of the word. They are more or less chosen by three or four consulting firms who are needed to provide *independent* advice on board membership and managerial salaries. The consultants are an intimate part of this self-indulgent, self-management system. Their firms are an integrated part of a process that overpays managers and sets them up to profit from the selling-off and breaking-up of the companies they have theoretically been hired to run. Instead of rewarding them for creating wealth, this system encourages managers to become personally rich by destroying their companies. This is legalized fraud. And to facilitate this, the consultants work toward recommending independent board members who are retired corporate managers and retired deputy ministers—all people who are useless when it comes to wealth creation, risk and crisis leadership. These people have been central to our loss of entire industrial sectors. In other words, corporate modernization in Canada has been all about reinforcing the internal management of what might just as well be called the contemporary Family Compact, except that it is less about families and more about interest groups. We should have been exploding these systems, not reinforcing them.

And this is not merely a private-sector phenomenon. We have fallen into judging cabinet ministers as if they should be managers, not leaders. Our now enormous collection of NGOs has begun to organize itself—faster than in any other country I know—into a *sector*, a compact of its own, carefully bureaucratized. One of the great strengths of Canada has been its volunteers—totalling somewhere between a quarter and a half of the population. This is more than in any other country. Most of the individuals have always worked through clubs and other public-service organizations. But now the idea of volunteers as engaged citizens is being converted into that of an administrative non-profit group that partners with other groups. Increasingly, becoming an engaged citizen is to become almost suspect because you are an unpredictable quantity. That individual, to be taken seriously, must be properly structured into a non-profit organization that has an entitlement to the area in question.

This whole idea of separating out control, which in turn guarantees benefits to those whose entitlement gives them control, lies at the heart of the growing problems of federalism. Compacts don't like overlapping areas of control. Of course, the real strength of federalism is precisely that. The tension of overlapping forces means that those with incomplete power must constantly demonstrate to the citizens that they are responsible. In René Lévesque's 1968 "An Option for Québec," he unwittingly adopted a classic Family Compact argument. The overlapping division of powers "creates a difficult problem in the rational planning of economic activity in general.... [T]his situation, along with the opportunity given one government to thwart the actions of [the] other, may lead to conflict" and "result in impotence in attacking the economic problems of the country with any kind of resolution or efficiency. Any duplication of institutions should be avoided...." We are so used to the contemporary dogma of efficiency that at first this argument makes perfect sense. But if you look closer you realize that real *economic activity* is not centred on *rational planning*. Governments do not have *to thwart the actions of the other* or fall into *conflict*. In fact, as the European Union has demonstrated, duplication is a disinterested way to create competition in the public good. Duplication encourages governments to co-operate, helps to create wealth and undermines the *impotence* that inward-looking, compliant arrangements bring to problems involving the broader public good.

We can see the effects of control and entitlement in today's "old friendship club." For a start, if you have self-confident leaders, they will be able to deal with being uncertain in public. They will not be afraid to show that they are thinking about situations and opportunities. Instead we have the false macho certainty of people trying to avoid discussions and deeply uncertain of themselves. Their view is that people with power should never really explain anything in public. In France, Britain, Germany or the United States, key leaders often discuss and explain problems in full public view. In Canada, leaders in most areas limit themselves to administrative replies, or off-putting one-liners designed to prevent discussion. When prominent public figures in Canada attempt to discuss something, they are pounced upon as if they are naïve or traitors to their corporation. Look at the treatment reserved for Peter Munk, who has built Barrick Gold into one of the most powerful gold-mining companies in history. When he attempted to raise the question of Canadian corporations being hollowed out, he was insulted and more or less shouted down by the columnists and others who speak up on behalf of the managerial compacts. The same was done on the same subject to Dominic D'Allesandro, one of the most successful financial leaders of contemporary Canada, one of the few who has a broad strategy.

The colonial mindset always prefers public silence as an expression of loyalty to the compact. And so, the RCMP brings a self-serving form of unnecessary secrecy to every subject. There is no admiration for the discussion of ideas in Ottawa among civil servants. There hasn't been for a quarter-century. Not being heard to think outside of the office is an expression of managerial professionalism, of loyalty. They are expected to help their ministers become as uncommunicative as they are. In spite of the importance of understanding the economic road we have taken over the last three decades, no useful public debate on economics is permitted by the economics community. Speaking up, debating issues: Both of these are signs of disloyalty.

This real silence is enforced by the idea that power must appear to lie in as few hands as possible—a prime minister or premier with his advisers around him, a single spokesperson for an organization or corporation. In some ways, this is an imitation of what appears to be the U.S. presidential system or the larger-than-life U.S. corporate leaders. But it is a childlike imitation, and what it hides is the possibility of differing ideas within each compact.

It is this belief in silence and public agreement as expressions of professionalism and loyalty that explain our toothless approach toward media concentration. It is intelligent, arm's-length public information and debate that has driven Canada forward over the last one hundred and sixty years. The strength of that intelligent debate is one of the ways you can tell whether we're in a period of self-confident leadership or one of insecure people who have slipped back into the old colonial mindset.

Gradually, since the mid-1980s, the idea of provoking debate by ensuring there is arm's-length, high-quality information available has been ground down. It began with the federal government's elimination of the Economic Council of Canada. What followed was a period of monolithic assertions from the economics community and the decline of such departments of economics as that of the University of Toronto, which had once been at the forefront of international thought.

Tied to this decline of economic thought in Canada we have seen a commercialization of the sort of questions Statistics Canada can ask. Its principal role is no longer to provide information to citizens. It is to support fee-paying corporations and organizations. The result is that a whole range of questions an independent country ought to pose about its existence are simply not asked. To take a single important example, the statistics relating to the shape of our economy and of our trade do not tell us how we are doing by sector. Or rather, the sectors have been redefined in such a way as to obscure understanding. It is very difficult, for example, to understand the full role of commodities. Yet, if we are becoming increasingly reliant on natural resources, then that would suggest our trade policy has failed as a motor of economic diversification. In which case, statistics should be organized in a manner that allows the country to judge the situation. What's more, the analysis of the service sector makes it very difficult to tell whether we are doing well at high-end communications services or at waiting on tables.

If I want to think about what our trade really looks like and whether we are doing well, I have to seek out often lesser-known, independent intellectuals. It should be added that most mainstream economic journals closed their pages to such non-conforming thinkers in the mid-1980s because they were non-conforming, that is, disloyal to the position taken by the economists' corporation.

Over the last two decades, government has been carefully removing funds from a broad range of areas where public organizations encourage independent thought, or rather thought, simply thought. In its place they reward structures of power or commerce. This is one of the outcomes of government moving to matching grant systems for much of the non-profit sector and for universities. And this is the intent of restructuring as many public institutions as possible on private-sector models, cost-recovery models or real-cost accounting models. So we have been replacing thought with low-level utilitarianism. This is not what has been happening in other Western democracies. They have tended to go in the opposite direction because enough people recognize the complexity of our times and the need to think deeply about what may be happening. Canada, by closing down many of the mechanisms of independent thought, regresses into the mental situation of a colony. To use a phrase of the writer and columnist Alain Dubuc, this is a refusal of intelligence—"un refus d'intelligence." And again, it is characteristic of a Compact system.

Recently, the position of National Science Advisor was abolished, the Canadian Nuclear Safety Commission was devalued, the independence of the Chief Electoral Officer of Canada was attacked, oil sands producers were included in a government delegation dealing with international environmental negotiations, and the maintenance of journalistic independence from their corporate owners was more or less transferred from the CRTC to the Canadian Broadcast Standards Council, an organization that is controlled by the corporate owners.

Perhaps the simplest illustration of our colonial roots at work through an elite convinced of its entitlement has been the treatment of our cities. Through the worst years of cities in the United States, most of ours managed to avoid gutting their downtown core and thus kept life at the centre. The reward for this success, which largely came out of citizen activism, was that the federal and provincial governments turned on them in the 1980s and began dumping the responsibility for programs on the cities, along with the costs, although the municipalities had little fundraising capacity.

At a technical level, this imbalance of power is usually blamed on a dysfunctional constitution that makes the cities powerless tributaries of the provinces. Certainly, those powers need to be redistributed. But the core of the problem has been the willingness of political parties and property developers to combine their interests, as if the cities were not real places. Toronto has suffered most. In urban affairs columnist Christopher Humes's words, it is "a city of vast private wealth, and civic impoverishment." While London is announcing a new $33-billion rail link across the city and Madrid is building "tens of kilometres of subway," Toronto is cobbling together a few bus lines and can't even build a rail link to the biggest airport in Canada.

This single example illustrates how disconnected the elites are from urban realities. Yes, they can manage a few exciting museums and theatres. And that is good. But what does it mean when private money can be found to supplement public money for such projects, while public money can't be found for public transit or even garbage collection? I'm not suggesting that it is an either-or situation. That would be the old populist argument that public money spent on a theatre means leaving children without a hospital bed. The argument of a colonial elite is always about control and domination. It always insists that choices are limited, that the pie is of a fixed size. Less is power. More is anarchy. In a healthy society, more is a larger circle with more happening inside.

If you were to look for an example of the heart of the Toronto problem, I would point to the Ontario Municipal Board (OMB), a body of developer-friendly provincial appointees. Their power to overrule the city's planners has made it impossible to develop any physical strategy for the city. Instead, the largest metropolis in Canada is held hostage by the unpleasant relationship between developer influence and provincial political parties. The city's official plan may set building heights at fifteen storeys on a street. The developer simply comes in and says he wants sixty. The city knows the OMB will back him. So after an expensive fight, they settle for fifty-five and even then the OMB may insist on sixty. And, if the complainant is a citizen body of volunteers, the OMB may insist that they pay the costs, just to teach them a lesson for trying to interfere.

The OMB is a modern recreation of the Family Compact and the interest-based politics that Robert Baldwin led the battle against one hundred and sixty years ago. It is as if the Jarvises and the Ridouts still controlled the city and so could remain boldly indifferent to anything except their personal interests. At the same time, this sort of unhealthy urban situation makes it impossible for city dwellers to understand their dependence on the wealth of the land that lies to their north. Instead, there is the same old north versus city anger that the Compacts have always used to play one against the other in order to protect their own position.

———

There is one factor partially beyond Canadian control that feeds the periodic return of colonial insecurity among our elites. There is no natural place in the international imagination for Canada. There is none in the imagination of the Americas, and there is no space at all in the North American imagination for Canada, except in Canada. Even there, that space is dependent on our capacity to imagine ourselves as we really are.

For the rest of the world the imaginative space, the mythological space of North America, is fully occupied by the United States. That is their strength, not our weakness.

The United States is the beloved child of European history. It is the full expression of the Enlightenment project. It announces itself, in its various declarations of independence and of constitutional order and of legal rights, to be the favourite child of the Western nation-state project. It was erected as the new Eden; a place where the apple-biting of the European could be eliminated. Central and South America have at various times attempted to embrace that same project, but for them the senior mythological space on this specific ground can't help but go to the United States. It could also be argued that much of the difficulty Latin American countries have had making this model work comes from their reality—an Aboriginal, Métis, immigrant tension—which is deeply unsuited to the Enlightenment project. Their reality has more in common with Canada's than with those of Europe or the United States. The rise of European-style nation-state nationalism in the early nineteenth century also was transferred with its most energetic expression to the United States and then to the rest of the Americas. If you add to that the broad temperate space the United States was lucky enough to be built around, you can easily understand how it came to so dominate the available imaginative space.

That Canada has tried at various times to go down the same road as our neighbour we know well. But the basis of this Enlightenment and nationalistic project is the monolithic nation-state, which Canada has never been and cannot become. For four centuries we have had repeated proof that attempts at a monolithic reconstruction of Canada can only bring internal strife and the real threat of disintegration. We have therefore gone down a highly original, even revolutionary, non-monolithic road.

Our successful thinkers, writers, creators, politicians, public servants and activists all understand this. Those with a colonial mindset are driven crazy by this complexity. They want good old-fashioned patriotism: Euro-U.S.–style patriotism. They want one people, one market, one whatever.

And by refusing the originality of the Canadian project they undermine it and confirm the mainstream North American, U.S. international position that there is no imaginative space for Canada. They insist on using monolithic language to describe, lead or manage a non-monolithic experiment. An exception is made for a handful of pro forma phrases—bilingual, multicultural, diverse. But these are linguistic and emotional window dressing when compared to the basic assumptions of governance used by our elites.

One of the clearest illustrations of this void is the difficulty we have projecting our history to ourselves. People will say that this is a factor of modern communications. They forget that Harold Innis, Marshall McLuhan, Glenn Gould and Northrop Frye are the inventors of the modern idea of communications. We ought to be able to handle it. People will say our history is boring, by which they mean it doesn't conform to the Euro-U.S. model. Difference and originality for an insecure person is frightening and therefore uninteresting, particularly if they worship the British way or the U.S. way. People will say that our competing regional interests cause us to erase large parts of our shared memory. The most obvious example is the washing-out in Quebec of the memory of French Canada's most successful and influential leaders, unless they pass the current nationalist litmus test. But that test is precisely a classic imitation of the Euro-U.S. model. LaFontaine, the first to extricate a colony peacefully from an empire; Cartier, the creator of a continental power; Laurier, the man who began the unravelling of the European empires, are washed out of the francophone memory precisely because of the originality of their success.

Looked at from the outside, the effects of Canadians refusing to embrace the atypical nature of the Canadian experiment are startling. It doesn't matter how many troops we put into a world war or how many die. That reality will be erased from international reality as fast as possible, in part by the U.S. projection of its saviour image, but also by the desire of countries such as Britain and France to imagine their dramas as involving a special, exclusive relationship with the United States. The more we do, the more annoying we become, like an uninvited third party at an intimate seduction ritual. When a Canadian wins a major international literary prize, he or she will almost inevitably be described as being from somewhere else or as if he or she comes from nowhere. To this day, international mythological figures such as Glenn Gould or Marshall McLuhan are not identified with this place.

But once you accept that the United States is rightfully the primary inheritor of the European ideal and that we don't fit into that model, you have the basic elements for a very different approach. We will not open up non-existent space by pressing our case as a similar model. The more we see ourselves backlit by soft Victorian melancholy, the more we use Euro-U.S. concepts, the more we project ourselves as a derivative sideshow, the more we then evaporate for anyone's imagination, including our own.

The only possible way out is to focus on what we really are and to develop the language and, more important, the imaginative language to express that. We are non-monolithic. We are not an extension of the European model. We are and always have been an experimental project. We are deeply anchored in this place because of our shaping by the Aboriginal part of us and their even deeper links to place. We are all about imagining a new way for people to live together—a way that embraces the capacity of humans to live with multiple personalities, to enjoy difference, to understand loyalty as an expression of human relationships, not fear of complexity. This book is about exploring how to express what this imaginative space is. If we cannot explain ourselves to ourselves, no one outside Canada will be able to imagine us. We need to be extremely clear, unromantic, comfortable with what is original or atypical about the Canadian experiment in order to create an imaginative space.

It has never been easier to express the meaning of our experiment. For the first time there is actually a real curiosity in many parts of the world about what we are doing. Why? Because they see that our ability to deal with difference has some real strengths. But again, if we don't learn how to explain what we are doing, that curiosity will wither away. And indeed our experiment may also falter if the colonial insecurity in so many of our leaders is allowed to drag us off onto utilitarian views of immigration and market-driven views of citizenship. Where do such misunderstandings come from? From elites that dream of disappearing into the absence of an imaginative space. What they seek is an emotional absorption into that monolithic project that is not ours.

PART IV

AN INTENTIONAL CIVILIZATION

23

From Perception to Action

What we become in our lives is often a matter of self-perception. So, too, for any society. If we can see how Canada has taken its unconscious shape from our Aboriginal experience and how we have organized that inspiration around the concept of peace, fairness and good government, we will approach our need to act in a different manner. We will feel ourselves justified in acting differently. It will seem to us that we are acting intentionally. And so, when we do act in a manner that reflects the foundations of our society, it will no longer be possible to present what we do as accidental or romantic or as merely the result of following a strong leader who took us momentarily off our old, orderly course. Instead, building upon fairness and inclusion, for example, or acting as if there is a natural and positive tension between people and place will feel to us like actions of continuity, in which we are building upon centuries-old patterns of behaviour that are true to this place.

Is it really only a matter of a few words? Is it as easy at that?

Why should it be easy? These concepts express what we are, and therefore what we can do, and how. Consciously absorbed and used they would bring our perceptions of ourselves in line with our reality. That means changing the way we think and talk about ourselves. Few things can be as difficult as that.

Confucius was the original theorist of social and governmental organization. Unlike today's consultants, whose words are expensive and in general quickly forgotten, Confucius is still with us twenty-five hundred years later. He was asked what he would do first if he were given power.

He replied that he would rectify the names. In other words, he would work on the way society talks about itself to ensure that the terms and concepts were accurate. "If the names aren't right, what you say will sound unreasonable. If what you say is unreasonable, what you try to do will fail."

If we go on insisting that Canada is an expression of the West and of its rational, Judeo-Christian tradition, we will be increasingly carried down a road with all that it contains—an obsession with clarity, a fear of social complexity, a horror of overlap, a constant confusing of moral rectitude and power, a conviction that the individual must dominate the place, a tendency to remove obstacles, such as minorities, minority ideas or minority languages. This linear approach makes no sense, given what Canada is. It does not help us make sense of what we have done, even when we have been successful.

The Aboriginal idea of society as a great circle works here. It is a mechanism of inclusion that absorbs new members, adjusting as it does so. It explains how we function. It explains why we seek balance rather than clarity. That balance is not a stand-alone human talent. It works because the circle is imagined as being one with the place. Witaskewin. Living together on the land. Seeking balance. Seeking a broader harmony. Accepting that this can only be multi-dimensional.

The word *welfare* has European origins. But *peace, welfare and good government* has slowly been reshaped in Canada. After all, we have had two hundred and fifty years to give it a Canadian sense. It has become an expression of the idea of a great circle. This has sometimes happened through a formal intellectual process, but it has largely been part of a constantly evolving mix of people learning how to live together, with as their guidance the non-European, non-linear, non-racial concepts of this place.

The novelist Joseph Boyden was asked in 2008 what he would tell people mattered if he was around in fifty years' time. He is young enough that he should get the chance to deliver his answer in person. Boyden replied, "The Land." Not the human view of the land or the urban view of the land, not even human responsibility for the land. It wasn't a romantic point of view or an environmentalist answer.

It was a sensible, balanced view. We are part of the land. We are included in it. And Canada is the sort of place—the sort of land—that can't be mistaken for background or decor or even necessarily for something of utilitarian use.

His reply was not in the Judeo-Christian tradition. It did not place humans at the front of the image. His two words jolted me into an acceptance that, in spite of the enormous role played by churches in Canada over the centuries, ours is not a civilization that emerged out of the Judeo-Christian line. Nor did we rise out of the opposite—the secular or the laïc. That, after all, would be a reflection of the Christian. One produces the other. If the central inspiration of our country is Aboriginal, then we are not, and never have been in the European or U.S. sense, a Christian country. This matters because in Europe and the United States, the assumption even among Marxists, agnostics and atheists is that the foundation of their world was Christian civilization. Of course, the churches did play a powerful role in Canada. For better and worse they controlled a great deal. But if the underlying explanation for why we act the way we do is the central role of Aboriginal culture, then the Judeo-Christian idea, with all its attachments, is shoved to a secondary position. In Quebec, the church was particularly powerful, but even in New France and French Canada, as in the rest of Canada, the foundations were not primarily Christian.

More precisely, the First Nations had never been, as Tomson Highway pointed out in the same conversation, expelled from the Garden of Eden. That means two things. No god has separated the people from the land. The land is therefore neither the enemy nor a lost paradise. Second, there is no built-in social concept of guilt.

It is no wonder that the early "official" settler reaction to this place was one of fear. Northrop Frye's garrison mentality was an attempt to recreate the tension of living in a state of permanent expulsion. You can almost think of it as the *populism* of its day. In other words, it repre-sented not so much the experience of the people as what the colonial, sedentary elite wanted that experience to be. So much of power in Judeo-Christian civilizations is built upon the tension of living in an emotional state of fear produced by a sense of permanent psychic expulsion. It is hardly surprising that an elite, attempting to function here, would instinctively set out to recreate that tension of expulsion. And no wonder that today's version of that need for fear is a rejection of the idea of place by attacking it as romantic. After all, what matters, or so the argument goes, is people.

Our ability to name what matters accurately was further twisted by the arrival of many among the Europeans who dreamt of building a new Eden here—they would escape the sin of Europe and regain entry to a state of purity. Nothing could have been more horrifying for them than to discover that this place was already inhabited by people who had never been expelled, and so lived without the appropriate guilt or shame or remorse. Here is one of the explanations for the determined denial, in the telling of our story, of the central Aboriginal role in Canada. This ought to have mattered less as more and more newcomers arrived and continue to arrive from places outside the Judeo-Christian world. Yet in some ways it matters more, because the newcomers are obliged to adapt to Canada by dealing with the official story they find in place. They are faced by the Confucian problem of a civilization inaccurately named.

This is worsened by the absence of any sustained conversation between Aboriginals and new Canadians. The assumption of the guardians of Canada's image of itself—long-established, now-urban Canadians—is shaped by the fact that most immigrants come to cities. Therefore, it is assumed the filter of their Canadianization should quite logically be those same long-established urban citizens. They are the source of continuity. This is not entirely wrong. New Canadians need and want to be drawn into the full meaning of their citizenship as fast as possible. But the missing conversation, which is desperately needed, is between Aboriginals and new Canadians. What's more, half of the Aboriginal population is now also urban.

The role of those among us who were not expelled makes perfect sense when we try to understand how Canada actually works. Our complexity is built on our comfort in the place, not on our fear of it. This is not a civilization of fear, in spite of the constant attempts by those who embrace the idea of *order* to impose the opposite. Our circular, non-Manichean, non-punishing approach is the product of a civilization that does not see itself as fallen or expelled.

In some ways this is a simple problem of geography. Do we imagine ourselves as being here? Or are we floating in a theoretically borderless world? Taken at face value, that sounds like an easy choice between a closed and an open world view. But what if the reality is the opposite? What if the theoretically borderless world implies not freedom but a return to the old fears of the expelled? What if that borderless world is a concept based upon a utilitarian, commercial view of human relations that uses the old mechanisms of expulsion and fear as an organizational principle?

And what does imagining ourselves as being here actually mean? Surely it means that if you can accurately describe yourself and how your society functions, you will then be able to deal with the world in a comfortable and successful, not fearful, manner. This is where the idea of the great circle joins that of fairness. And together they form the basis of our long-term public policies. They are as relevant to health policy and foreign policy as they are to a wealth-creating market and a creative rather than defensive approach to the environment.

And yet, imagining ourselves as being here is more difficult than ever. Most of us live in cities and know little else. These cities can be wonderful places. But they can also become the new garrisons. With this urban life comes two contradictory perceptions of ourselves. One is a modern version of the old fear attached to the expelled Judeo-Christian world view. People are what matters. People are in the cities. The rest is romanticism.

But since the land is seen as separate from the city and is not known, the urban view itself takes on a romantic view of what lies out there, out of sight: The land is to be feared. Therefore, however severely it is mined or pulped, so much the better. Humans are cutting it down to size. We are taming it. Thus severe exploitation makes us, a frightened and insecure people, feel superior.

The other possibility is that the land is to be feared, but in a dark, romantic way, and must be protected, as if it were a mysterious, off-limits space. This is an unexpected response to the very real environmental crisis that we face, a setting aside of reality rather than an engagement with it. You cannot be a part of a place if you feel you cannot engage with it. The city must therefore be a garrison in order to protect the place stretching away outside its walls of suburbia.

This takes us right back to the medieval European concept that also combined fear with a commercial view of civilization. Sophisticated trading cities once dotted coasts, usually at river mouths, in less settled areas. They were built with walls on their backside, to protect them against the unknown hinterland, and ports on their front side, to link them to one another, city dwellers of the world. In the eighteenth and nineteenth centuries, this same idea was used by the European empires as a cheap way to handle uncontrollable foreign markets. Thus there were treaty ports around the edges of China, of much of Asia and, until European armies penetrated the African continent, all along Africa's coasts. If you look at today's cities in this light, you can see the link between the old fear and a certain kind of environmentalism. The result is a distanced, linear projection out from the city walls of what the land should be.

This is the exact opposite of a balanced, inclusive approach. Take as an example the Haida Gwaii experience. There, the Haida have set about freeing their archipelago from the borderless, linear world of maximum resource extraction. They are reorganizing Haida Gwaii in order to live in a different way. That will still involve extraction, but with two elements in mind: remembering the relationship between the people and the land; and taking a long-term view, which implies a value-added approach to that extraction.

And yet the way most of us have come to think and talk about ourselves prevents us from doing what we need to do. Why? Because it is not true to this place. If we make the enormous effort needed to think and talk in a more accurate way, we will see ourselves living within a society that wishes to be inclusive and balanced. And we will see that society, that circle, as an integral part of the place.

24

The North

The ice was melting. The Northwest Passage might open for commercial traffic. The United States wanted part of our great Arctic Archipelago declared international waters so that they could take cargo through when and how they wished. Even oil tankers. Russia made a physical claim on the floor of the Arctic Ocean, right under our nose, sending a clever submarine to deposit proof of its presence. That ocean bed contains a wealth of untapped natural resources. Perhaps 20 percent of the world's oil. The Danes were claiming territory we know to be ours. The Swedes were probably with the Danes. All of this—who owned what, what was national, what international—would be decided by an international tribunal. We were falling behind in the proof of our claims. No, surely we were not making claims. We were falling behind in the demonstration of our sovereignty.

Finally, Canada was going to have to pay attention to the Arctic.

Plans were announced for an arctic fleet capable of breaking thin ice. Thick-ice ships would take too long to build. The matter was urgent. They would also be expensive. Too expensive for what was not clear. After all, sovereignty implies a long-term state of affairs requiring stable, long-term policies. And other countries, such as the United States and Russia, have quantities of thick-ice ships. There were nevertheless signs that this was finally being understood. A military base was to be built well to the north. Research was to be jacked up.

All of this is perfectly sensible. It should have been done decades ago. In fact, some of it had already been done during one of our earlier periods of Southern enthusiasm. After all, the base was going where there had once been one. All sorts of research projects had been started up decades before and then had gradually slipped into limbo—all initiatives done and then undone as the enthusiasm waned. In any case, these new policies, from the point of view of sovereignty, all came rather late in the day. The immediate challenges have been public for a long time. Other countries have been slowly, carefully, building their Northern policies and institutions, while we were doing more important things: keeping our taxes low, cutting back on all sorts of wasteful government programs, attacking debt. Northern initiatives in such an atmosphere apparently ranked quite low. In 1985, following an earlier sovereignty scare, our elites had announced a solid and clear six-part program to solidify our arctic position. We then forgot about most of it. Indeed, today we can be proud that our rigorous economic policies have been so successful that we may have set the stage for losing a good part of our Northern sovereignty. When faced with choices between economic theory and poverty, economic theory and housing, economic theory and citizen health, economic theory and taking responsibility for your country, which includes the North, the choice is obvious. Far better to have children at food banks and lose control of a large part of your country than to risk upsetting the Department of Finance economists. But perhaps it is not too late for the Arctic.

The curious thing about these new Northern policies is that they have an almost-charming retro air about them. It is as if some old-style imperial government huddled in the temperate South were cranking itself up to send ships and soldiers off to a distant, mysterious, threatened frontier of the empire. Not that it isn't a good idea.

There was one Northern-centred element among the initiatives: the strengthening of the Rangers, a militia regiment spread all around the North. In the Arctic, its members are largely Inuit hunters, men and women, their training conducted by devoted regular-force warrant officers. They come under the Commander of the North, a general in Yellowknife, a few thousand kilometres away. But then everything is far away in the North. And what else could the army do? The regiment, indeed the forces in the North, had been deeply underfunded for decades. There were no officers on the ground with the men. No Northerners were being trained to create a permanent leadership base at a senior level. On the other hand, the warrant officers and the Rangers love their work. And do it well. And now there was real enthusiasm in the South for change in the North.

That phrase—*enthusiasm in the South for change in the North*—sums up all the arguments in this book. The words could equally read *progress in the North* or *action* or *new initiatives.* They all deliver the same message: Canada as a whole insists on seeing the North through Southern eyes. And this perspective is the extension of an essentially Western European view. It is an expression of *order*: The South has solutions for the North. The South will shape the North in an old-fashioned, monolithic nation-state manner.

At first this may seem odd, given the efforts that have been made to ensure self-government for the Inuit. But making efforts is not the same as seeing the North in its own terms, as seeing the Inuit or the Dene or the Gwich'in or other Northerners as the Canadians of the North. The rest of the country is punctilious about seeing Alberta from an Alberta point of view and Quebec from a Quebec point of view. But Northern cultures and points of view are treated as marginal, as if Northerners were not really citizens, not really the primary custodians of the land on which they have lived for thousands of years.

There seems to be little understanding in the South, and certainly no sustained understanding, that Canada as a whole benefits and is truer to itself when there are strong Northern communities that stand out as expressions of our country. This is quite different from communities artificially pumped up by solutions conceived in the South and imposed by Ottawa or organized by Southern universities or departments of education or researchers working in the South and visiting the North in the summer to check out their theories. All of these Southern initiatives are what they have always been—expressions of *order*. No matter how well-intentioned, they undermine the reality of the North and so undermine the truth—that Northerners are Canadians and therefore the real custodians of our sovereignty there. Put another way, there is very little understanding in Canada's elite structures that the basis of sovereignty is the *welfare* of the community and not the *order* with which it is organized.

Sheila Watt-Cloutier, former elected chair of the International Inuit Circumpolar Council: "As Canadians seek to assert our sovereignty in the Arctic, we must remember that history is on our side, that Inuit traveled an icy highway through the Northwest Passage long before more recent arrivals even considered a fast route west. [T]hriving human communities speak stronger than any fleet of ice breakers or barracks full of soldiers." Mary Simon, president of the Inuit Tapiriit Kanatami: "Canadian Arctic sovereignty must be built from the inside out." If we want the world to understand and accept our sovereignty as self-evident, we need that same world to see Northern Canada in good part through the eyes and the words of our Northern leaders. The more the world sees Northern Canadians building up their communities, and operating in ways true to the North, the more they will see our vast North as Canadian.

This implies myriad elements. A successful Northern strategy means Northern communities made stronger in a Northern way, which means approaches not imitative of Southern urban beliefs, but approaches naturally integrated as a blend of old and new Northern ways. We will be judged by the success of the individual lives of Northerners—lives successful in ways appropriate to both the North and to small, isolated communities, which is the reality of more than half our country. All of that will depend on the appropriateness of their local infrastructures to their geographical reality, on whether their economy is an innovative response to that reality. Perhaps most important, all of us will be judged on how successfully the expression of citizenship and democracy throughout the North is adapted to Northern realities.

These are all practical matters and matters of perception. For example, oil companies have been absent from the Arctic for several decades. As the price of oil goes up, so they are becoming eager to start up their exploring again, and the federal government is busily auctioning off exploration rights in the Beaufort Sea and the Mackenzie Valley. Inuit leaders have complicated views on all of this. They worry about the environment. But they also worry about generating an income for their people. The federal government and the oil companies on one side and Southern environmental organizations on the other do not suffer from such complexities. They are proceeding to battle as if there were no Northern Canadian reality. Nellie Cournoyea, the long-time Inuvialuit leader in the Western Arctic, has struck out at the World Wildlife Fund for interference in Northern affairs. "The Inuvialuit are sick and tired of having their future economic well-being blindsided by southern-based environmental organizations that poke their self-righteous noses into someone else's backyard without either having the decency to consult with the people that live there or offer any realistic alternative to their economic challenges." In other words, Southern structures of power offer only two possibilities to Northerners: Either they can earn some income off old-fashioned commodity exploration or they can earn no income off no-commodity exploration. No one in any place of power in the South bothers considering how Canadians are going to live in the North. They don't ask what that phrase might mean: to live in the North.

Take the example of education. Everyone in the Arctic recognizes that education is the key to what happens next. And the classic Southern line is that *What Aboriginals need is to escape the cycle of poverty through education*. But what kind of education? The Canadian model is based on largely urban assumptions. Applied in the Arctic, it is largely irrelevant. Yet in its first years, Nunavut found itself obliged—in the absence of any other curriculum—to rely on that of Alberta. You could say that success in that model meant for most students that if they wanted to use their education they would have to leave their communities. But the purpose of education is not to empty the Arctic of its citizenry. Nor is it to undermine their self-confidence as Northerners. The Southern system in place couldn't help but do both.

There is a formal, carefully thought-through movement in the Arctic to reshape education into appropriate Inuit ways. There is a whole concept, known as IQ, which refers to that *Inuit way*. The principles of IQ have been carefully laid out with the idea that "we must incorporate the government into [Inuit] culture," not the other way around. Yet the territorial government of Nunavut has had trouble applying IQ in any integrated way. Why? Because in 1999, when Nunavut was set up, they had little choice but to "borrow a model of public government from the Northwest Territories"—a Southern model put in place by Southerners who had worked in Yellowknife. Even with the best will in the world, IQ often ended up as a series of ad hoc initiatives pinned onto this borrowed model.

Over the last decade, Northerners have been hard at work trying to change this situation. They have started developing curriculum from the early grades up. They have introduced traditional learning into the courses. They have begun training Northern teachers and are moving toward a bilingual education system. If they can't get Inuktitut into the core of the system, English will simply act like a bulldozer knocking over Northern realities. There is now a plan to build IQ into the entire educational approach. Justice Thomas Berger, in his 2006 report on "The Nunavut Project," summarized this situation clearly: "What we have to get into our heads is that the loss of language and educational under-achievement are linked. The strengthening of Inuktitut in the school, the home and the community can bring improvement in achievement in both Inuktitut and English. The Inuit have decided that this is their only choice, and I believe it is Canada's only choice."

It won't be easy. But if education is not relevant to life in these communities, with no road access, far from one another, then it simply becomes an emotionally isolating force. After all, life is largely about where you live. And real life in the Arctic has to be in good part about the land that surrounds the communities. Studying and hunting on the land cannot be seen as separate functions. The new model of education is trying to put schooling together with that reality of Northern life. This is difficult. But it is also one of the most exciting initiatives in education anywhere.

And schools are only one factor in the broad reinvention of Arctic life. Northerners have been gradually installing their own sorts of systems in other areas. The legislature in Iqaluit is organized around Inuit ideas of consensus and so has no political parties. The administration has been decentralized to several distant communities and runs on high-tech communications. The premier is chosen by secret ballot in the assembly.

He or she then chooses his or her cabinet. In the Northwest Territories
there is also a consensus system. The new Nunavik territory, accounting
for one-third of Quebec, has another version of this. In its electoral
system, the five who are elected with the most votes will make up the
cabinet. And in all these territories they are hard at work creating
curriculum in Inuktitut as well as Dene and other languages, beginning
at the primary school level.

The greater problem lies with how the vast majority of Canadians
imagine this North. Until around 1900 we were too busy organizing the
Southern third of the country and knew nothing of the Arctic. Early in
the twentieth century we began sending out the North West Mounted
Police to establish *order* and, presumably, *good government*. What the
Inuit and long-established traders recorded was the heavy-handed and
ill-informed arrival of the police, who insisted on treating the Inuit in a
patronizing manner. They didn't seem to grasp that these Northern
Canadians had been dealing with whalers and traders from various parts
of the world for a long time. They had lived together, had families
together. The Inuit had already taken full advantage of the essential
Western technical advances, such as rifles. They had helped both the
whalers and a mixed bag of foreign explorers. Those foreigners who
survived did so in good part thanks to the Inuit. And then our police
arrived and enthusiastically distributed woollen underwear while talking
of the great white mother. The Inuit were perhaps grateful for some
unexpected comic relief. As late as 1953, Louis St. Laurent admitted that
Canada had administered the North "in an almost continuing state of
absence of mind." And even then the capital of the Northwest Territories
remained Ottawa until 1967. There were some administrators on the
spot, but as the Northern judge Jack Sissons put it, "Many of these civil
servants were in the north but not of the north, and Ottawa was their
spiritual home...." Only in the 1960s did Ottawa begin to take its role
seriously, establishing real services, but again in a heavy-handed way:
registering people as numbers because we found their names difficult,
hanging these numbers on discs around their necks to simplify

administrative processes, and inoculating them against Southern diseases but often forcibly and without any serious attempt at explanations.

~

The source of our difficulties through all of this was how we perceived ourselves. Southern Canadians and our government saw themselves as the inheritors of the early Europeans in the North—the British and other foreign explorers and the Hudson's Bay Company. Their quest for a northwest passage was our quest. Their adventure was our adventure. Their tragedy, ours. Their triumph, a victory for our Western civilization, as they/we defeated the fearful, frigid ice. They saw the North as a place to be crossed, not to be lived in. The Inuit, Métis, coureurs de bois appear in this saga as at best supporting actors, more often as bit players. Their roles are to amuse, to frighten, to pull, to carry. If you look coolly at today's arguments over sovereignty, they are still about cutting through the Arctic, not living in it. They are about protecting access and passages, perhaps about extracting resources through these passages. But only tertially about Canadian citizens living permanently in the Arctic.

But what were those foreign explorers except the expression of rich, settled countries? They were a foreign indulgence. As individuals, they were escaping the monotony of a stable life at home. They were trying to fulfill the dreams of foreign empires. These were short-term foreign visitors, uninterested in Canada as a place, obsessed by cutting through it. They did take the few minutes required to claim the land. After all, they were usually stuck somewhere in the ice for a long winter. They had lots of time to do that. And we inherited those claims from the British. The Inuit thought this was comic and vaguely barbaric. One of their words for the visitors was *people who stick poles in the snow*, that is, flagpoles. These explorers were often so egotistical or comically unadapted—in concrete terms, stupid—that they died of their self-indulgence. From the Canadian point of view, they were just uninvited passersby. Before their arrival, there had been people of the place. After the visitors were gone the Northerners were still there. These Northerners are the originators of Canada in the Arctic. They are the source of our sovereignty. As Canadians, we are all the descendants of the Inuit, the Dene and the other peoples of the North. We are not the descendants of Sir John Franklin or of Sir Edward Parry. In the same way, in the mid-north, miners have come and gone, money has been dragged out of the ground and evaporated. Villages have prospered and vanished or stagnated. But again the Canadians of the North are those who see themselves as belonging there and so are responsible for it.

There is little in recent Canadian Northern policies to suggest that we have learned to see ourselves in this way. We still act as if we were more excited by ignorant visiting failures such as Franklin than by the real North. And like his kind, we come and go with almost seasonal enthusiasms.

It seemed in the 1990s as if all of this were changing. Driven in good part by Canada, the Arctic Council was created in 1996. In 1997, the Parliamentary Foreign Affairs Committee proposed an integrated approach to policy in the North. In 1999, Nunavut was created. In 2000, Ottawa released a serious Northern Foreign Policy, which dealt with the role of Aboriginal Canadians, the environment, climate change, nuclear waste, security, the prosperity of Northerners, sovereignty and an active circumpolar coalition with Canada as a leader. The University of the Arctic—a circumpolar virtual approach toward education—was created with a great deal of Canadian leadership. In 2003, a series of elaborate circumpolar state visits was organized to advance this new Canadian role in the most public manner possible, with Aboriginal, political, as well as cultural and business leaders volunteering to put aside their own interests in order to support Canada by taking part.

By 2004—only a few months later—the new foreign policy had been mislaid. No one seemed to know quite where. Canada then picked a series of stupid fights with our closest Arctic neighbour, Denmark, which includes Greenland, when Denmark ought to have been the strategic key to our circumpolar coalition. We then sent an insultingly inappropriate ambassador to Copenhagen. The state visits were cancelled for internal political reasons in a way calculated to insult Denmark, Sweden and Norway. Various elected officials made denigrating remarks about our Arctic neighbours. Since then, only a scattering of cabinet ministers has bothered to visit the circumpolar countries. They would rather go to London or Paris or New York, where the restaurants and theatres are more to their taste, where they can concentrate on international issues that may be important but have little direct relevance to Canada as a real place. All the while, the question of sovereignty has been there for anyone to recognize. All the while, we should have been busy building circumpolar coalitions.

Meanwhile, Denmark, Norway and Sweden developed a joint northern foreign policy. They chair the Arctic Council one after the other from 2006 to 2012. For these six years they have placed the roving secretariat of the council in northern Norway in Tromsø. They will then probably try to settle the secretariat there permanently. We could probably have had it permanently in Canada in one of our Northern capitals as of 1996. But we were too busy saving money to be serious leaders. And no one with power in Southern Canada imagines the possibility of Northern cities being the site of real power. Norway also moved its Polar Institute to Tromsø in the 1990s. There are now two hundred and fifty people in it, leading in the development of arctic policy with a budget of more than $40 million. As well, they have a good university in the same town. And there is an international university research station farther north at Svalbard with one hundred research spots for students, half of them foreigners, twenty full-time professors, twenty-one assistant professors and a hundred and twenty arctic specialist guest lecturers. As for the international University of the Arctic, it is centred in northern Finland. One of the reasons it isn't in Canada is that we have no appropriate Northern institutions. Besides, we wouldn't have wanted to invest the small amount of long-term money that would have been necessary.

What does Canada have in the North, with its population seven times that of Norway, six times that of Finland? Well, we have all sorts of Northern study centres in the South. We have Southern experts visiting the North in the summer. God forbid that they should have to live in the North in the winter. We have the Polar Continental Shelf Project, which has been stagnant for years. And it is a branch, astonishingly, of the Department of Natural Resources, a fact that betrays the narrowness of how we view the Arctic. Meanwhile Italy, France, Japan, Korea and China are all setting up arctic research stations based out of Norway. On a more practical level, we did invent the snowmobile but haven't bothered to develop or build any designed for the Arctic. These are designed and built instead in northern Finland. We haven't even developed goggles that work in the high arctic cold. There is a great deal of puffed-up talk from mining companies developing in the North. They say this is a new era. They are training Aboriginals to do many of their jobs. When you examine the training, it is virtually all at the manual or machine-operating level, driving big trucks, operating cranes. Why are they not training managers? Usually they insist that it's all generational, that the next generation will have managerial jobs. This is nothing more than old-style paternalistic prevarication. Above all, it's all about seeing the North as somewhere far from the real world, the South.

And, most revealing, we are the only circumpolar country that has no university in the Arctic. If anyone were serious about the next genera-tion, why is it that we are the only circumpolar country without such a university? The answer given is usually that we lack the population density in the Arctic. No other circumpolar nation has used that argument. Yet they don't have large arctic populations. The other answer is that we are waiting for sufficient demand—that is, we are combining the population density argument with the next generational argument. Thus, we are building up that demand from the elementary school level. These attitudes are hardly worth crouching low enough to be responded to. The density argument merely betrays a lack of commitment to the North. And the next generation argument is just about Southerners holding on to power. What we know is this: Education requires push and pull. You must push on from kindergarten up, while you pull from the most advanced university levels.

The real answer is that we don't look at the North from the North, in its own terms. There are three training colleges in our three Northern capitals. It would be easy to build on to these. For example, we could create one arctic university with three campuses, each specializing in fields relevant to particular territories. The federal government could anchor these with three or four national research chairs on each campus.

Some of these research chairs could deal with indigenous cultures and languages, others with the specific development and environmental needs of the territory. There would be no lack of Northerners and Southerners eager to teach and research on these campuses. Young Northerners would quickly feel encouraged to find their place in such a university. This would be a great magnet for Inuit high school students, who so often drop out, to stay on to grade twelve. This would also be a real attraction for Southerners wanting to settle in the North. An arctic university would be the single-most eloquent statement we could make about Canada as a place in the North.

Why eloquent? Because the North, like all of Canada, needs a voice that is true to the people and to the place. That is what Inuit leaders seek with their IQ concept. The *Inuit way*, they are saying, should become the concept for imagining the modern North. This is, in Confucian terms, all about *rectifying the names*. And an arctic university, bringing together Northern concepts and languages with the study of everything from the environment to mining, could be the motor for a modern Canadian idea of the North. We need theoretical and practical work on how to live and work in the Arctic. We need to be thinking about what we build in every detail. That is true at every level. Houses, for example, no longer look quite as if they were picked up from Southern suburbs and dropped in the Arctic. But the progress has been ad hoc, without any serious, continual thinking about architecture and engineering in the North. Canada has hundreds of communities with no road access, yet they are obliged to bring in at great expense diesel oil to heat themselves and run their machinery. There is no serious, integrated work being done on how else these isolated settlements should be powered in an era of soaring oil prices and global warming.

I remember hearing Chief Darrell Beaulieu of the Taidene Corporation speaking in Yellowknife in 2004. He talked of how the North was "peripheral and vital." Vital to security, energy, economic growth and climate change. "Historically, the periphery has been a place of safety, freedom and isolation." But above all, the Arctic, because of its fragility, has always obliged Northerners to live with severe limitations, that is, to adapt to them in order to "live with them." Now Southerners should be paying attention in order to do the same. First, they should be thinking of the North in Northern terms. But more than that, they should be using the Northern perspective of limitation and care to think about Canada as a whole.

And that perspective does indeed turn on the non-Judeo-Christian, non-rational, non-linear idea of limitation and balance between people and place and a circular view of society that assumes inclusion and being careful. An arctic university would be the right place to work out what such a view might lead us to.

I realize that it is a Southerner who is making these arguments. But Northerners have been making these same sorts of arguments for a long time, just as First Nations leaders were making their equivalent arguments throughout the eighteenth, nineteenth and twentieth centuries. What is astonishing is how Southerners have organized themselves intellectually and emotionally not to hear what is said. In part it is because we insist on listening in a European manner and so cannot digest the full meaning of what Northerners say. They talk of place in a manner that suits that place. We persist in evoking the Northern place in our version of the old explorer perspective.

How is it that we are focusing on the North once again, yet still in that old European manner? Part of it is our addiction to the European version of the story of Canada, which reduces the North to a place to be crossed. Part is the failure of most of us to see ourselves and our Northernness as expressed by the Inuit, Dene, Northern Cree and other Northern peoples, and Southerners who have become Northerners and Northern Métis. In other words, we can't seriously focus on the North and maintain that focus unless we see ourselves through them. Part of it, as a result, is our desire to see the North in old-fashioned frontier terms, instead of as a society offering a possible expression of welfare, of fairness.

And part of it, again as a result of all of the above, is Ottawa's obsession with Washington, whether loving, hating or fearing. Fixated by what the United States might want or do, we have fallen into the classic state of colonial insecurity. We seek constantly to mollify our neighbour, when thousands of years of diplomatic history tell us that large powers don't respect smaller powers they can take for granted. The most powerful nations respond best to friends who regularly annoy them. Not infuriate them—but they need to feel the tensions of a real relationship. Look at whom Washington listens to with respect: Berlin, Tokyo, Jerusalem, even Paris. All these countries regularly yank the chain that links them in friendship to the United States. Paris occasionally takes itself too seriously and slips into infuriating behaviour, but that only makes the kiss and make-up drama that inevitably follows all the sweeter for both sides. Tony Blair's Britain was a perfect example of what happens to the compliant ally. They slip into irrelevance and then are treated with indifference and eventually contempt. Canada never goes quite that far and so is merely treated with indifference.

The arctic chain that Canada has with which to yank the United States consists of the other circumpolar countries. To do that, we would have to build real relationships with our Northern allies. Instead, we have mismanaged our relations with all of them, even Russia. In May 2008, the Danes convoked a meeting to come up with a shared arctic position over the various claims being made to arctic territory. They handled the meeting well and the outcome seems to have been reasonable. But why did it take Denmark to convoke it in their distant territory of Greenland? Why was Canada little more than a passive player, hoping for the best?

Our constant trepidation over what Washington might do or say is central to what prevents us from seeing the North in its own terms. Instead we project ourselves up from our southern border. We constantly forget that our geopolitical reality has several elements to it. True, one is our single and long-shared border. But the other is our coastline—the longest coast of any nation-state. We are a gigantic peninsula on three oceans. Our reality is as much if not more maritime as it is continental. Yet we struggle with this concept of ourselves. We can't remove our imagination from that linear border. We remain fixated by our southern, linear projection of Canada. We seem frightened by the great spatial idea of our civilization, in which almost half of our place is truly Northern.

We have got as far as saying, "from sea to sea to sea," but haven't bothered to actually change our motto. And the proposed French version—d'un océan aux autres—and the proposed Latin version— A mari usque ad maria—are both vague and abstract, as if there might be four or twenty oceans involved. As if no one cared. These translations are impossibly European: If the country can't be linear, then it must be an abstraction. They miss completely the conceptual idea of the space, of the circle, of the turtle. They miss the reality of a country living within three oceans.

Somehow this maritime idea of Canada has gradually withered, as if we have slowly been drawn by our insecure elite into looking only one way. And so we came out of the Second World War with one of the greatest merchant marines in the world but merrily sold it off. As if it were pretentious for us to be a great shipping nation. Why would we want to own all those ships? Surely someone else could own them for us. It would be so much less work, so much more agreeably modest, even inferior. As for our various governmental navies—the RCMP, the Coast Guard and the navy itself—we gradually reduced them to almost invisibility around our shores. Why would coastline matter? Only that southern border counts. Only the utilitarian process of trade to the south matters.

And again, our elite's obsession with Washington makes us all forget that our greatest neighbour in the north is Russia, just across the arctic pond. Again, early in this century, there was a short-lived attempt to build a polar relationship with Moscow. As so often, Ottawa's foreign policy enthusiasms lasted two or three years. And then a critical mass among the civil servants and the lobbyists dragged us back to what could best be described as their need for a colonial reality in which all important thoughts must be projected in one direction. And so we let the Russian initiative drift away into a relationship of indifference, even though the environmental stability of the Arctic—our Arctic—is far more dependent on what Moscow does or does not do than on vague imperial plans from Washington.

But foreign policy is only the outer shell of our Northern role. We could easily change our patterns of behaviour. We could try to think of the Scandinavians as real and essential allies. We could place ourselves vis-à-vis Russia as if Washington were not the arbiter of such relationships. We could stop speaking of ourselves as if Canada only exists huddled along the southern border. We could accept our reality as a coastal and largely Northern nation. We could accept that our legitimacy in the North is dependent upon the well-being of Northern Canadians. In less than a year we could set in motion the creation of national Northern institutions, such as a university, and begin building the infrastructure needed to think in a Northern way.

All of that would be possible, even easy, if we could convince ourselves of our own reality. But at the heart of such a change is our need to see ourselves in this new way—a way in which non-Aboriginals accept that Aboriginal concepts of place and of culture will be the determining factor in our success or failure. This is not romance. This is our reality.

What does that mean? That we must begin not with old-fashioned ideas of profit or of market determinism. Instead we must start with the fragility of the North, the unforgiving outcome if we make a mistake, such as a shipping accident with oil slipping under the ice. We need to drop the facile *for and against* economic debates of the South in favour of a more open and realistic attempt at consensus in the North in the Northern way. There may well be various sorts of resource extraction to be undertaken, but the conditions will have to be honest and transparent in a way our commodities industries have never accepted.

And the key to these realizations is the legitimacy of Northernness as the core of the Canadian idea in the North—Northern ways, not vaguely adapted methods from the South.

Again this is all about perception, about rectifying names. Think of today's debate over whether the Northwest Passage will open up as temperatures rise and what we should do about it. The core of this argument—of our fear for our sovereignty—is the classic Western concept of land and anyone's ability to own it. The international debate is structured around such land as opposed to its opposite—water—

through which you may pass. Ice is just frozen water, through which you may be able to break your way.

Our legal claims are based in good part on our inheritance of owner-ship from British explorers. We actually base our sovereignty on the dubious historic claims made during those imperial trips. This leads us to a dependence on Law of the Sea arguments, which may work in temperate areas but are inappropriate in the Arctic.

The explorers claimed the land. The European tradition is that you can own land, while you merely pass through water. The question, there-fore, is how much water lying off your land you can claim as yours.

The Northern view is quite different. It is special. Territory is a space in which you live, and in that space land and ice are one. Most of the year you travel on ice rather than on land. Ice is your road. It is the source of much of your food. Early in this chapter I quoted Sheila Watt-Cloutier on the real source of our legitimacy in the Arctic. It was, she said, the long history of Inuit travelling on the ice. They have always used the ice as land. Ice is valuable because it allows you to move easily from island to island. Even when melted, water has historically been an element that unites, not separates Inuit life.

This is a point of view that resembles the argument of oral over written in which our Supreme Court has recognized the possible supremacy of the oral. Yet in its defence of arctic sovereignty, Canada continues to advance arguments that are outcomes of the European view. That is, we continue to argue as if we were completing the logic of the explorers, who saw ice as uncooperative water getting in the way of their drive to find a passage through Canada. In other words, we argue as if we believed that arctic waters were a separation between land. And in doing so, we undermine our own claims of sovereignty. Worse still, in these arguments we also use an old colonial argument: that we need to control the Arctic in order to protect the Inuit and their culture. What could be more patronizing? We undermine our own sovereignty position by presenting Inuit citizens as fragile survivors instead of as the source of Canada's power and legitimacy.

If we thought of ourselves as Canadian—as a people of this place, as a nation that operates in the Arctic through the legitimacy of the Inuit—

then we would present the arctic waters as a form of land—as one with the land and legally inseparable from it. We would draw our role in the Arctic from the people of the Arctic. There are those who would reply that the Inuit did not live throughout the Arctic Archipelago. But they lived and live through a good part of it and the rest was their hinterland. After all, there are large parts of the United States, Brazil, northern Scotland, even of France and Germany and so on that are not lived in. No one says that the deserts of Nevada or the Massif Central or the Highlands should therefore be treated as less than fully sovereign lands of those countries, with all that that implies.

And if we were to take on our Northernness and argue from the position of Inuit legitimacy and Inuit concepts—of stable life involving a joining together of land and ice or water, how would the rest of the world react? Would international tribunals and courts have trouble with this rectification of names? Of course they would. They would be amazed and confused, at least at first. But they would be obliged to consider it and therefore to consider differently the very nature of the opposing arguments. And they would discover that this approach is both useful and accurate as all countries attempt to deal with the environmental challenges facing the North. In fact, the Law of the Sea is remarkably unsuited to the modern situation of the Arctic. The Law of the Sea is derived from old European ideas of ownership, starting from how far a cannonball can be shot across water from a coastal fortress. Today's realities are about shared problems and relationships and needs that cross the boundaries of ownership, just as fish do, and pollution, and climates. And so the tribunals and courts might find such an indigenous and integrated approach refreshing. As for Canadians, we would find ourselves for the first time thinking about our legitimacy in a way that is true to this place and to its people.

25

A Circle of Fairness

How rarely do we link our ability to imagine with our ability to act. Perhaps that is because we confuse simply doing our job, managing situations or focusing on the short term with the concept of action. Perhaps this is because so many of us are somehow employed or feel employed rather than feel that we are free to act. And that atmosphere of *order* impinges on our real desire as individuals, as citizens, to get things done.

And yet we do imagine our society and we do know what ought to be done. And there is enormous energy caught up in that imagination.

When Canadians are asked—as citizens, not as representatives of interest groups or as employees—what lies at the heart of their civilization, they are most likely to reply: fairness and inclusion. This response cuts easily across what are often presented as dividing lines of Aboriginal and non-Aboriginal, francophone and anglophone, established and new citizens. Where this comes from is less clear, because our intellectual and moral history has been so artificially tied to Britain, Europe and the United States.

When James Orbinski—long-time head of the international organization Doctors Without Borders and now living back in Toronto—was asked to identify the core of Canadian civilization, he replied that it was fairness. "I think it's a principle—what's good for me should be good for you...."

How successful we are at embracing that principle is another matter. And our success may vary from era to era. But societies function on the basis of how they imagine themselves. The colonial mindset is always easy to identify in Canada because it attacks fairness and inclusion as soft and romantic notions. They are neither. I can't think of anything harder to achieve. It is far easier to glory in class difference, financial difference, racial difference, insiders versus outsiders. I can't think of a more romantic notion than to believe that a stable society can be built on the celebration of disadvantage.

Fairness has always been the intent of the Aboriginal circle. In the Great Peace of Montreal in 1701, that oral concept was turned into a text stating that we should all be "eating from a common bowl." In that founding document of the Canadian idea, the *we* is indigenous and non-indigenous together. This was LaFontaine's egalitarian message in his *Address to the Electors of Terrebonne*, as it was Nellie McClung's conceptualization of Canada as "a fair deal," as it was Tommy Douglas's intent with medicare, and that of a series of governments, accelerating with St. Laurent, Diefenbaker, Pearson and Trudeau, putting in place a broad system of fair programs. Here and there a mix of provincial governments in Saskatchewan, Ontario and Quebec kept up the pressure of fairness and sometimes led the way. And then, as governments at all levels fell behind in the 1980s and 1990s and on into this century, so a growing number of citizens turned to non-profit organizations to try to slow the growing unfairness and exclusion in our society.

The idea that drove them was one that stretched back to the idea of the *common bowl*. You cannot have a democracy that functions on the legitimacy of the citizenry and then have citizens eliminated from that society by their condition, by poverty, for example, or homelessness. Citizenship implies inclusivity. An inclusive society cannot accept the idea that exclusion is normal. This is what Baldwin was warning about in his resignation speech in 1851: The consequences of the "reckless disregard of first principles, if left unchecked [will be] wide spread social disorganization with all its fearful consequences."

What is fascinating about the first principles of fairness and inclusion is how much energy such intentional ideas produce. Compare two recent studies driven by these ethics on the one hand with the expensive and long federal government study on corporate hollowing out on the other.

The Community Foundations of Canada and the Law Commission looked at what was holding immigrants back. In fifty pages, they laid out a clear analysis and a clear and doable program. Not too complicated. Not expensive. Dealing with every aspect of society. They perceived immigrants as citizens in waiting and therefore took a long-term investment view: Any money spent now would be more than earned back by society over the long term.

This was the attitude we took in the 1780s when Loyalists were given up to twelve hundred acres, plus two hundred acres for each son and daughter on majority or marriage, plus two years' worth of agricultural implements, food and clothing. Today's equivalent would include, for example, proper extended language training. As it is, we don't even have shared standards across Canada in English as a Second Language (ESL) programs or their French equivalent, and the federal government has frozen funding for much of the last decade. Any government could take the recommendations in this study and solve the problems.

Equally, a six-part study in 2008 by a few journalists at *The Globe and Mail* analyzed and laid out a program for the mental health crisis in Canada. Again, the twelve solutions are doable and touch everyone from schools to all three levels of government to the business community and the universities to citizens' groups. You feel the energy—the desire for problem solving—in every word.

Then you turn to the lengthy, year-long study commissioned by the federal government from a group of senior industry managers on the crisis in corporate hollowing-out. The result is not entirely without interest. There are one or two useful ideas. But the central theme is what everyone should do for the business community. There is scarcely a word about what they themselves should do to do better. It is mainly a moan for less taxes, less regulation and more support. In a country that has more foreign ownership than in any other democracy, their solution is to lower barriers in order to encourage more foreign ownership in order to encourage a competitive spirit. They don't explain why what hasn't worked up to now would work if pushed further. They don't explain why we should lower what few barriers remain while the United States, Brazil, China and so on keep theirs up. They recognize the failure of the private sector to do even a reasonable amount of research and development but offer no solutions. They suggest that Canada compete in the wide world in order to get away from dependence on the United States, but then call for us to harmonize with—that is, convert to—U.S. rules. This would be more likely to shut us out of other markets by making us a secondary market shaped by the United States. And, of course, market rules are part and parcel of broader social rules. They have to do with the nature of fairness and inclusion.

I read documents like this with a determined hope that something new or original or risky is going to be said. Instead there is a curious atmosphere mixing entitlement with passivity, almost pessimism, which is even more curious given the report's call for a competitive spirit.

That same atmosphere surrounds most of our elites' attitudes toward the environment. While there are energy and ideas in the population, most of the leaders are worried that if we get ahead of the pack of developed countries on environmental reform or even keep up with them, we put ourselves at risk. But if the West is on the edge of turning toward a new economics, the worst place to be is behind. You want to be in the advance guard, if only because there is always great wealth creation when societies change direction.

Within a week of the hollowing-out competition report, a major Paris magazine ran a long interview with Paul Desmarais Sr., chair of Power Corporation, one of the largest investment groups in Canada. He was on the cover because he has international clout. He was in the advance guard of investors in China. His group controls strategic corporations on three continents. His tone is one of clarity, humour and self-confidence. You sense his long-term view. You may agree or disagree with his opinions, but this is what a business leader—indeed a capitalist—is supposed to sound like. If you then turn back to the lugubrious managerial report on hollowing-out, it is as if you have fallen into another world. One is active, the other passive. One wants to own, control, shape, carry its power around the world. The other wants stock options and thinks a meeting in New York is an assertion of global ambitions.

Our approach toward energy over the last quarter-century highlights that passive and frightened atmosphere. Think of our situation sequentially. First, with NAFTA, we sign an energy deal that guarantees the United States access to our resources at the level that meets their needs. We cannot reduce what we supply. This was meant to be a clever way to protect our markets. But it doesn't. It protects their access, not ours. They can cut back any time. We can't. Second, this leaves the eastern half of Canada dependent on unsecured imported energy. Third, cushioned by our short-term energy profits, we have since done less than almost any other democracy to develop alternate energy sources. Fourth, we have been selling off our unrenewable energy as fast as possible, while collecting as few royalties as possible. The theory is that an enriched business community will cause a general trickle-down to society. Instead, even Alberta has developed a rich-poor divide. Raw numbers aside, what does a growing rich-poor divide resemble? For a start, we might look at the number of jobs needed to support a family. Or we could judge the percentage of Canadians working weekends—in other words, the loss of the five-day workweek that it took a century to achieve. In 1990, 11 percent of Canadians worked weekends. Now more than 20 percent do. The government in Edmonton obscures its failures to spread wealth and build infrastructure by constantly fanning an *us against the rest of Canada* atmosphere. Meanwhile, fifth, the money drifts away, just as commodity money always does unless you carefully invest it. Yes, some big buildings are built in Calgary. But those are just buildings. They don't even represent infrastructure. Across the Atlantic, Norway, with a similar population, in the same petrodollar-rich situation, has been building up one of the world's largest investment funds and has become a player with international clout. Alberta remains a mere provincial source of raw materials and has won no influence at all outside of Canada. None. Zero. When you go to Norway, the difference is obvious. They have real infrastructure, have spread the money around the country and are investing in interesting projects around the world, in particular in the North. Sixth, as the environmental wave continues to rise and in particular begins to focus on the oil sands as a problem,

Alberta and Canada simply slump into denial. The old *us against them* routine, which works inside Canada, is coming to the fore. But outside Canada nobody is interested in the idea of Alberta as a victim. What they are interested in is the environment. As for the United States, if it decides to cleanse itself of dirty fuel, it will do so. Those in the business community who are true believers in the U.S. free market doctrine have neglected to notice that the power of the political mechanisms of the U.S. government is enormous. If it decides the oil sands are a symbol of dirty fuel that pollutes river systems and causes global warming, it will act accordingly. Washington may even choose the oil sands as an example of worldwide importance; an example the United States can set. After all, not exploiting the oil sands does not hurt U.S. jobs or the U.S. economy. And building a new U.S. energy profile will be a wealth-creating enterprise at home. Their home. We have two recent examples—the beef industry and the wood industry—of how that sort of politics works. There is, nevertheless, a persistent idea that if we can just fully integrate our economy into the U.S. economy, then we will disappear from their nationalist sights and so be protected. This is a perfect example of colonial naïveté. Besides, U.S. investment, or the lack of it, can as good as shut the oil sands down, with the knowledge that twenty or thirty years later the same corporate investors can change their minds. That is what they did with their oil and gas explorations of the 1970s. If you add up these six points, you have a perfect example of self-destructive policy making.

Energy is perhaps the most extreme example of the Canadian elite's seeming incapacity to act in an interesting or original manner. With proper royalties, urgent research could perhaps have altered the world's view of the oil sands and made Alberta an international centre of cutting-edge approaches to the greening of oil. Ethics aside, the best place to be when there is a change of direction is on the cutting edge. That's where money is made. The most expensive attitude is that of the defender of an unpopular old cause. With a sensible Heritage Fund investment policy, Alberta could have been a major international financial force, creating broadly based wealth at home while influencing the policies of others abroad. With a sensible east-west energy policy, Canada would be stable during the difficult economic times ahead, while Alberta would not have been shackled to policies set in Washington for U.S. purposes, which are not Edmonton purposes. All of these things were entirely possible—possible for a self-confident elite that wished to lead.

And it would still be possible, even today, to change the face of our beef, lumber and fish industries by taking a value-added approach. All it would require is the desire to own, invest, control and shape these industries in order that they earn at their full value. These are easy problems to solve.

As is homelessness. You put money into assisted housing. You focus on what kind of special housing assistance the half of the homeless population with mental health issues need. This costs a bit of money, but nothing compared to the ethical cost of humiliating a crucial mass of citizens; and nothing compared to what the current crisis is both costing us and losing us. That first step of creating housing makes a range of other practical steps possible.

Even health care is not such an obscure problem. You begin by removing the most obvious barriers—the shortages of doctors, nurses, beds and operating rooms. But you do it fast, as a broad intentional policy, not the way we are now. Having denied for years that that was the problem, our various governments, universities and medical associations are now moving in a painfully slow and uncoordinated way, all the while pretending that the real problem lies elsewhere, in our single-tier system. And while you are at it, you deal with health at schools, get rid of the junk food, multiply the exercise students do. This is a simple way to begin rethinking health care as being first about health, not sickness, and the first step toward increasing the prevention part of the health-care budget from its current 1 percent. Tommy Douglas's original health-care idea was all about balancing investments in health with investments in treatments for sickness. He was right about that from the beginning.

The point I'm making is that what we see as our problems are more often merely the result of our problems. We are a mid-sized, middle-class country living next to a behemoth. We need to take every advantage of every situation. We cannot afford to waste lives or be lazy and sloppy. We know we need better-educated students, intellectually prepared for a society in constant change. We need them to have the self-confidence to be open to questioning, to ideas, to risk. The skills of management and reactions are theoretically easy to put in place. The capacity to create and carry out strategies is a far more complicated matter. Management can only function at a high level when there is a powerful strategic capacity operating above it. To accomplish this, the emphasis in our education needs to be on content, on thinking. That means smaller classes, more teachers, more professors, more bilingual students, more trilingual students. We need our universities to be working hand in hand with our high schools. We need the opposite of call-centre education. The last thing we need to do is promote training over education. We can't afford that sort of unimaginative, mechanical approach. Yet that is exactly the approach we're taking. Or rather, we are putting a great deal of money into a small percentage of high-level positions, then flatlining the rest. On paper, this appears efficient. In reality, it is a provincial and unbalanced imitation of what we wrongly think to be the U.S. system. Whatever their system actually is, it has been shaped for a very different population and economy. Our current approach to education has heavy long-term costs, particularly, once again, in a mid-sized, middle-class democracy.

We still have no strategy on international university exchanges. We could, should be trying to get Canada into Europe's Erasmus Program, which in two decades has moved more than a million university students through exchanges across the continent. That would be a meaningful strategy if we seriously want to shift Canada out of our monolithic relationship with the United States toward something more balanced.

We have gone to a lot of trouble to create a body of professors. Yet we still insist on encouraging a form of tenure that shuts most of them into a quiet life, isolated from the society they should be helping to lead. This could be changed with a simple expansion of the qualifications for tenure. We need only add to the current three inward-looking qualifications one that is based on involvement in society at large. People have suggested it be called Social Impact.

These are not complicated or even original observations or suggestions I am making. Most of them are widely understood. Many of our difficult problems are not particularly difficult. The point that we need to be thinking about is what holds us back.

I dealt earlier with the origins of our faulty elite, its insecurity, its colonial cringe. I talked of how the British Law Lords undermined not the power of the federal government but the capacity of Canadians to act. Who today are the equivalent of the Law Lords? Who are their successors? The answer seems to be that a large part of our elite has inherited that fear of action, which has caused us to slip backward into the slough of charity.

Studies show that Western democracies that maintained their social programs over the last twenty-five years also maintained a large and healthy middle class. Those that cut back seriously saw their middle classes shrink—the United Kingdom, Sweden, the United States—and the rich-poor divide explode. Canada held on longer than most so that our middle class was spared. But slowly it is being pressed by the cuts imposed from the mid-1990s on. What this reminds us of, along with the rich-poor divide and the return of charity, is that egalitarianism is not a natural state of social organization—certainly not, at any rate, in the European tradition. It was not so in the Middle Ages or the Industrial Revolution. And even now, even in those countries in which there are careful protections for citizens, the slippage is always toward more sophisticated definitions of class. So the natural state of being in an organized society, certainly in the Western, Judeo-Christian, rational tradition, is likely to be one of division and of the celebration of disadvantage.

Perhaps our own focus on egalitarianism—and therefore on fairness—was so tied to our Aboriginal past and the long-standing poverty of our immigrant society of minorities that it could not survive as we became a wealthy commodity-dependent society, obsessed by our Western status. And we have never been as much that as we are today. Perhaps we have been irrevocably separated from our foundation. If so, we are a fragile society, unlikely to last much longer. Civilizations, no matter how old or how changed, are built upon their foundations. If they slip off, they collapse. That is the Haida warning: *The world is as sharp as a knife. If you don't watch out, you'll fall right off.*

That is why the collective unconscious has meaning. And that is why I cannot help but feel that the Canadian collective unconscious flows with a strong current. No matter how unconscious we have been of our origins, we have continued to act upon the basis of our original foundation, even if we have been unable to explain how we have come to put fairness and inclusion first in our self-image.

In some ways we are closer to our origins now than we have been for a long time. Twenty percent of Canadians are immigrants, which takes us back to the 1911–1931 period of heavy immigration. As in the past, almost half of Toronto is foreign-born. Now 16 percent of Canadians are part of visible minorities. All of that is bringing us closer to the way we were in the seventeenth and eighteenth centuries. We were a deeply complex mix and no one then could pretend that this was a particularly British place, as was done in the late nineteenth century.

Today, when other Western countries are developing largely "false fears," to use the Gérard Bouchard–Charles Taylor phrase, about the possible divisive effect of immigrant groups on society's cohesiveness, Canadians seem to be doing better than ever at making the emotional adjustments necessary to live together. Our failures, once again, have to do with our elites' incapacity to deal with administrative barriers to integration or adjustment, such as clarifying credential issues and providing enough long-term language training. It is almost as if our leaders and administrators wish to provoke, by their utilitarian immobility, an emotional backlash from the citizens, new and old.

A few localized and short-term flashpoints aside, this backlash has not come. And we do not find ourselves seeking to live in isolation in separated ethnic communities. In fact, multiculturalism operates—to the extent that it does operate—further and further away from its original meaning of *separate but together*. Established and new Canadians simply don't think of themselves that way. The demographer Michael Adams points out that there are no signs of *groups* trying to use *multiculturalism* as a legal concept to avoid becoming an integrated part of Canada's citizenry. Even Quebec's vastly preferable term of *intercul-turalisme* is beginning to sound a little too rigid to absorb the originality with which Canadians, whether francophone or anglophone, whether long established or recently arrived, are figuring out how to live together. The intellectual problem of defining nationality anywhere is always the same. It is relatively easy to define the ethical shape of a civilization. *Fair* and *inclusive* is a solid foundation. But social scientists—carried away by their image of themselves as scientists—would also like to define the social behaviour of each civilization. And they no sooner put a definition in place than the citizenry alter their social behaviour. That's why laws defining the meaning of words such as *multiculturalism* and *intercultur-alisme* rapidly become irrelevant or problematic, getting in the way as real people simply move on in their real lives and real relationships. In the meantime, however, I am much more comfortable using the term *interculturalisme* than *multiculturalism* to describe how Canada works. It isn't quite right, but it comes close.

What is fascinating, in Canada's development of an inclusive ethos out of the original Aboriginal model, is that only once in our history has an immigrant group garnered enough power to attempt to change the direction of Canada in its own interests. Perhaps the better way of saying this is that only once has an immigrant group believed it had both the right and the power to remake Canada in its own image. And that was attempted by the wave of Irish Protestants in the second half of the nineteenth century, with the soft support of the English immigrants. They saw Canada through British blinkers and brought with them a hatred of Catholics, a resulting angry incomprehension before the French-Canadian reality, a rejection of the possibility of Aboriginal culture and contempt for immigrants coming from other than Britain. To back them up, they had the energy and confidence drawn from the global power of the British Empire—then at its mytho-logical high point. It is hard to imagine today the emotional force of that globalist mythology, except that it had a similar effect to the U.S. mythology of today.

The outcome of their attempt to remake Canada was not entirely negative. But at its worst it included the European concept of the nation-state as a monolithic being. And this brought exclusionary race laws and anti-French educational restrictions and Aboriginal assimilation policies. Most damaging in the long run has been their success in erasing much of our conscious memory of Canada as an experiment, original in its adaptations to this place, with our métis mindset at the heart of that experiment. In its place, they attempted to lodge in everyone's mind that this was a European-derived civilization. Their attempt culminated with our explosive internal tensions during the First World War. But then their drive to change everything here slowly shrank back as the British began to fit in to Canada as a real place, while new immigrants from other places began to speak up and so changed the balance of power. Out of this shift came the opening of a new wave of ethical policies. And these allowed Canadians to focus on their country's deeper intent.

All of these earlier negative incidents lie far behind us. So far behind that we forget the extent to which their effect is still obscuring our understanding of Canada's real foundation. In spite of this we continue to draw closer to our original model. For example, we are now recreating that most basic métis atmosphere of early Canada, with the number of mixed-race couples growing five times faster than couples in general. The national number is still a little over 4 percent, but it is moving fast into the territory of a critical mass. Even more important, this métis factor is above all growing in the big cities, where it is at least 10 percent, creating an interesting link between our new urban life and the original Canadian reality. In some professional circles, it's more like 50 percent. Perhaps these new métis will in turn help to provoke those Aboriginal–new Canadian conversations that we so desperately need. But such conversations are not about mixing races. They are about a métis mindset, which could be seen as an embracing of social complexity.

When we talk about cohesion in Canada, it is not at all the same as talking about agreement. We still have a rough way of arriving at national or regional agreements. Our politics are rude and tough. That has always been the way. It is part of maintaining the tension between individuals and groups, between the national and the regional. Cohesion in a context of fairness and inclusion has always required a balance between individual and government action. This is a modern form of the old First Nations idea of the necessary tension between individualism and the group. That this is still working can be seen in the levels of volunteerism backed by personal donations. This is not old-fashioned charity, rightly condemned by New Brunswick poet Alden Nowlan:

> But, above all, I said, don't act
> from a desire to be loved. Don't ask
> so great a payment for your services.

Instead I believe it arises from a long-held belief that the state must do all the citizens can make it do. But in such a complicated place, with so much territory, such a climate, so many fresh arrivals, this will never be enough. And so volunteerism is in truth just a non-governmental form of citizen engagement. It is true these days that an epidemic of thank-youitis has overtaken us, creating the impression that we are dealing with self-interest and charity. In part, this is the result of corporate donation departments needing a formal public justification for their spending of shareholder money. But this, too, will pass and we will again be able to sit in seats and rooms dedicated to the public good, not to a fizzy drink or a cellphone.

Much more important is that every study shows new Canadians to be volunteering and donating as much as, often more than, other citizens. The ways in which this is done and the causes may vary, but 85 percent of those who come to Canada make donations, only one percentage point less than those born here.

What this testifies to is the success of our traditional immigration policy that invites to Canada people in need, refugees, the lesser educated. Even today they represent three-quarters of those who immigrate. The elite position is often that we should be concentrating on people with education and skills. Their belief is that we are now largely bringing in elites, and this conviction has coincided with their actions to weaken general public services available to those in need. This was particularly obvious in the severe 1990s cutbacks of theoretically *soft* aspects of public school education in favour of a narrower, more utilitarian approach. Those soft aspects of education were, in fact, the elements essential first to the adaptation of new Canadians and second to the development by all students of their historical, physical and ethical sense of the country. But there is no proof in our history that such an elite-oriented immigration policy would serve us better. We are a country built on working-class, farming and refugee immigrants. Our public school system and services have enabled these new Canadians to find their way as fast as possible. This immigration of the less fortunate goes back to the French Canadians, the Loyalists and to LaFontaine's first law as prime minister in 1848, aimed at supporting poor immigrants. That is our historic secret. We have not built Canada by robbing poorer countries of their scarce elites. We have done it by offering an opportunity to those with the courage to seize it and we have backed up our offer with government support programs and the more personal support of established citizen engagement.

Any part of our elite that gets in the way of such programs is standing in the way of our country's evolution. It is their responsibility to help, whether that involves paying taxes, personally volunteering, contributing to non-governmental programs or hiring new Canadians. One group that needs particular attention paid to it is made up of the thousands upon thousands of young new Canadians who have limited financial resources and no contacts. They need academic support in their education because their parents may be weak in English or French and may not have had an equivalent education. These young people need summer jobs. They need real jobs. They need a hand up. They need the friendship of established citizens to help them find their way into the mainstream of Canadian life.

There are those among us who will talk of how lucky immigrants are to be able to come to Canada. This sort of self-evident self-congratulation is not helpful to anyone. What is more interesting is to examine the heart of our secret method. We invite not immigrants but future citizens. More than 85 percent become citizens. This is more than double the U.S. rate and it is multiples higher than any European rate. In other words, our invitation is based on the assumption that the newcomer will quickly come into the circle and join our family. Immigration is an engagement leading to marriage. The psychological assumption is one of dignity based on the inevitability of a future family relationship. This is the old Aboriginal idea.

But there is a second, even deeper heart in our method. What we know is that most people who decide to change countries in order to build a new life have already shown themselves to be highly conscious and have proved a certain courage. No matter how impossible the situation at home, to leave it and make a new home requires conscious consideration and courage. Even the most desperate of refugees must struggle with such a profound change. It is that proven consciousness and courage that has driven Canada forward for centuries. There lies our real source of renewable energy.

In 2007, an apparent outbreak of nerves over immigration appeared in mainly small-town Quebec. And yet a year later two remarkable thinkers, Gérard Bouchard and Charles Taylor, produced a report that seemed to carry the ethos of Quebec. And what you could find in it was a classic expression of those original Canadian ideas of fairness and inclusion. "The wisest and most effective method of dealing with cultural differences is not to hide them but to show them." "A particular responsibility falls upon the ethno-cultural majority" to build relationships with immigrants. "Our society must struggle against under-employment, poverty, inequality, unacceptable conditions of life and forms of discrimination." And how are immigrants to be dealt with? On the basis of "four civic virtues." *Equité*—equity or fairness; *welcome*, getting to know *the other*; *moderation and wisdom*; *patience*. After all, such great changes of life require time in order to be digested by all sides. I can't think of a finer summary of the founding Canadian ideals of egalitarianism, inclusion and fairness within the circle of a welcoming community.

In fact, I can't think of a time in our modern history when Canadians, whatever their political or constitutional views, whatever their language or region, have been so aligned on their shared ethical foundations.

Part of this may indeed be because we have slowly over the last half-century begun to talk about our Aboriginal origins, even if we have tended to see it as a failure by non-Aboriginals and off to the side of our theoretical mainstream. Nevertheless, we have been less and less in denial of this historic reality. And even though we tend to deal with the rapid growth in the Aboriginal population above all as a *challenge*, meaning a problem, we know at some unconscious level that large groups of citizens cannot simply be discounted as a problem. Our democracy can't work that way. It would take very little now in the rethinking of how we imagine ourselves—all of us—to re-centre our civilization on that Aboriginal reality.

When I describe the tension between the individual and the group as an essential element of our ethic of fairness and inclusion, what is the implication? That if we are true to ourselves we are not engaged in a classic Euro-U.S. struggle between the citizen and the state. Rather, we are dependent on the personal engagement of the citizen, both as an individual and as a bulwark of the state.

If our elites are failing it is because they don't understand this model. They are fixated on the imported idea of oppositions. And so I find our education is increasingly one aimed at training loyal employees, even though the state and the corporations are increasingly disloyal. What we should be doing is quite different. It turns on our ability to rethink our education and our public expectations so that we create a non-employee, non-loyal space for citizenship. After all, a citizen is by definition loyal to the state because the state belongs to her or him. That is what frees the citizen to be boisterous, outspoken, cantankerous and, all in all, by corporatist standards, disloyal. This is key to the success of our democracy.

The Aboriginal idea of a circle is based upon that idea of tension. We need to redesign our education to do the same. When I say it needs to be about thinking, not training, I could equally say it needs to be about engagement and aggressive debate, not about smooth expertise and passive service.

One other element that is helping us along the way is the gradual rise of the voice and influence of people with what are traditionally thought of as disabilities. They share with immigrants the consciousness and courage that circumstances have forced upon them. They bring that force to the public table. In some cases the speed at which they bring it may be in some way slower than the managerial or productivity norm. But then speed has never been a characteristic of civilization. Even in war, speed is more often than not a characteristic of foolishness and immaturity. Consideration is the most often shared characteristic of a successful civilization. Speed brought us mad cow disease and fished-out oceans and global warming. The arrival of more conscious voices at the public tables, voices less likely to be swayed by fashion, is a step toward the ethic of fairness. In all of these examples—the Aboriginal, the immigrant and new Canadian, those with disabilities—the result is a certain toughness born of experience. They have a sense of strategy and an understanding of how to act. And that is where our society is now weakest.

If you examine the way the state organizes itself, you find that utilitarianism has reduced creative economics down to instrumental economics and even further down to classic bookkeeping. In this mindset, every action is a cost. The concept of investment is merely another cost. It is a non-conceptual approach that would have made every historic Canadian breakthrough in public policy appear to be an impossible extravagance.

It is this corner-store approach to cost that prevents us from dealing with poverty or health care or education. This is what shapes our narrow and short-term view of the environment. What is presented as *being careful with the public's money* is more often than not a simple failure of imagination. That means those in charge are frightened to act because real action can only be presented as a cost. This is not really an economic theory. It is well below theory. But if it were theory, it could be described as a linear approach to cost based on the assumption that society is driven by self-interest.

We built our society in quite a different way. Our ideas of fairness and inclusion have been based on an economic theory of investment, in which you create new possibilities of wealth by changing the conditions in which our society operates. To do this does take courage, consciousness, imagination, a taste for risk and an ethical sense of purpose. It is about conduct not contract. It is a way of thinking and acting.

What form could it take today? The most obvious strategic initiative from a governmental point of view would be to create what is usually called a guaranteed annual income. This is an idea that cuts across all political lines. It can satisfy an ethical fiscal conservative because it consolidates a vast range of bureaucratically cumbersome support programs into this one simple policy. A great deal of administrative waste is saved. It can satisfy classic socialists or social democrats because it is a policy that treats citizens with dignity. This is the opposite of the nosy managerial desire to dissect the details of the life of the poor. Instead, it can lift them out of poverty. Above all, it bears a family link to the long Canadian history of egalitarianism as a civilizational goal. Perhaps most interestingly, it could break down that public and private corporatist structure that makes people feel they are caught in a series of employee or dependent relationships.

What form could such a different approach take outside of government structures? It would depend on our ability to create citizen structures that are driven neither by profit nor by non-profit. Both of these are valuable and essential. But they fail to provide citizens with the space they need to function as engaged citizens.

Yes, there is a need to encourage much more citizen engagement in public causes. Canada is healthy by international standards at a national volunteer rate of 45 percent, although Quebec lags 11 percent behind that national average and 20 percent behind Saskatchewan and 16 percent behind Ontario and Manitoba. This is perhaps the inheritance of a statist Catholic Church passed on to a statist provincial government. By statist I mean the European model, in which there is little positive tension between the engaged citizen and the state. But Quebec compensates to some extent with other, more co-operative mechanisms such as the Caisse Desjardins. In any case, the national average itself is not high enough.

And on the private front there is a desperate need to develop the courage and energy of ownership and risk and cutting-edge action in every size of corporation. Our business schools need to be radically rethought or simply shut down. The last things we need are more managers or more consultants.

But the key to change in both the public and private sectors may lie in opening up another space for engagement. What would it look like? Its purpose would relate somehow to a shared public good. It would be free-standing and citizen based. It would create wealth, enrich citizens, reinvest profits, yet involve community stability.

In other words, such structures would avoid the weight of government, the short-term drive of the market and the passivity of charity. Unlike NGOs, it would not be focused on influence. It would be locally based and therefore feed off the energy of communities, yet belong to larger structures that could function at any level, regional, national, international.

In 1824, at the Sharon Temple just north of Toronto, the Children of Peace, a highly prosperous community of breakaway Quakers, created the Farmer's Storehouse. It was an early co-operative designed to band farmers together so that they could avoid the destruction caused by bank and merchant loans. It was, if you like, a co-operative agricultural marketing board. This idea re-emerged much later in the United Farmers movement and the Coop movement, including the Caisse Desjardins. In 1832, the Children of Peace created a permanent fund—a small loans credit union—with flexible terms and open credit. In the 1840s, this same group and their Sharon Temple—a magical building, miraculously still standing—became the centre of the anglophone democratic movement. They organized Robert Baldwin's campaigns. And when Orange Order mobs prevented Louis-Hippolyte LaFontaine's election in Terrebonne, he was welcomed into the Sharon Temple and elected in the constituency of York North.

I can't help but feel that the strategic key to our rediscovering our four-century-long path toward fairness and inclusion lies in a rethinking and relaunching of the co-operative movement. Over the last quarter-century, most co-ops and marketing boards have been pushed toward conforming with the managerial private sector. Our elite structures did everything they could to encourage this. It was a terrible mistake that undermined the space of citizenship and the idea of geography in an enormous country. We should instead have been experimenting with how to take this movement further away from the unimaginative conformity of the contemporary corporation. Here was an opportunity to build powerful, grassroots, citizen-based structures. These are organizations that can thrive on discussions, ideas and strategies. We should have been thinking, and still can, about how this model could both anchor our communities and help us move away from mass commodity extraction toward the highest levels of value-added production in any domain, whether related to commodities or not. This is equally true about our need to anchor ourselves as communities in our biggest cities. The employee atmosphere of the contemporary corporation or state undermines the idea of fairness, inclusion and an engaged citizenry.

Canadians do indeed live in the broad world and in a large country. But they also live precisely where they live. And if our economic and social system exists in denial of our physical reality, then our society simply won't function. That is the source of the frustration and anger that can be felt in smaller communities, but even in our cities, when people cannot imagine how to shape their communities, how to shape their democracy in a real way or how to create real long-term wealth.

None of what I am suggesting should be seen as a solution or an answer. These were simply what could be called expressions of common sense or common sense playing off our imagination and our ethics and our memory.

At the core of the Canadian civilization there do exist ideas used and shaped over four centuries. Our idea of citizenship as a circle that welcomes and adapts. Our conviction that fairness and inclusion are the keys to how we function. These also are simple ideas. But all successful civilizations are built upon simple realizations, usually dragged out of difficult circumstances. Our ideas are particular to our experience. But then the realizations of any civilization are built upon their personal and local experience. There is nothing universal in the national theories of our friends and allies except their ambition and capacity to convince others that these are universal theories. A citizen of China today or a citizen of Rwanda is as far away from the experiences of an eighteenth-century British parliamentarian or French revolutionary or American rebel as anyone could possibly be. Much farther, I would suggest, than from the experiences of those Canadian Aboriginals and immigrant minorities seeking desperately how to live and how to live together in the seventeenth and eighteenth centuries in difficult circumstances. Canada has no model for the world. But the long Canadian experiment with complexity and fairness has never appeared more modern.

NOTES

PART I: A MÉTIS CIVILIZATION

1. WHAT SHAPED US

p. 5 **As Sandra Laronde of Red Sky Theatre**
Sandra Laronde, onstage conversation at Luminato: Toronto Festival of Arts and Creativity, Toronto, 8 June 2008.

2. MARRYING UP

p. 11 **The strength of the Acadians**
Nicolas Landry and Nicole Lang, *Histoire de l'Acadie* (Sillery, QC: Septentrion, 2001), 49–52.

p. 11 **This was "calculated to mediate"**
Jeannette Armstrong, "Early Relations Between the Okanagan and Settler: A Missed Opportunity for a Civilized Colonial Process," paper presented at the Fifth Galway Conference on Colonialism: Settler Colonialism, Galway, Ireland, June 2007.

p. 15 **James Douglas found**
Jean Barman, *The West Beyond the West: A History of British Columbia*, rev. ed. (Toronto: U of T Press, 1996), 46–47, 85.

3. DOUBLE DENIAL

p. 21 **Renée Dupuis, chief commissioner**
Conversation, 19 August 2007. "L'histoire de l'Amérique du nord n'est pas encore écrit. Elle est écrite en anglais du point de vue anglophone et de ses origines coloniales, francophone du point de vue français et colonial, etc. Une des raisons qu'on n'arrive pas à s'en sortir c'est qu'on n'arrive pas à la manière collective de regarder ensemble les racines. On est toujours sur les racines colonisateurs."

p. 21 **Author Thomas King**
Thomas King, *The Truth About Stories* (Toronto: Anansi, 2003), 2.
Tomson Highway, onstage conversation at Luminato: Toronto Festival of Arts and Creativity, Toronto, 8 June 2008.

p. 22 **To put this in the straightforward language**
Jack Sissons, *Judge of the Far North: The Memoirs of Jack Sissons* (Toronto: McClelland & Stewart, 1968), 65.

p. 22 **I give these historic but practical examples**
Thomas King, *A Short History of Indians in Canada* (Toronto: Harper Perennial, 2005), 12–13.

p. 23 **By the end of the nineteenth century**
"Report of the Royal Commission on Aboriginal Peoples" (Ottawa: Canada Communications Group, 1996). See Vol 1, Ch 2: "From Time Immemorial: A Demographic Profile"; See also Ronald Wright's classic *Stolen Continents: Conquest and Resistance in the Americas* (Toronto: Penguin, 1992). An eloquent description of the European treatment of the First Nations.

pp. 23–24 **In the words of Mi´kmaq poet Rita Joe**
Native Poetry in Canada, eds. Jeannette C. Armstrong and Lally Grauer (Peterborough, ON: Broadview, 2001), 17.

p. 24 **In 1996, the Royal Commission on Aboriginal Peoples**
"Report of the Royal Commission," Vol 3: Gathering Strength, 57, 59, 60.

p. 24 **Two Inuit elders**
Interviewing Inuit Elders, Volume 2: Perspectives on Traditional Law, eds. Jarich Oosten, Frédéric Laugrand, and Wim Rasing (Iqaluit: Nunavut Arctic College, 2002), 26, 27, 50.

p. 25 **"Treaty promises were part of the foundation"**
"Report of the Royal Commission," Vol 2, Pt 1, Ch 2: Treaties, 37.

p. 26 **Twice in his ruling**
Delgamuukw Case, 1997, paras 85 and 106.

4. WHY WE STUMBLE

p. 27 **It justified this sort of language**
Amor de Cosmos, *British Colonist*, 8 March 1861.

p. 30 **John Mills Jackson wrote**
John Mills Jackson, "A View of the Political Situation of the Province of Upper Canada."

p. 31 **And there they were**
King, *The Truth*, 79.

p. 31 **"I have never yet heard"**
Quoted in a fascinating book by Daniel Coleman, *White Civility: The Literary Project of English Canada* (Toronto: U of T Press, 2006), 61.

p. 32 **What this demonstrated**
There is a good description of this collision in Robert S. Allen, *His Majesty's Indian Allies* (Toronto: Dundurn, 1992), 202–5.

p. 32 **And so Thomas King asks**
King, *The Truth*, 121.

p. 33 **The Aboriginal response to the sympathetic pessimism**
Jeannette Armstrong, "Early Relations."

p. 33 **He puts it down instead**
Jack Anawak in *Nunatsiaq News*, 18 October 2002, 14.

pp. 33–34 **Octavio Paz argues that**
Octavio Paz, *The Labyrinth of Solitude*, trans. Lysander Kemp, Yara Milos, and Rachel Phillips Belash (New York: Grove, 1985), 362.

5. LEARNING TO SEE OURSELVES

p. 38 **Aboriginals considered any society**
See, for example, C.E.S. Franks, "In Search of the Savage *Sauvage*: An Exploration into North America's Political Cultures," *The American Review of Canadian Studies* (Winter 2002): 556.

p. 38 **Writer John Jennings has demonstrated**
John Jennings, *The Canoe: A Living Tradition* (Toronto: Firefly, 2002).

p. 40 **It became the British-Loyalist-Canadien strategy**
See especially Allen, *His Majesty's Indian Allies.*

p. 41 **It is all about harmony**
See "Report of the Royal Commission," Vol 2, Pt 1, Ch 3: Governance, in a paper by Greg Johnson of Eskasoni discussing arguments made by the Mohawk philosopher Taiaiake Alfred, 9, 111–12, 117.

6. PROGRESS

p. 45 **One-third to one-half of the men**
See Franks, "In Search of" from page 565 onwards, but the entire essay is very useful and of a parallel relevance.

p. 48 **The second has been laid**
Hugh Brody, *The Other Side of Eden: Hunters, Farmers and the Shaping of the World* (Vancouver: Douglas & McIntyre, 2002), 6–7, 97–8, 123, 306. See also Jennings, *The Canoe,* 18–19.

p. 49 **In Jeannette Armstrong's words**
Armstrong, "History Lesson," in *Native Poetry,* 110.

p. 49 **And they needed to see themselves**
Jennings, *The Canoe,* 18.

p. 51 **In all of their formal sessions**
The description of Cree words, here and later, are drawn largely from a fascinating conversation among Saskatchewan Elders in *Treaty Elders of Saskatchewan,* by Harold Cardinal and Walter Hildebrandt (Calgary: University of Calgary Press, 2000). In particular, I am drawing from Elders Simon Kytwayhat, Jacob Bill, Norman Sunchild, Peter Waskahat, Danny Musqua, Gordon Oakes, Jimmy Myo, among others, and Judge David M. Arnot, then treaty commissioner for Saskatchewan.

p. 51 **One of the oldest Inuit traditions**
Robert G. Williamson, "In the Search for 'A People': The Inuit, their Habitat, and Economic Politics," in *Self-Determination: International Perspectives.* eds. Donald Clark and Robert Williamson (London: Macmillan, 1996), 313.

7. LEARNING TO IMAGINE OURSELVES

pp. 57–58 **Marie Brent, from a well-known B.C. Métis family**
Armstrong, "Early Relations."

p. 58 **In 1623, Brother Gabriel Sagard**
Franks, "In Search of," 555, 556.

p. 58 **As Leonard Nelson of the Roseau River Anishinabe**
"Report of the Royal Commission," Vol 2, Pt 1, Ch 3: Governance, 115.

p. 58 **This balance of individualism**
"Report of the Royal Commission," Vol 2, Pt 1, Ch 3: Governance, 119.

p. 58 **According to Nisga'a leader Joseph Gosnell**
Dr. Joseph Gosnell, "A First Nation, Again: The Return of Self-government and Self-reliance in Canada's Nisga'a Nation," speech to the Harvard Faculty Club, Cambridge, MA, 3 March 2003.

p. 59 **For example, Inuit women tended**
"Report of the Royal Commission," Vol 2, Pt 1, Ch 3: Governance, 122–25.

p. 61 **Many of the nations had ritual adoption**
Allan Greer, *Mohawk Saint-Catherine Tekakwitha and the Jesuits* (New York: Oxford University Press, 2005), 13–14.

p. 62 **Guy Buchholtzer, an independent scholar**
Guy P. Buchholtzer, "Multiculturalism and Canada's Pacific Northwest Coast Aboriginal Societies: An Overview in Context," *Intercultural Communications Studies* 5 (February 2002): 121–36. See especially 124, 125, 129, 131.

p. 62 **The royal commission pointed out**
"Report of the Royal Commission," Vol 2, Pt 1, Ch 3: Governance, 238.

pp. 62–63 **"We are," Thomas King says**
King, *The Truth*, 24–25.

p. 63 **He is us.**
See, for example, Michael Angel, *Preserving the Sacred* (Winnipeg: University of Manitoba Press, 2002), 21–24.

p. 64 **Our non-monolithic idea of society**
Cardinal and Hildebrandt, *Treaty Elders*, 14–18.

p. 65 **And negotiations were all about**
Jean-Pierre Morin, "Peace, Order and Good Government: Indian Treaties and Canadian Nation Building," paper presented at the "First Nations, First Thoughts" Conference, U of Edinburgh, 5–6 May 2005.

p. 67 **Jean Friesen, the historian**
Conversation, 22 August 2007. See also her paper "Magnificent Gifts: The Treaties of Canada with the Indians of the Northwest 1869–76," *Transactions of the Royal Society of Canada* 5.1 (1986): 41–51, which brilliantly pulls many of these elements together. A key book that lays out this process of adaptation is Arthur J. Ray, Jim Miller and Frank J. Tough, *Bounty and Benevolence: A History of Saskatchewan Treaties* (Montreal and Kingston: McGill-Queen's Press, 2000).

p. 67 **Renée Dupuis, chief commissioner**
Conversation, 19 August 2007. "Dans le système juridique, les racines autochtones sont dans les racines des deux autres qui sont mélangées." See also Renée Dupuis, *Le Statut Juridique des Peuples Autochtones en Droit Canadien* (Scarborough: Carswell, 1999), Chapter 3, in particular 87.

p. 68 **You will find this idea of consensus**
For example, *Mohawk Saint*, 97.

p. 68 **During the Mackenzie Pipeline debate**
Mel Watkins, "My Own Personal North," unpublished paper, 2006.

p. 68 **But their concern and a more general concern**
For an interesting comment, see "Report of the Royal Commission," Vol 2, Pt 1, Ch 3: Governance, 134–36.

p. 69 **Here an approach was developed**
See an interesting interpretation in *Treaty Implementation: Fulfilling the Covenant* (Saskatoon: Office of the Treaty Commission, 2007), 116–222.

p. 70 **"The issue was not one of contract"**
Bill Henderson, a lawyer well known in the area of Aboriginal legal work, in his "Annotations" on the *Guerin* case.

p. 71 **Decades before, Justices**
William G. Morrow, *Northern Justice: the Memoirs of Justice William G. Morrow*, ed. W.H. Morrow (Toronto: U of T Press, 1995), 201.

p. 73 **He "viewed his work"**
Alexander John Watson, *Marginal Man: The Dark Vision of Harold Innis* (Toronto: U of T Press, 2006), 399–400.

p. 74 **"A shift from oral to written"**
Robert Bringhurst, *A Story as Sharp as a Knife* (Vancouver: Douglas & McIntyre, 1999), 193.

p. 74 **If you come from the oral tradition**
Brody, *The Other Side of Eden*, 205.

p. 75 **Taiaiake Alfred is an Aboriginal philosopher**
Taiaiake Alfred, *Wasáse: Indigenous Pathways of Action and Freedom* (Peterborough, ON: Broadview Press, 2005), 2, 3, 4, 5.

p. 75 **A very different indigenous philosopher**
Dale Turner, *This Is Not a Peace Pipe: Towards a Critical Indigenous Philosophy* (Toronto: U of T Press, 2006). Quoted in Taiaiake Alfred, 200.

p. 77 **This in turn was to be seen**
Leon E. Trakman, William Cole-Hamilton and Sean Gatien, "R. v. Oakes 1986–1997: Back to the Drawing Board," *Osgoode Hall Law Journal* 36.1 (1998): 83–149; Andrée Lajoie and Henry Quillinan, "The Supreme Court Judges' Views of the Role of the Courts in the Application of the Charter" in *Protecting Rights and Freedoms: Essays on the Charter's Place in Canada's Political, Legal, and Intellectual Life*, eds. Philip Bryden, Steven Davis, and John Russell (Toronto: U of T Press, 1994), 102, 101, 99.

8. THE MINIMAL IMPAIRMENT OF THE ENVIRONMENT

p. 81 **More precisely, the southern, urban, human-centred**
Stephen J. Augustine, "A Culturally Relevant Education for Aboriginal Youth," master's thesis, Carleton University, 1998. Augustine is a native history researcher for the Canadian Museum of Civilization and hereditary chief on the Mi'kmaq Grand Council.

p. 83 **The concept of government as "our way of life"**
"Report of the Royal Commission," Vol 2, Pt 1, Ch 3: Governance, 118.
"Treaty Implementation," 18. Elder Peter Waskahat is from the Frog Lake First Nation.

p. 83 **As Big Bear put it**
Big Bear, quoted in Rudy Wiebe, *Big Bear*, Extraordinary Canadians series (Toronto: Penguin, 2008).

pp. 83–84 **In case this does not sufficiently**
Quoted in King, *The Truth*, 114.

pp. 84 **It is a philosophy centred on how things**
"Report of the Royal Commission," Vol 5, "Renewal: A Twenty-Year Commitment," Appendix C.

p. 85 **Then in a moment of straight violence**
Charles G.D. Roberts, *The Heart of the Ancient Wood*, intro. Thomas Hodd (Halifax: Formac Publishing, 2007), xiv.

p. 86 **Meanwhile, people around the world**
Tim Flannery, *An Explorer's Notebook* (Toronto: HarperCollins, 2007).

9. MINIMAL IMPAIRMENT ON THE BATTLEFIELD

p. 90 **In 1753, when it looked as if they might lose**
Quoted in Wright, *Stolen Continents*, 133.
Allen, *His Majesty's Indian Allies*, 13. The entire book lays out the First Nations' role.

p. 94 **We wanted "greater consultation"**
John English, *The Worldly Years: The Life of Lester Pearson*, Vol II (Toronto: Knopf, 1992), 108, 116, 121, 145. English, in his remarkable biography, lays out how the modern form of this consultation strategy took form.

p. 94 **Gunnar Jahn, the chair of the Nobel**
Ibid., 145.
See also Andrew Cohen, *Lester B. Pearson*, Extraordinary Canadians series (Toronto: Penguin, 2008).

10. WITHIN AN EVER-ENLARGING CIRCLE

p. 98 **David Arnot, for a long time**
Treaty Implementation, 56. See also Cole Harris, *Making Native Space* (Vancouver: UBC Press, 2002), for example, 323: "In my optimistic moments, I almost convince myself that this province [B.C.] and country are finally coming to terms with what they are."

p. 99 **It was wonderfully laid out**
Quoted in Robert Bringhurst, *The Tree of Meaning* (Kentville, NS: Gaspereau, 2006), 191.

p. 99 **"The Nisga'a people"**
Gosnell, "A First Nation Again."

p. 99 **Robert Bringhurst: Our "literature"**
Thérèse Rigaud, *Translating Haida Poetry: An Interview with Robert Bringhurst* (Vancouver: Douglas & McIntyre, 2002), 21.

p. 100 **Some thirty-five years ago**
Native Poetry, 1. From *Akwesasne Notes*, 1970.

p. 102 **As we struggle with the complexity**
"Report of the Royal Commission," Vol 5, "Renewal: A Twenty-Year Commitment," Appendix C.

p. 103 **In the words of James Dumont**
"Report of the Royal Commission," Vol 4, Ch 3: "Elders' Perspectives," 114.

p. 104 **James Prentice, a few years before**
James Prentice, before the Canadian Bar Association, 28 April 2000.

PART II: PEACE, FAIRNESS AND GOOD GOVERNMENT

11. ONE WORD

p. 115 **In 1489, he instructed**
With particular thanks to Ian Wilson for this idea and information. See G.R. Elton, *The Tudor Constitution, Documents and Commentary* (Cambridge: The University Press, 1960), 462–63: *An act for justices of the peace, for the due execution of their commissions* (1489: 4 Henry VII, c. 12); And in general for the research in Part II, many thanks to Chief Justice, the Right Honourable Beverley McLachlin; the Honourable J.E. Côté, Justice of Appeal, Alberta; Ian Wilson, National Archivist, who has worked with me on these sources for years now; Patricia Kennedy and Timothy Dubé of the National Archives.

12. COLONIAL FAIRNESS

p. 117 **This led to a local disagreement**
W.P.M. Kennedy, *Statutes, Treaties and Documents of the Canadian Constitution 1713–1929* (Toronto: Oxford University Press, 1930), 9.

p. 117 **And there in late 1763**
This text is often thought to be lost. See Major-General R.H. Mahon, *Life of General The Hon. James Murray, A Builder of Canada* (London: John Murray, 1921), esp. Ch 14.

p. 120 **That is what Claude Lévi-Strauss meant**
Bringhurst, *The Tree of Meaning, 105.* See also *A Story as Sharp as a Knife.*

p. 123 **Their names appeared on the treaties**
See, for example, Patricia Dumas, master's thesis, York University, 2004. "La naissance de la traduction officielle au Canada et son impact politique et culturel sous le gouvernement militaire et civil du général James Murray, Québec (septembre 1759 à juin 1766)."

p. 124 **Today we often describe this**
Matthieu Richard, *Happiness* (London: Atlantic, 2007), 108, 171.

p. 127 **At the same time, then as now**
George Elliott Clarke, *Odysseys Home: Mapping African-Canadian Literature* (Toronto: U of T Press, 2002), 12, 74.

p. 128 **Smith avoided recommending change.**
See the biography of Sir James Monk in the *Dictionary of Canadian Biography.*

p. 129 **In *The Book of the Bible Against Slavery***
See Clarke, *Odysseys Home*, 93–94.

p. 132 **As had been clarified in Canada**
See on this Frank Underhill, *In Search of Canadian Liberalism* (Toronto: Macmillan, 1960).

p. 134 **"All the histories of all peoples"**
Octavio Paz, *The Labyrinth of Solitude*, trans. Lysander Kemp, Yara Milos, and Rachel Phillips Belash (New York: Grove, 1985), 291.

p. 135 **A week after the victory**
Letters of Agar Adamson, 1914 to 1919 (Nepean, ON: CEF Books, 1997).

p. 135 **The story of slavery**
See L'Hon. Sir L.H. LaFontaine and L'Honorable D.B.Viger, "De L'Esclavage en Canada" in *Mémoires et documents relatifs à l'histoire du Canada* (Montreal: La Société Historique de Montréal, 1859); Marcel Trudel, *L'esclavage au Canada Français* (Quebec: les Presses Universitaires Laval, 1960); Robin W. Winks, *The Blacks in Canada* (Montreal and Kingston: McGill-Queen's Press, 1971); James W. St. G. Walker, *The Black Loyalists: The Search for a Promised Land in Nova Scotia and Sierra Leone* (Toronto: U of T Press, 1992); Clarke, *Odysseys Home*; Lawrence Hill, *The Book of Negroes* (Toronto: HarperCollins, 2007).

p. 138 **He meant "harmonized"**
Thomas Jefferson, Second Inaugural Address, 4 March 1805.

pp. 138–39 **He argued that the United States**
Ibid.

p. 139 **James Madison was the U.S. public figure**
The Federalist Papers, No. 45, intro. Clinton Rossiter (New York: New American Library, 1961), 290.

p. 139 **He saw "the universe as a harmonious system"**
Frederick S.J. Copleston, *A History of Philosophy* (New York: Doubleday, 1985), Vol IV, 266–67; Vol V, 172.

p. 139 **The architect Douglas Cardinal**
See also Douglas Cardinal and Jeannette Armstrong, *The Native Creative Process* (Penticton, BC: Theytus, 1991), 12.

p. 139 **It was an all-inclusive view**
See, for example, Patrick Macklem, *Indigenous Difference and the Constitution of Canada* (Toronto: U of T Press, 2001), Conclusion; and Allan Greer, *Mohawk Saint; Catherine Tekakwitha and the Jesuits* (New York: Oxford University Press, 2005), 33.

13. IMAGINING A FAIR COUNTRY

p. 141 **It involved serious taxes or duties**
Provincial Statues of Canada, Vol III, First Session, Third Parliament (Montreal: Stewart Derbishire and George Debarats, 1848). With thanks to and in memory of Dr. Henry Best.

p. 144 **He was referring to the utopian idea**
Débats parlementaires sur la Confédération (Quebec: Hunter, Rose et Lemieux, 1865), 59. "Une nationalité politique indépendante de l'origine nationale, ou de la religion d'aucun individu." "Nous sommes de races différentes, non pas pour

nous faire la guerre, mais afin de travailler conjointement à notre propre bien-être." See also La très honorable Beverley McLachlin, "Dualité Linguistique et Pluralisme," Les Conférences J. Fernand Landry, 8 March 2004.

p. 144 **This is what Harold Innis**

Harold Innis, "Political Economy in the Modern State," *Political Economy in the Modern State* (Toronto: U of T Press, 1946), 132–33.

Madam Justice Rosalie Silberman Abella, "A battle that never ends," *Globe and Mail* (Toronto), 5 July 2003, A15.

p. 146 **The philosopher Will Kymlicka**

For example, Will Kymlicka, *Liberalism, Community and Culture* (Oxford: Clarendon, 1989).

p. 147 **They concluded that more should be made**

Gérard Bouchard and Charles Taylor, *Fonder L'Avenir: Le temps de la conciliation* (Quebec: Gouvernement du Quebec, 2008), 20, 242, 265. See also a very fine and complete report on interculturalisme by Professors François Rocher, Micheline Labelle, Ann-Marie Field and Jean-Claude Icart of UQAM: "Le Concept d'inter-culturalisme en contexte Québécois : Généalogie d'un néologisme," 21 December 2007. See especially pages 6, 9, 10, 11, 12, 14, 18, 21, 22, 24, 26, 27 38, 39, 46, 49 on the real similarity of interculturalisme and multiculturalism.

p. 152 **This sounds more like a continuation**

Anthony Kroeger, *Hard Passage: A Mennonite Family's Long Journey from Russia to Canada* (Edmonton: U of A Press, 2007), 183. Kroeger offers a wonderful portrait of the Mennonite immigration story.

p. 153 **In September 1864**

Again, with particular thanks in this section to the Chief Justice, the Right Honourable Beverley McLachlin; the Honourable J.E. Côté, Justice of Appeal Alberta; Ian Wilson, National Archivist; Patricia Kennedy and Timothy Dubé of the National Archives. Great thanks to Stephen Eggleston for his remarkable work in this area. His essay "The Myth and Mystery of POgG" (*Journal of Canadian Studies*, Winter 1996–97) was a major breakthrough. Also to Jordan Birenbaum, for his continuing work in this area and his very fresh analyses, in particular his international comparisons. As for myself, I began looking at this question in this period during the 1990s. I feel that when the work of this group is put together we have a solid base, for the first time, from which to understand what happened in the 1860s around Welfare versus Order and what the implications were.

p. 155 **"Nothing," he wrote, "will satisfy"**

Murray to Lords of Trade, 29 October 1764.

p. 155 *Welfare* **was used to describe**

Jordan Birenbaum at the University of Ottawa has compared the uses of Order and Welfare throughout the British Empire.

p. 156 **They said it referred to the scope**

Deb v Roy (1942) L.R. 69 IA.76, 90 (P.C. [Cal.]).

p. 156 **A clear sign that this is independence**

With thanks to Timothy Dubé at the National Archives.

14. ORDER AND FEAR, FEAR AND ORDER

p. 160 **"Symmetry in any narrative"**

Northrop Frye, *The Great Code* (New York: Harcourt, Brace, Jovanovich, 1982), 43.

p. 164 **"But we felt not less"**

Richard Burdon Haldane: An Autobiography (New York: Doubleday, Doran, 1929), 101–2.

p. 164 **His job was "to make the part"**

Jean Graham Hall and Douglas F. Martin, *Haldane: Statesman Lawyer Philosopher* (Chichester, U.K.: Barry Rose Law Publishers, 1996), 174. See also 76–78, 170–79.

15. THE EDDY LINE OF FAIRNESS

p. 167 **They saw them as tools**

Katherine Fierlbeck, *Political Thought in Canada: An Intellectual History* (Peterborough, ON: Broadview, 2006), 71.

pp. 167–68 **There in 1902**

Paul Whitney, "A Refuge and a Sanctuary: Vancouver's Carnegie Library as Civic Space," paper presented at the Canadian Academy of Independent Scholars Symposium, Vancouver, 25 May 2008.

p. 168 **There she was in 1915**

Nellie McClung, *In Times Like These* (Toronto: U of T Press, 1972), 97. Originally published in 1915.

p. 168 **Striding back and forth on stage**

Charlotte Gray, *Nellie McClung*, Extraordinary Canadians series (Toronto: Penguin, 2008), 105.

p. 169 **"The land and the myths"**

Shlawtxan (1860–1935), "So goes the Myth," quoted in Bringhurst, *A Story*, 371.

PART III: THE CASTRATI

17. SIGNS OF FAILURE

p. 180 **Even then you would have to examine**

2004 numbers in a study co-authored by Dr. Joel Lexchin of York University, 2008.

p. 188 **The playwright René-Daniel Dubois**

Daniel et René-Daniel Dubois, *Entretiens Janvier–Avril 2005* (Montreal: Leméac, 2006), 79–83.

p. 199 **In 2007, $15.3 billion was drawn out**

See Andrew Nikiforuk, "Alberta's Gamble with Gambling," *The Walrus*, November 2006. See also "Catholic bishop says all bets are off," *Globe and Mail* (Toronto), 23 June 2006.

p. 201 **The historian Jocelyn Létourneau**

Jocelyn Létourneau, *Que Veulent Vraiment les Québécois?* (Montreal: Boréal, 2006), 147. "Pour permettre à la société québécoise de poursuivre sa route, il est certainement nécessaire … de cesser de la concevoir comme étant en crise, au bord de l'effondrement, en voie d'être absorbée, glissant sur une pente descendante ou à la veille de disparaître.…"

p. 201 **Roy Romanow, the former premier**
Roy Romanow, "A House Half Built," *The Walrus*, June 2006.

p. 204 **"Why take risks when there are people"**
Robert Milton, quoted in *Toronto Star*, 9 February 2008, B1.

p. 207 **Nothing prevented our owners and managers**
International Herald Tribune, 16 November 2007, 14.

p. 210 **In February 2008, a study prepared**
The report was prepared by Secor Consulting for the Federal Competition Policy Review Panel. See also an interview given by the Secor chairman Ken Smith in *Globe and Mail* (www.globeadvisor.com), 27 February 2008.

p. 212 **This is one of those cases**
See, for example, *Financial Post*, 2 February 2008, online. Even someone obsessed by the ideology of marketplace freedom found this transaction inconceivable in a normal world.

p. 213 **When you lose ownership**
For a thorough analysis of this, see *Globe and Mail* (Toronto), 21 February 2008, "Report on Business," 1, 6.

18. WHAT DOES ALL OF THIS MEAN?

pp. 215–16 **Thomas Caldwell, one of our leading investment advisors**
Toronto Star, 28 July 2007, ID8.

p. 216 **"A head office of a subsidiary"**
Scott Hand, 19 February 2007, Action Canada evening. Dominic D'Alessandro, ibid.

p. 216 **These protected employees, who rarely leave**
The Conference Board of Canada, February 2008 Report: "Hollowing Out—Myth and Reality."

p. 216 **The economists in the Ministry of Finance**
3 May 2007. Confidential briefing for the deputy finance minister. See *Globe and Mail* (Toronto), 20 June 2007, 1.

p. 218 **As the philosopher Hannah Arendt**
Hannah Arendt, *Considérations morales* (Paris: Rivages, 1993), 26–27. Originally published in *Social Research* (1971): "Thinking and Moral Considerations: A Lecture." ("Les clichés, les phrases toutes faites, l'adhésion à des codes d'expression ou de conduite conventionnels et standardisés, ont socialement la fonction reconnue de nous protéger de la réalité, de cette exigence de pensée que les événements et les faits éveillent en vertu de leur existence.")

p. 218 **And using those very public numbers**
Erin K. Weir, "Lies, Damned Lies, and Trade Statistics: North American Integration and the exaggeration of Canadian Exports," *Canadian-American Public Policy*, 63 (July 2005).

p. 221 **Meanwhile, *The New York Times***
New York Times, 24 October 2006.

19. HOW DID THEY COME TO BE THIS WAY?

p. 225 **Tom Kent immigrated to this country**
Conversation with Tom Kent, Kingston, ON, 25 June 2007.

20. THE COLONIAL MIND

p. 230 **Or, in the words of economist**
Amartya Sen, *Identity and Violence* (New York: W.W. Norton, 2006), 89.

p. 232 **Roy MacGregor laid this out**
Canadians: A Portrait of a County and Its People (Toronto: Viking, 2007), 134–139.

p. 233 **Theirs was to be what Northrop Frye**
Northrop Frye, Conclusion to "A Literary History of Canada." *The Bush Garden: Essays on the Canadian Imagination* (Toronto: Anansi, 1971), 213–51. Originally published in 1965.

p. 234 **But perhaps because he saw culture**
Ibid., 219, 233.

p. 237 **Emily Carr described the English-born**
Emily Carr, *The Book of Small* (Toronto: Clarke Irwin, 1966), 116. Originally published in 1951.

p. 238 **The female explains to the still-confused male**
James De Mille, *A Strange Manuscript Found in a Copper Cylinder* (Toronto: McClelland & Stewart 1996), 116. Originally published in 1888.

p. 241 **LaFontaine in 1840**
"C'est une erreur trop générale de la part des partis politiques, dans les colonies, que de croire qu'ils ont de la sympathie à attendre de tel ou tel ministère Impérial."

21. TWO COLONIAL TALES

p. 247 **A few years later, in 1860**
Wilfrid Eggleston, *The Queen's Choice* (Ottawa: NCC, 1961), 129.

p. 247 **And he brought it all together**
David B. Knight, *Choosing Canada's Capital: Conflict Resolution in a Parliamentary System* (Ottawa: Carleton University Press, 1991).

p. 248 **In *The Unfinished Canadian***
Andrew Cohen, *The Unfinished Canadian: The People We Are* (Toronto: McClelland & Stewart, 2007).

p. 250 **At the core of the colonial mindset**
I want to particularly thank three people for what I say in this section. The general interpretation is mine. But Father Yves Abran was remarkably generous with his time and his research skills. It is thanks to him that I understood the role and the implications of Zachariah 9:10. I would also like to thank Old Testament scholar Walter Deller for helping me to understand the implications of the use of

Psalm 72. And the Most Reverend Michael Peers for, as ever, his guidance and sense of meaning. And finally Jean-Pierre Lussier, p.s.s., Directeur, Département des livres rares, Université Culturel de Saint-Sulpice, Grand Séminaire de Montréal; also there, Marie-Hélène de Montigny.

p. 251 **As for the insecure colonial-minded**
Ravi J. Gunno, "La Constitution canadienne en traduction: quelques pistes de réflexion." This essay is a good example of the foolishness of a certain school of translation, then as now.

p. 253 **Besides, as a still indignant**
See Gunno. See also *Translators Through History*, eds. Jean Deliste and Judith Woodsworth (UNESCO: John Benjamins Publishing Co., 1995), Ch 5.

p. 255 **And within four years of Confederation**
Alastair Sweeny, *George-Étienne Cartier* (Toronto: McClelland & Stewart, 1976), 180. Sweeny's interpretation of Cartier is the best there is.

p. 258 **And in 1951**
See the debate in the House of Commons, 8 Nov 1951.

22. THE ROOTS OF FAILURE

p. 261 **Only one journalist—James Travers**
Toronto Star, 16 February 2008, A15. And 3 April 2008, A6.

pp. 261–62 **The Globe and Mail's Jeffrey Simpson**
Globe and Mail (Toronto), 6 January 2006, A15; 21 January 2006, F1; 16 February 2007, A17.

p. 266 **In 1878, he launched his new policy**
Speech in the House of Commons, 14 March 1878.

p. 268 **In René Lévesque's 1968 "An Option for Québec"**
René Lévesque, *Option Québec* (Montreal: Éditions de l'homme, 1968).

p. 271 **To use a phrase of the writer**
Alain Dubuc, *La Presse* (Montreal), 28 October 2007, A17.

p. 272 **In Christopher Hume's words**
Christopher Hume, *Toronto Star*. See 6 July 2007, A8, and 23 July 2007, A9. In these two columns he lays out the anomalies of the situation.

PART IV: AN INTENTIONAL CIVILIZATION

23. FROM PERCEPTION TO ACTION

p. 280 **He replied that he would rectify**
Confucius, *The Analects*, trans. D.C. Lau (Hong Kong: Chinese University Press, 1992), Book XIII, 3. Confucius lived 551–479 BCE.

p. 280 **Boyden replied, "The Land."**
Joseph Boyden, onstage conversation at Luminato: Toronto Festival of Arts and Creativity, Toronto, 8 June 2008.

24. THE NORTH

p. 288 **Sheila Watt-Cloutier, former elected chair**
Sheila Watt-Cloutier, *Ottawa Citizen*, 29 April 2007.

p. 288 **Mary Simon, president of the Inuit**
Quoted by Franklyn Griffiths, "Camels in the Arctic?" *The Walrus*, Nov 2007.

p. 289 **Nellie Cournoyea, the long-time Inuvialuit leader**
Quoted in *Globe and Mail* (Toronto), "Report on Business," 2 June 2008, 1.

p. 289 **There is a whole concept**
IQ: Inuit Qaujimajatuqanginnut.

p. 289 **The principles of IQ**
First Annual Report of the Inuit Qaujimajatuqanginnut (IQ) Task Force (Iqaluit: Government of Nunavut), 12 August 2002, 9.

p. 291 **And then our police arrived**
Shelagh D. Grant, *Arctic Justice: On Trial for Murder, Pond Inlet, 1923* (Montreal and Kingston: McGill-Queen's University Press, 2002), 27.

p. 291 **As late as 1953, Louis St. Laurent**
Sherrill Grace, *Canada and the Idea of the North* (Montreal and Kingston: McGill-Queen's, 2001), 46.

p. 291 **There were some administrators**
Sissons, op. cit., 58.

p. 301 **We actually base our sovereignty**
See, for example, a major paper by the leading Canadian expert on this subject: Donat Pharand, "The Arctic Waters and the Northwest Passage: A Final Revisit." *Ocean Development and International Law*, 38.3 (2007): 3–69; Robert Dufresne, A Report on "Canada's Legal Claims Over Arctic Territory and Waters," Ottawa: Parliamentary Information and Research Service, 6 December 2007; and the Government of Canada, The Speech from the Throne, 16 October 2007.

25. A CIRCLE OF FAIRNESS

p. 303 **"I think it's a principle"**
See Michael Valpy, *Globe and Mail* (Toronto), 1 July 2008, A9.

p. 305 **The Community Foundations of Canada**
Sarah V. Wayland, *Unsettled: Legal and Policy Barriers for Newcomers to Canada* (Ottawa: Law Commission of Canada and Community Foundations of Canada, 2006).

p. 305 **Equally, a six part study in 2008**
André Picard, *Globe and Mail* (Toronto), 23–28 June 2008.

p. 305 **Then you turn to the lengthy**
Compete to Win: Final Report (Ottawa: Competition Policy Review Panel, June 2008).

p. 306 **Within a week of the hollowing-out**
"Exclusif: Une légende du monde des affaires parle. L'avenir selon Paul Desmarais," *Le Point* (Paris), 26 June 2008.

p. 309 **Tommy Douglas's original health-care idea**
See Tom Kent, "Healthy Children First" in *Medicare: Facts, Myths, Problems, Promise*, eds. Bruce Campbell and Greg Marchildon (Toronto: Lorimer, 2007).

p. 310 **We could, should be trying**

See a good argument in favour of this by Peter MacLeod, *Toronto Star*, 16 August 2007, AA8.

p. 311 **Studies show that Western democracies**

See Steven Pressman, "The Decline of the Middle Class: An International Perspective," *Journal of Economic Issues*, XLI(1) (March 2007): 181–200. See also Doug Saunders, *Globe and Mail* (Toronto), 4 August 2007, F3.

pp. 312–13 **The demographer Michael Adams**

See Michael Adams, *Toronto Star*, 1 July 2008, AA6.

p. 315 **This is not old-fashioned charity**

Alden Nowlan, "The Social Workers Poem," *Selected Poems*, eds. Patrick Lane and Lorna Crozier (Toronto: Anansi, 1996), 96.

p. 317 **And what you could find in it was**

Bouchard and Taylor, *Fonder L'Avenir*, 241–42. Translated by the author, as the official translation was not yet completed at the time of this book's publication.

ACKNOWLEDGMENTS

This has been a complicated book to write, with a great deal of invaluable advice and ideas and research coming from all directions. Much of that researching and thinking with others has gone on for close to a decade. When I have explained the three basic ideas to others, they have often become excited about helping. As the saying goes, they may or may not agree with my conclusions, but the generosity and enthusiasm with which people have helped has made this whole project both fun and sometimes a virtual community project.

I first want to thank Dr. Thomas Hodd for his support, ideas, research and firm hand getting me to the end. Also Jonathan Weier, who has a magical eye for research and who has also brought his ideas to the table.

And then there is the remarkable Michael Levine, Diane Turbide, David Davidar and all the patient and talented people at Penguin; my old friend Pascal Assathiany and Jean Bernier of Boréal. Publishers who push you to think harder and enjoy risk are a rare commodity. But none of this would have been possible without the sharp eye and determination of Sandra Tooze.

Margaret Conrad, George Elliott Clarke, Émile Martel, Frank Cunningham, Alain Dubuc, Gerald Friesen, Anne Golden, Rudyard Griffiths, Bob Jickling and Jocelyn Létourneau with all of their ideas.

Part I is in good part the outcome of hundreds of conversations over the years with Aboriginals and non-Aboriginals all over Canada. A small number of the people who have helped me are Dr. Joseph Gosnell, Georges Erasmus, Giindajin Haawasti Guujaaw, David Chartrand of the Manitoba Métis, Tomson Highway, Thomas King, Jeannette Armstrong, Lally Grauer, the Honourable David Arnot, Lachlin McKinnon, Pita Aatami, Siila Watt-Cloutier, Mary Simon, Peter Irniq, Philippa Ootoowak, Norman Simonie, the youth of the Nunavut Sivuniksavut program, Brad Chambers, Rudy Wiebe, Joseph Boyden, Lorena Fontaine, the Honourable Jean Friesen, the Honourable Graydon Nicholas, Renée

Dupuis, David Garneau, Guy Vanderhaeghe, Norman Price and Diane Brown of the Skidegate Haida Immersion Program, Katherine Barber of the *Canadian Oxford Dictionary*, Roger Boucher of Le Village Historique Acadien, Aritha van Herk, Mel Watkins, Bill Henderson with his expertise on the *Guerin* case, Guy P. Buchholtzer, Robert G. Williamson, John Jennings, C.E.S. Franks, Shelagh O. Grant, Franklyn Griffiths.

For Part II, regarding the whole question of Peace, Welfare and Good Government, many thanks to the Right Honourable Beverley McLachlin, the Honourable J.E. Côté, Ian Wilson, who is as passionate about this as I am, Patricia Kennedy, Timothy Dubé, Stephen Eggleston and Jordan Birenbaum, Andy Orchard of Trinity College, Edward Andrew. Regarding the questions of Dominion/Puissance, particular thanks to Father Yves Abran, who understood the Zachariah 9:10 link, Walter Deller, the Most Reverend Michael Peers, Jean-Pierre Lussier and Marie-Hélène de Montigny. Regarding the choice of Ottawa as the national capital, special thanks to David Knight.

For Part III, Monica Patten, Thomas Caldwell, David Olive, Sean Geobey, Dominic D'Alessandro, Peter Munk, the Honourable Donald Macdonald, Jennifer Welsh, James Travers, Erin K. Weir, Alyson Atkinson, Al Etmanski and Vickie Cammack and the people at PLAN, everyone at Rossbrook House in Winnipeg and the artists at the Nina Haggerty Centre in Edmonton. Particular thanks to Tom Kent and to the youth and staff at the Pelham Park Youth Resource Centre in Toronto.

Finally, many thanks to Robert McKellar, Robert MacMillan, Tim Welke, Olga, Ken and Judy, who kept me going.